War and Revolution in Catalonia
1936–1939

Historical Materialism Book Series

The Historical Materialism Book Series is a major publishing initiative of the radical left. The capitalist crisis of the twenty-first century has been met by a resurgence of interest in critical Marxist theory. At the same time, the publishing institutions committed to Marxism have contracted markedly since the high point of the 1970s. The Historical Materialism Book Series is dedicated to addressing this situation by making available important works of Marxist theory. The aim of the series is to publish important theoretical contributions as the basis for vigorous intellectual debate and exchange on the left.

The peer-reviewed series publishes original monographs, translated texts, and reprints of classics across the bounds of academic disciplinary agendas and across the divisions of the left. The series is particularly concerned to encourage the internationalization of Marxist debate and aims to translate significant studies from beyond the English-speaking world.

For a full list of titles in the Historical Materialism Book Series available in paperback from Haymarket Books, visit:
www.haymarketbooks.org/category/hm-series

War and Revolution in Catalonia 1936–1939

Pelai Pagès i Blanch

Translated by
Patrick L. Gallagher

Haymarket Books
Chicago, IL

First published in 2014 by Brill Academic Publishers, The Netherlands
© 2014 Koninklijke Brill NV, Leiden, The Netherlands

Published in paperback in 2014 by
Haymarket Books
P.O. Box 180165
Chicago, IL 60618
773-583-7884
www.haymarketbooks.org

ISBN: 978-1-60846-412-8

Trade distribution:
In the US, Consortium Book Sales, www.cbsd.com
In Canada, Publishers Group Canada, www.pgcbooks.ca
In the UK, Turnaround Publisher Services, www.turnaround-psl.com
In all other countries, Publishers Group Worldwide, www.pgw.com

Cover design by Ragina Johnson.

This book was published with the generous support of
Lannan Foundation and the Wallace Global Fund.

Printed in Canada by union labor.

10 9 8 7 6 5 4 3 2 1

Library of Congress Cataloging-in-Publication data is available.

Contents

Foreword vii

Introduction 1

1 Precursors to War and Revolution in Catalonia 5

2 The Military Uprising and the Failure of the Rebellion 20

3 Political Transformations: the Crisis of the *Generalitat* and
   the Formation of the Militia Committees 32

4 The Formation of the Popular Militias and the Aragon Front 44

5 Public Order and Political Repression in the Rearguard 54

6 The Republican Justice System: From Popular Tribunals to
   Special Tribunals 64

7 Social and Economic Transformations 76

8 The War Economy and the War Industries 84

9 Forming the Unity Government and the First Political
   Disagreements 93

10 The May Events of 1937 105

11 The Consequences of the May Events 117

12 The Republican Military Offensives, Summer 1937 126

13 The Negrín Government in Barcelona and the Rupture of
   the Catalan Front 136

14 The Battle of the Ebro and the Deterioration of Conditions in
    the Rearguard 149

15 The Occupation of Catalonia and Losing the War 160

Conclusion: The Historical Significance of the Republic's Defeat 160

Appendix of Documents
 A 'The Failure of the Military Insurrection in Barcelona',
    La Vanguardia, 22 July 1936 176
 B Manuel Moragues, 'The Formation of the Catalan Central
    Committee of Anti-fascist Militias', *La Publicitat*, 2 August 1936 ... 183
 C 'Popular Militias on the Aragon Front', *Crònica diària*,
    24 July 1936 186
 D 'Public Order in the Catalan Rearguard', *Crònica diària*,
    24 October 1936 188
 E 'The Municipalisation of Housing', *La Vanguardia*, 19 June 1937 ... 190
 F The Fatarella Incidents:
       From the CNT's *Solidaridad Obrera*, 26 January 1937 200
       From the UGT's *Las noticias*, 28 January 1937 202
 G The May 1937 Events. From *Crònica diària*, 3, 4 and 5 May 1937 ... 204
 H 'Repression Against the POUM', letter from jailed members of
    the POUM 207
 I Francisco Franco and Ramón Serrano Suñer, 'The Abolition of
    the Catalan Autonomy Statute', *Boletín Oficial del Estado*,
    8 April 1938 211
 J 'The Battle of the Ebro', *La Humanitat*, 30 July 1938 213
 K 'Disagreements Between the *Generalitat* and the Republican
    Government', *La Vanguardia*, 1 October 1938 216
 L 'Bidding Farewell to the International Brigades', *La Humanitat*,
    29 October 1938 221
 M 'The Last Armed Resistance', editorial published in the PSUC
    daily newspaper, *Treball*, 21 January 1939 224
 N Franco occupies Catalonia:
       Fidel Dávila Arroyo, *La Vanguardia*, 27 January 1939 226
       Elíseo Álvarez Arenas, *La Vanguardia*, 28 January 1939 228

Bibliography 233
Index 239

Foreword

Despite its valuable contribution, this book by Pelai Pagès i Blanch is virtually unknown outside of Spain. Under Franco's government, the history of the Spanish Civil War was exclusively written by the victors, and so most academically rigorous studies of the Republic and the revolution were conducted by non-Iberian writers. Today, even though academic freedom is alive and well in Spain, and state-sponsored censorship has been left behind, foreign academic works are still commonly translated into Spanish, while alarmingly few works by Spanish and Catalan writers have been translated into English. Consequently, many of the best studies in the field are not accessible to non-Spanish or non-Catalan readers. My hope is that this translation will make Pagès's book – originally published in Catalan in 1987 and then greatly expanded for the Spanish edition in 2007 – accessible to many more people.

Pagès, a professor at the University of Barcelona, is a leading Catalan historian of the Civil War and the foremost biographer of Andreu Nin, a leader of the POUM (*Partido Obrero de Unificación Marxista*), the 1930s Spanish communist party opposed to the official Stalinist-controlled PCE (*Partido Comunista Español*). His book offers a dynamic and sympathetic portrait of the revolution and its aftermath as experienced in Catalonia. Many writers today, opponents of revolutionary politics, portray the revolution in Catalonia firstly as unfortunate and strategically disastrous, and secondly as an exclusively Catalan affair and therefore of little importance other than the nuisance it caused to Spain as a whole. Of those who do recognise the pivotal historical importance of the revolutionary left in Catalonia, many have only dedicated book chapters to the Catalan events. In fact, until now, George Orwell's *Homage to Catalonia*[1] is the only book in English dedicated to the war and revolution in this region.

Pagès's study has a great deal in common with Orwell's work. It has always struck me as odd that Orwell's account, despite its enormous fame and international readership, illustrates a side of the war, and draws conclusions about it, that sharply contradict the most commonly held assumptions regarding the conflict. Orwell wrote about how the bourgeois press and the international communist press of the time persisted in misrepresenting and misunderstanding the war and revolution. Seventy-five years later, however, it is their accounts that dominate both popular and academic understandings of the war – not Orwell's. It would appear that the ideological motivations behind such portrayals of the war still prevail, affected only slightly by the prism of subsequent events.

Some of the most striking images in Orwell's narrative describe the contrast between two Barcelonas: the one Orwell first experienced in December 1936, while the social revolution was still visible in the streets, and the one he returned to a few months later, at the end of April 1937, when the Catalan bourgeoisie had made great advances towards retaking power from the workers. In December, Orwell had observed the red and red and black banners hanging from buildings, the disappearance of forms of speech that signalled social distinctions, the absence of the bourgeoisie from the streets of the city, and the energy of a confident working class inspired by revolutionary speeches and music. Orwell punctuated his powerful description of revolutionary Barcelona with an admission still marked by his own recent arrival and status as an outside observer: 'All this was queer and moving. There was much in it that I did not understand, in some ways I did not even like it, but I recognized it immediately as a state of affairs worth fighting for'.[2]

Orwell knew that his first impression of Barcelona in December 1936 was already months after the peak of workers' power had passed: after all, the central organ of the revolution, the Catalan Anti-fascist Militia Committee, had already disappeared by October 1936. Nonetheless, when Orwell returned in late April 1937, the changes he observed were remarkable. Instead of a city where the entire population appeared to be dressed in the blue coveralls of the worker, elegant dress had reappeared. Distinctions of rank were being reasserted in the rearguard under the guise of the new 'Popular Army'. Perhaps most tellingly, the civilian population seemed to have lost the enthusiasm of the revolution. Orwell learns that from the beginning of January 1937, as the power of the

---

1. Orwell 1952.
2. Orwell 1952, p. 7.

workers' organisations had declined in Catalonia, the number of volunteers for duty on the front had plummeted. In this book, Pagès tells us how and why Catalonia moved from that state of revolutionary optimism to the state observed by Orwell on his second visit. Like Orwell, the author shows the extremely high stakes involved in uniting the leftist forces to fight the fascists, as well as the consequences of reversing the progress of the revolution as a strategy to win the war. After a general introduction to the social and political circumstances that brought war and revolution to Spain and Catalonia in the 1930s, Pagès offers a detailed account of separate but overlapping processes. One begins with the revolution itself, emerging from the Catalan workers' reaction to the military rebellion. He gives a step-by-step account of everything from the street battles that stopped the military uprising in its tracks to the workers forming militias to extend their defensive efforts to other areas of Catalonia and neighbouring Aragon, collectivising the economy and housing, and building a collectivised war industry almost from scratch. The revolution created circumstances that are often referred to as 'dual power', where workers' organisations ruled in the streets and organised the defence of the revolution, while bourgeois and republican institutions continued to exist, although sometimes only in name. Pagès also addresses the most controversial aspects of this revolutionary stage: the repression of class enemies, the actions of the 'uncontrollables' and anti-clerical violence.

One of the fascinating realities of the revolution in Spain is the variety of solutions that workers and peasants adopted in order to reorganise production while they were mobilising for war. As Pagès shows, in some instances revolutionary transformations were magnificently successful. In other instances, social transformation was forced into retreat before it ever had a chance to succeed. Pagès makes sense of Catalonia's revolutionary experience, showing that revolution is an infinitely complicated and contradictory affair.

An understanding of these details greatly clarifies the process of republican counterrevolution that began to take significant steps as early as September 1936. The author describes the progressive imposition of bourgeois power over the workers and their organisations – first by the republican government in Catalonia, backed by the PSUC (Unified Socialist Party of Catalonia), and then by the Spanish republican government, backed by the Spanish Communist Party.

As Pagès points out, the need to centralise efforts to fight against the military rebellion allowed the Catalan government to gain representation on the Catalan Anti-fascist Militia Committee and begin to co-opt the revolution and regain the power they had lost to the anarchists with enormous efficiency. The anarchists' refusal to centralise power on a strictly working-class basis resulted in the creation of a 'cross-class' committee with members who, from the beginning, were attempting to increase the Catalan government's power at the expense of the Anti-fascist Militia Committee.

Throughout the book, close attention is paid to the different crises suffered by the parliamentary governments of Catalonia and, in some cases, of Spain. During the war, legislation in Catalonia was largely confined to the cabinet (*consell executiu*), or to decrees from the president, who was the first minister of the government cabinet. The author pays close attention to the ever-changing appointments and reappoinments, the shuffling and re-shuffling of cabinet positions: he often includes detailed lists of the appointed ministers and their party or trade union affiliations. In most cases, these moves reflect a change in the political balance of power within the broad array of the anti-fascist forces represented in the Catalan government. These forces are often simplistically referred to as the 'republican' side, a view that this book challenges in several ways. These changes are referred to as 'governmental crises' because of the need to reconstruct the cabinet. Following the revolving door of ministerial appointments and the ministers' political affiliations is one way to see the gradual imposition of republican strategies and politics over those of the revolution.

Another process Pagès describes, played out between Spain and Catalonia, is signalled by the author's careful lexical choices. Throughout the text, both in the original and the translation, Catalonia is not referred to as a mere region within Spain. For clarity, my translation refers to Spain's government as the 'Government of the Republic' or the 'Republican Government' and to Catalonia's (republican) government as the '*Generalitat*'. Whatever one's own sympathy or antipathy towards Catalan nationalism, it is important to recognise that aspirations for Catalan autonomy and/or independence conditioned important processes in the war. These aspirations were felt – although not always in the same way or with the same vigour – among Catalan workers, the peasantry, the middle class, and even important sectors of the Catalan ruling class. They were also an important factor in the military uprising against the Spanish Republic, because the military opposed what they saw as the Spanish Republican Government's disastrous lenience towards Catalan nationalism between 1931 and 1936.

Pagès shows that, in spite of what the military believed, the politicians of the Republican Government felt little support for Catalan nationalism, and, in fact, their opposition to Catalan nationalism became much more intense during the course of the war. Like the *Generalitat* in its struggle for power *vis à vis* the workers, the Republican Government stressed that it was taking over the war effort because coordination and centralisation were needed in order to take on the enemy. Still, in its efforts to fight the military rebellion and wrest power from the workers, the *Generalitat* actually broadened its autonomy through much of the first year of war.

From the perspective of the Spanish Republican Government, Catalonia was extremely important because of its economic strength and its relative distance from the fronts that could have threatened its industrial might. Catalonia's position relative to the fronts has been described as 'lucky', but it was, of course, the result of material conditions. Catalan industry was an important factor in the strength and maturity of the Catalan working class. In turn, the workers' high level of political organisation and their ability to mobilise had contributed substantially to the defeat of the military *coup* in Catalonia and made possible the early successes of the revolution. It is true that there were military forces loyal to the Republic in Catalonia that played an important role in defeating the *coup*, but it is inconceivable that they would have defeated Franco without the spontaneous and massive mobilisation of the Catalan working class.

In the end, the Spanish Government of Madrid, which had moved to Valencia by November 1936 and then to Barcelona itself in October 1937, was wary both of the social revolution that had placed republican rule as a whole in jeopardy, and also of the independence gained by the *Generalitat* as it recaptured more and more power for republicanism from the Catalan workers. In this book, then, we see a dual dynamic unfolding in the conflict in Catalonia: republican opposition, both Spanish and Catalan, to worker and peasant revolution, which threatened republicanism as the liberal defender of the capitalist state; and the Spanish government's opposition to Catalan autonomy. The final chapters of *War and Revolution in Catalonia* tell the tragic tale of the increasingly desperate circumstances in Catalonia from the summer of 1937 to its capture by Franco in January 1939.

Finally, another of this book's important contributions is an Appendix that collects many fascinating documents from the war. Until now, most of these documents could only be found in their original language in the Spanish or Catalan archives. Pagès introduces each of these documents – newspaper articles, correspondence, legislation and decrees.

A Few Notes on the Translation

As has already been mentioned, an attempt has been made to write about Catalonia as an independent entity as much as possible. A few other lexical choices are worth noting. Pagès does not refer to the enemy of the Republic – the rebellious army that will soon be led by Francisco Franco – as the 'Nationalists', as is often the case in histories of the war. The 'Nationalist' label was devised by the insurgent army, appropriating for themselves a legitimacy that their insurrection against the Republican Government did not necessarily merit. Not surprisingly, Franco and his generals label their enemies 'criminals' or 'rebels'. While calling Franco's forces 'Nationalists' may be a convenient way of referring to those who took up arms against the Spanish Republic, this work uses various words: 'rebels', 'insurrectionists', 'insurgents', 'Francoists', 'fascists'.

Geographical locations in this book span both Catalan-speaking and Castilian-Spanish speaking areas. Catalan is the primary language of the *Generalitat* and Castilian (*Castellano*) the language of the Republican Government. Therefore, sources, place names, parties, offices, and even the names of important participants in the events can be written in Catalan, Castilian, or translated into English. Although I have sometimes followed conventions established in other English-language histories of the Civil War, in general I have left Catalan sources and place names in Catalan, Spanish sources and place names in Castilian. The Catalan city Lleida, for example, which is Lérida in Castilian and Lerida in English, is referred to as Lleida throughout the book. Offices and parties usually referred to in English are, when first mentioned, given their names in Catalan (if they are Catalan), or in Castilian (if they are Spanish). One exception to this is in quotations: if a Spanish politician is speaking about a Catalan party or place and uses the Castilian term, I have left the name in Castilian. Finally, there are a few instances where important source texts can be found in English. Where that is the case, I have provided bibliographical information so that the English-language text can be consulted.

Special Acknowledgements

I would like to express my gratitude to Kent State University's Research Council for the grant that made possible the completion of this translation.

Patrick L. Gallagher
Kent State University

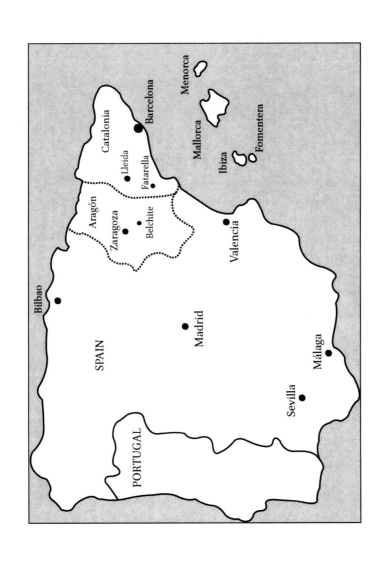

Introduction

In 1986, on the occasion of the fiftieth anniversary of the Spanish Civil War, I was asked to write a book in Catalan about the war in Catalonia that, while maintaining methodological rigour, synthesised current research for the general public. The idea was to write a new history that would contribute to our understanding of the war in Catalan territory by bringing together new research from the monographs published in the previous two decades. In the introduction to that book, published one year later, I commented that the Spanish Civil War was still intensely debated. With the fiftieth anniversary came a multitude of conferences, expositions and debates. Ten years later, the second edition of the book was published. I again talked about how much interest there was in the Civil War, and I discussed the popular and critical success of Ken Loach's film *Land and Freedom* when it came out in 1995. Also noteworthy at the time were the new historical sources that became available to historians due to the fall of the Soviet régime. Nevertheless, the second edition made few changes to the edition published in 1987.

Now, on the occasion of the English translation of the book, itself based on the 2007 edition published in Spanish for the seventieth anniversary of the Civil War, I find myself once again remarking on the continuing relevance of the Civil War and its lasting sociopolitical weight. In 2007, Prime Minister Rodríguez Zapatero's government approved the Historical Memory Law, which challenges earlier attempts, during the transition period, to shut the door on the trauma of the war in Spanish society. As a consequence, it seems that a day does not pass without the Civil War appearing in the country's newspapers for some reason or another. This is a new phenomenon in our history, and it shows that the war still casts a long shadow on both the present and the future. This is not the place to debate why the war is still an issue, but it does seem clear that, even without the enormous and growing literature on the subject, the Civil War is the most important event in contemporary Spanish history.

Something else has happened over the last few years: a collection of conservative authors has begun publishing books re-examining the Civil War and questioning its left-wing 'myths'. A few things should be mentioned about these 'revisionists'. They are not professional historians but rather ideologues of the right. Their books have failed to offer anything new: instead, they have merely reproduced what Franco's historians said about the war in their day – albeit in a more modern prose. Their access to the media explains why their books have been successful, but, with few exceptions, the debate they hoped to re-launch has had little impact on historians.

With the exception of the Second World War, the Spanish Civil War (1936–9) continues to be the event of the twentieth century with the most extensive bibliography. With all that continues to be published on the topic both inside Spain and beyond, it is difficult to keep up – even for a specialist. This interest undoubtedly reflects the immense echo the war produced at the time: its enormous international implications, its role in leading up to the second European conflagration of the century, the participation of Italy and Germany on Franco's side, the international volunteers that came to fight for the Republic, the final outcome, Franco's long dictatorship after the war, the peculiarities of the Spanish transition to democracy, and finally, the war's contemporary implications. Interest is still strong internationally: in just the last few years, for example, I have participated in conferences on the Civil War in Italy, Switzerland, and France. The Spanish Civil War might be the last 'romantic' war in history: it was certainly fought over economic and social spoils and over power in both Spain and Europe, but it was also a battle of ideals. In many respects, it was history's last ideological war.

I believe that this ideological aspect is fundamental for understanding why the war has stirred passions so deeply and why it continues to do so. As I have pointed out on other occasions, these ideological questions crystallise around the social revolution that developed in the Republican zone as a result of the outbreak of war. That is to say, without the far-reaching economic and social transformations in the first months of the war, the ideological questions would have been less significant. And without recognising the importance of the social revolution, it would be difficult to understand the political evolution of the

Republic during the war, the positions taken by international forces, and the war's outcome.

Of all the Republican zones following the outbreak of war, Catalonia experienced the most profound revolution. The strength of the workers' movement and popular organisations explains not only why Catalonia was considered the 'bastion of the Republic' beginning in 1931, but also why the popular classes saw in the profound crisis created by the war a chance to realise the social transformations to which they had dedicated themselves. Under workers' power, Catalonia achieved revolutionary change and considerable political independence, and this eventually set the stage for a conflict on the Republican side that became, within the greater war, a kind of mini-civil war among the anti-fascist camp. Due to the extent of this social revolution, some have claimed that Catalonia somehow stayed out of the war. Catalonia did experience a social revolution, but at the same time it organised a significant war effort to help defeat the military insurrection. Others, such as certain Catalan nationalists, have claimed that the war was imported to Catalonia from Spain, and that Catalonia ignored the problems and exigencies in the Spanish Republican zone that were caused by the war. All these ideas about Catalonia's role in the war will be challenged here.

One must consider countless facets of the Civil War in order to understand how it played out in Catalonia. In this book, I have attempted to look at them globally: the Catalan circumstances that led to war, the 19 July events that led to the failure of the military coup, the revolution itself, the political and religious repression, the evolution of the political conflict, the military aspects of the war, and the final defeat and its repercussions. My intention has been to consider everything that determined the history of those two-and-a-half years of war in Catalonia. I have attempted to present this history from a perspective that is both critical and self-critical, that hides no details, and that makes no concessions to the heightened emotions this history stirs. This is not a book that makes any attempt to play to the gallery.

One last thing. The 2007 edition of the book, of which this edition is a translation, has little in common with the Catalan edition of 1987. In the newer edition I not only corrected some errors in the original, but also brought it up to date and included a consideration of new work that has since appeared on the war. I have made ample use of the *Crònica diària*, a daily publication of the office of the president of Catalonia's *Generalitat*, currently located in the Tarradellas Archives of the Poblet monastery. From the same archive, I have used documentation from the War Industries Commission, and I have drawn on research from various other archives like the one in Salamanca and the National Archive of Catalonia (*Arxiu Nacional de Catalunya*). I have also made ample use of the daily press, especially *La Vanguardia*, documents from the former Comintern archives in Moscow, and, when necessary, official sources of the Catalan government and the government of the (Spanish) Republic. The result, with all of these new sources, is practically a new book. It is based on the Catalan version, but this can hardly be recognised. The twelve chapters from the original are now fifteen, and the documental appendix has been entirely restructured. My intention has been to include aspects of the war, like the important questions of the War Industries and the Justice Tribunals, that had hardly appeared in the Catalan version of the book.

As I said in my introduction of 1986, I wrote this book in order to offer a critical approach to a period of our history that has had an enormous impact on many generations of Catalans and Spaniards, and even on the lives of thousands of international combatants. Whatever its value, I would like to dedicate this small work to these many people.

Chapter One
Precursors to War and Revolution in Catalonia

One school of Spanish historians has repeatedly argued that the outbreak of Civil War in Spain had little to do with Catalonia or its history. According to this school, Catalonia, on the eve of the military insurrection of 19 July 1936, was enjoying a political and social peace – sometimes referred to as a 'Catalan oasis' – that contrasted sharply with the profound tensions experienced throughout the rest of the Spanish Republic. For these historians, Spain imposed the Civil War on Catalonia, imposing it on the region against the wishes of both the left and the right.[1]

At the very least, this analysis – still defended today by certain groups of Catalan nationalists – is superficial, and not just because the notion of the region being fundamentally at peace in the spring of 1936 needs careful qualification. To understand fully the war and revolution in Catalonia, we must focus not only on the few months preceding the war's outbreak, but also on the structural causes originating further back in time. Both the Republican period between 1931 and 1936 and the tense international circumstances of the 1930s shaped the histories of Spain and Catalonia. In addition, we cannot ignore the complex relationship between Catalonia and the Spanish Republic, with their closely related, yet nonetheless distinct, histories.

---

1. [Translator's Note, hereafter, TN] Throughout this study, 'Spain' is used to refer to the larger nation whose capital (at least at the beginning of the war) was Madrid: Catalonia has a strong history of aspiring to independence and/or political autonomy from Spain. See the Translator's Introduction for a fuller description of this aspect of Pagès's analysis.

The Civil War should even be understood in conjunction with Spain's other civil wars, the Carlist Wars of the nineteenth century.[2] Those wars were not, as is commonly thought, merely a conflict between Carlists and Liberals, with the Liberals representing progress, modernisation, and the introduction of capitalist relations, and the Carlists representing the *ancien régime* and economic, social, and political intransigence.[3] A third socio-political force also played a role in the conflicts, a force that appeared early in the nineteenth century and contributed to the tensions leading to civil war in the next century: Spanish republicanism. A popular movement obviously distinct from Carlism, republicanism also distinguished itself from Spanish liberalism by supporting a social and political project that reached beyond the boundaries of liberal capitalism. In fact, Spain's original republicanism, already strong by the 1840s, had ties to the Utopian socialism that had begun to appear in Europe, and, in contrast to the liberal aim of building a strongly centralised state, it fiercely defended federalism. Also during the 1840s, the first signs of a workers' movement appeared. The movement was still weak, and it lacked solid organisation at the national level; however, its appearance in some regions, particularly in Catalonia and parts of Valencia, set in motion the historical forces that would eventually challenge the capitalist social relations that were themselves just gaining a foothold in Spain.[4]

The social and political contradictions produced by the confluence of all these forces reached their breaking point during the six years between 1868 and 1874, known by historians as the Revolutionary Sexenium, which began with the progressive bourgeoisie's 'pseudo-revolution' in September 1868. The Sexenium culminated in Spain's first experience of Republican rule from 1873–4, when – as had happened repeatedly earlier on in the century, in 1835, 1840–3 and 1854–6 – popular forces from below overwhelmed the bourgeoisie's timid political aims.[5]

---

2. [TN] There were three Carlist civil wars in the nineteenth century. The Carlists were Catholic conservatives who had defended the interests of the *ancien régime* in the name of Carlos Isidro. Carlos was passed over for the Spanish crown in 1833 in favour of his three-year-old niece, Isabel II, the daughter of Fernando VII.

3. There are many analyses of the Carlist Wars that offer this perspective, but we should not forget that these wars represented something more, since they also saw Spanish peasants react strongly to the negative effects of introducing capitalist relations into the agricultural sector. See the classic study of these effects by Jaime Torras (Torras 1976). See also Fradera, Millan, and Garrabou (eds.) 1990.

4. See Pagès et al. 2001.

5. The year 1835 marks the first offensive of liberalism after Isabel II inherited the throne [TN: first her mother, María Cristina, and then General Baldomero Espartero, served as Regents until 1843], resulting in the definitive establishment of liberalism in Spain. It is also the year of the first stage of the great '*bullangues*' (insurrections) in Catalonia, culminating in the burning of convents, monasteries, and the Banaplata factory. During the years of Espartero's regency (1840–3), an important popular movement in Catalonia led to the 'Jamància', an enormous popular rebellion. Finally, the two years between 1854 and 1856, known as the Progressive Biennium, was a period of popular rebellion in all

This First Republic represented a victory for the republican impulses that had so often failed before. Meanwhile, the first Workers' International was also gaining a presence throughout the Spanish state, and anarchism, recently introduced in Spain, was coalescing rapidly into a worker and peasant movement with distinct regional characteristics in places like Catalonia and Andalucía. These factors combined to undermine two of the most important objectives of nineteenth-century bourgeois hegemony: order and stability, which, along with the doctrine of private property, were the foundation on which the liberal bourgeoisie had hoped to base its new capitalist system. In the demands of social sectors marginalised by the new political system and of new social classes that had emerged with industrialisation, Spain's hegemonic classes perceived a clear threat. And so, during the Sexenium, the struggles of workers and republicans – those forces that stood to benefit most from social, economic and political change – impelled Spain's hegemonic classes to set aside their own conflicts, the very conflicts that had motivated the previous century's succession of military coups, or *pronunciamientos*.[6]

More than anything else, the restoration of the monarchy in 1874 represented this consensus between the new and the old ruling classes, joined together by a shared interest in defending their privileges. This new hegemonic class developed a Spanish form of speculative capitalism which was radically anti-industrial and fundamentally based on large agricultural interests. Until the agrarian crisis at the end of the century – and even outliving it, given that few alternatives existed for the accumulation of capital – the Spanish bourgeoisie's hunger for land remained constant, and culminated in the rise of the great landowners as the definitive class that would rule Spain. In this context, where the rise of capitalism was mediated by a ruling class that embodied the most retrograde sociopolitical interests, the new Liberal and Conservative parties of the Restoration period represented little more than two sides of the same coin.[7] And even though the state showed an impulse to modernise for the first time, it was also clear that the social changes desired by popular forces would once again be postponed.

Conservative party leader Antonio Cánovas del Castillo succeeded in establishing a relatively stable political order during the final decades of the nineteenth century, and during this time the army remained quiet in its barracks. However, the new system experienced frequent crises during the Restoration.

---

of Spain and Catalonia, during which the first general strike was organised. The characterisation of the revolution of 1868 as a 'pseudo-revolution' comes from the classic study by Josep Fontana, 'Cambio económico y crisis política: Reflexiones sobre las causas de la revolución de 1868', in Fontana 1973.

6. [TN] See chapter 2, note 2 for a description of the Spanish *pronunciamiento*.

7. This political dynamic repeated that of the Moderates and Progressives (*moderados* and *progresistas*), earlier in the century.

The revolutionary crisis of 1917 was the most profound, but the crisis of 1898, known as 'the disaster', paved the way for a wave of reform-minded critics advocating 'regeneration'. There was also the crisis of 1909, characterised by protests over forced conscription for a military adventure in Morocco and culminating in Barcelona's Tragic Week, during which seventy-eight people died and around five hundred were injured. And there were endless labour strikes and social protests. These crises brought into relief the basic incompatibility between the ruling social sectors, who opposed any kind of change that might affect their privileges, and those sectors of Spanish society interested in modernising the state as well as effecting social and economic change. Even the Catalan bourgeoisie, which since 1898 had supported 'regeneration' through a conservative variety of Catalan nationalism, abandoned the pretence of reform when it saw the wolf's ears: the massive strikes in August 1917, when the workers' movement opted for revolutionary struggle in the face of the Catalan bourgeoisie's calamitous failure to make reforms.[8] The aggravation of political tensions after 1917 forced Spain's ruling classes to resort to the military dictatorship of General Miguel Primo de Rivera in 1923. Those years had been marked by the 'Bolshevik Triennium' in the Southern region of Andalucía and *pistolerismo* in Catalonia, when Catalan bosses hired gun-toting thugs to assassinate labour leaders and to violently repress the workers' movement, sparking retaliation from radical workers.

Much of the history of Spain's Second Republic, proclaimed on 14 April 1931 after a prolonged crisis of the monarchy, is a history of the contradictions and antagonisms between the two incompatible social blocs that had confronted each other so fiercely during the years leading up to Primo de Rivera's dictatorship. The situation gained even more complexity within its new conjuncture. The reform-minded republicans – Azaña, Domingo, Giner de los Ríos, and the Socialists – held a majority in government, and they managed to pass reformist legislation during the first two years of the Second Republic. But after November 1933, the reformists had to confront the conservatives under worsening circumstances: the conservatives had already attempted their first anti-republican coup, led by General Sanjurjo, in the summer of 1932; meanwhile, significant popular forces had become disillusioned with the timidity of the reforms of the first two years and had concluded that their aims could only be won by going beyond such limited measures. Most of these workers were in the anarchist-led National Workers' Federation (*Confederación Nacional del Trabajo*, or CNT), the Iberian Anarchist Federation (*Federación Anarquista Ibérica*, or FAI), and the socialist-led General Workers' Union (*Union General de Trabajadores*, or UGT), but those in the smaller communist groups were also drawing revolutionary conclusions.

---

8. The crisis of 1917 has been analysed in detail by Juan Antonio Lacomba in his classic book *La crisis española de 1917* (Lacomba 1970).

Immediately before the war, these conflicts coalesced around a triple stand-off: republican reformists against the reactionary right, the revolutionary left against the republican reformists, and the revolutionary left against the reactionary right. Throughout the republican years, tensions grew among these groupings, becoming even more intense when the right-wing bloc won the 1933 election and set about halting the reforms passed during the first two years. In addition, the international situation stemming from the Great Depression of the 1930s had a negative impact on the developing Republic. Beginning with the New York stock market crash in October 1929, the structural crisis of international capitalism had led to a second anti-democratic wave in Europe (the first having occurred in the 1920s, as a consequence of the First World War). Most notably, in January 1933, Hitler and the National Socialists were voted into power in Germany. In October 1934 the Spanish Federation of the Autonomous Right (*Confederación Española de Derechas Autónomas*, or CEDA) was called to form a government in Madrid, and workers feared that Spain was following the example of Germany, where Hitler, once in power, had rapidly dissolved democratic institutions from within, abolishing the Weimar Republic and establishing an iron-clad fascist dictatorship.

Of course, the Spanish Civil War cannot be explained without considering what some see as its immediate antecedent: the 1934 October Revolution. This revolution was, at least initially, intended to prevent the anti-republican forces from forming a government, but it quickly took on extraordinary social dimensions. The Spanish Socialist Workers' Party (PSOE) proclaimed a general strike throughout the country, and the strike grew into a revolutionary movement among the miners of Asturias. After two weeks of resistance by the miners, the military suppressed the revolution, giving the Chief of Military Staff, General Francisco Franco, his first opportunity to employ repressive measures.

In Catalonia, the general strike became an insurrection led by Lluís Companys, the Catalan president. It has often been held that this insurrection was strictly political, lacking the social content of the events in Asturias. Certainly, when Companys proclaimed the new Catalan State of the Federal Republic of Spain on 6 October, his affirmation of Catalan nationalism was primarily political in nature. In addition, the CNT had abstained from the strike. However, in many Catalan cities, like Lleida (Lerida), Girona (Gerona), Palafrugell, Vilanova i la Geltrú and Granollers, the rebellion was both nationalist and social in character.[9] This dual character is confirmed in the accounts of contemporary witnesses as ideologically removed from one another as Aymamí Baudina, of the

---

9. [TN] For many writing during or about the 1930s in Spain, 'social' aims or 'social' conflict refers specifically to class and to the conflicts or political contradictions that show the opposing interests of different social classes.

Catalan Left Republicans (*Esquerra Republicana de Catalunya*); Ángel Estivill, of the Workers and Peasants' Bloc (*Bloc Obrer i Camperol*, or BOC); and both Costa i Déu and Modest Sabaté, of the conservative Catalan League (*Lliga Catalana*).[10] In fact, social tensions in the Catalan provinces had recently worsened due to the contentious *Llei de Contractes de Conreu*,[11] which for much of 1934 had caused landowners to face off with tenant farmers (*arrendataris*). In some cases, social tensions rose even higher in the country than in the urban centres.

This description of the relations that existed in small towns, written by Costa i Déu and Modest Sabaté, the *Lliga*'s journalists, essentially predicted what would happen in rural areas all across the region in July 1936: 'With regards to the towns, where the most contrasting social classes had to experience political and social tensions while in constant proximity with one another, the outbreak of a revolutionary period made the hatred and passions of the anarchists for those associated with religiosity and high social rank more acute. And it is true that when these passions are unleashed in the darkest moments of a rebellion, they unfailingly produce the greatest catastrophes, because they entail the barbarity of fights between brothers'.[12]

Certainly, this right-wing presentation of the events shows its bias: it exaggerates the malice of the revolutionaries and gives all agency to the anarchists, and when the writers claim that in the provinces 'the first victim, the victim that encompassed all the hatred, was the temple, and with the temple, the priest', they are only repeating the axiom present in nearly all the popular revolutions in Catalonia since the nineteenth century.[13] However, the journalists' assertion that 'the events that occurred in the provinces were essentially social' was fundamentally correct.

The 1934 October Revolution was the most important and most immediate precursor to the Civil War, not only because of the events themselves but also because of their consequences. It is important, however, to reject accusations made in the last few years by right-wing 'revisionist' historians, who assign prac-

---

10. Aymaní i Baudina 1935; Estivill 1935; Costa i Déu and Modest Sabaté 1935 and 1936.

11. [TN] Llei de Contractes de Conreu (The Cultivation Contracts Law) is an example of a Republican reform that infuriated Catalan landowners. The law provided some security for tenant farmers as well as an avenue for peasants to gain ownership of any land they had worked for eighteen years.

12. Costa i Déu and Modest Sabaté 1936, pp. 15–16.

13. Unlike other areas of Spain during the Second Republic, Catalonia did not experience violent popular protests against the Church until October 1934. Of course, historically, the first demonstration of popular anti-clericalism took place in July 1835, when several monasteries were burned. The immediate antecedent of the anti-clericalist demonstrations during the Second Republic and then, in particular, at the outbreak of the Civil War, was the events of Tragic Week of 1909, when monasteries, churches, and other religious structures were set on fire.

tically all responsibility for the outbreak of the war to the PSOE, citing as evidence its role during the events of October 1934. Franco apologists like Pío Moa are merely reproducing the excuses elaborated by the Franco régime itself during nearly forty years of dictatorship – claims that the 'military uprising' was intended to prevent the revolution that the communists, anarchists and socialists had been advocating since 1934. The history of Spain's Second Republic up to 1934, however, shows that the revolution was a response to the failure of reforms, and that the reforms were failing precisely because of the obstructionism of the right and the privileged classes, who had already demonstrated in August 1932 that they were moving toward military insurrection. The origins of the officers' insurrectionism thus long predate any socialist revolutionary project. In addition, at this time some political organisations in Spain were proposing their own version of European fascism. As early as October 1931, Ledesma Ramos and Onésimo Redondo had organised the Assemblies of National Syndicalist Offensive (*Juntas de Ofensiva Nacional-Sindicalistas*, or JONS), and their newspaper, *Conquest of the State (La Conquista del Estado)*, made their intentions explicit. Two years later, in October 1933, José Antonio Primo de Rivera, son of the 1920s dictator, created the Spanish Phalange (*Falange Española*) after meeting Mussolini. The JONS and the Phalange united in February 1934, and by the end of the year they had clarified their tactical and strategic objectives, and their new philosophy would soon become the 'dialectic of fists and pistols'.[14] On the question of 'responsibilities', then, it is very clear where one ought to look to find who was to blame.

After the October Revolution, the path to conflict was irreversible. The first consequence of the revolution was repression: in addition to those killed during the events themselves, especially in Asturias, tens of thousands of revolutionaries landed in jail. In February 1936 the number rose to thirty thousand. In Catalonia, far fewer were arrested – three thousand four hundred in December 1934 – but they included the entire Catalan government (the *Generalitat*), even President Companys, and all were given thirty year sentences.[15] Commander Pérez i Farràs and Captain Frederic Escofet, chief of the *Mossos d'Esquadra*, Catalonia's autonomous police, were condemned to death by a military tribunal, although the government later commuted the sentences. Furthermore, Catalonia lived under martial law until April 1935. The Autonomy Statute was suspended until February 1936, as were most of Catalonia's municipal governments.[16] New authorities

---

14. Primo de Rivera 1966, pp. 61–9.
15. [TN] The Catalan Republican Government is known as the *Generalitat* in Catalonia. It is sometimes translated into Spanish as *Generalidad*. In *Homage to Catalonia*, Orwell calls it the 'Generalité'.
16. [TN] In 1932, Catalonia gained an important measure of self-government when the Republican Government passed the Autonomy Statute, allowing Catalonia to form

were appointed by the Republican Government: in January 1935, Manuel Portela Valladares was named governor of Catalonia. Joan Pich i Pon, a conservative politician of the Republican Radical Party (*Partido Republicano Radical*), was appointed mayor of Barcelona. In April 1935, Pich i Pon replaced Portela Valladares as governor.

Another consequence of the October 1934 events was played out in the Catalan agricultural sector, where tensions were already high due to the *Llei de Contractes de Conreu*. Landowners took advantage of their 1934 victory to throw hundreds of workers off the land. By the time the law was annulled, more than a thousand land workers had been expelled from their land in Catalonia. Between October 1934 and February 1936, fourteen hundred trials were held to evict both *rabassaires* (peasants in the vineyards) and *parcers* (sharecroppers). The resentment generated among peasants and workers in response to the landowners' drive for revenge helps to explain much of what would happen after the military insurrection of July 1936.

Additionally, Spain's republican government was now in the hands of the conservatives. With the growing governmental presence of José María Gil Robles's CEDA coalition, Manuel Jiménez Fernández, the agricultural minister, approved throughout 1935 a series of agrarian laws that, in effect, made it easier for landowners to expel land workers under the pretext that the owners themselves would work the land. The construction of schools was suspended under another pretext: that of reducing the government deficit. Furthermore, with the obvious goal of placating the Spanish Church, the government returned to it those properties confiscated from the Jesuits during the first two reformist years of the Republic.

Events in Europe and the rest of the world exacerbated tensions in Spain and Catalonia. Capitalism's profound crisis hit Spain especially hard after 1933, when unemployment rose sharply. Meanwhile, fascism was gaining power in Europe, challenging the stability of parliamentary democracy across the continent. Dollfus's ascent to power in Austria in 1932, and Hitler's in Germany in January 1933, increased international tensions to dangerous levels. Fascism's aggressiveness contrasted with the progressive weakness of Europe's democracies, especially that of France, which faced not only its many internal political and social problems but also the external threat of Italy and Germany.

The threat of fascism led nearly the entire European workers' movement to look for viable alternatives to block its advance. For many workers, Joseph Stalin's Soviet Union offered a positive model throughout the 1930s, and Stalin

---

a parliament. Though its powers were limited, any measure of Catalan autonomy infuriated Spanish conservatives, who saw it as a disastrous step towards the disintegration of traditional Spain.

and the Communist International would end up playing a crucial role in the events of the 1930s. The Seventh Congress of the Comintern, held in Moscow in July and August of 1935, adopted the popular-front strategy to fight fascism. This new strategy – whose chief theoretical exponent was Comintern secretary-general, Georgi Dimitrov – was designed to advocate alliances among all political and social sectors interested in defending democratic systems, alliances he called 'popular fronts'. At the organisational level, this approach would be carried out through electoral fronts bringing together the entire left, including both workers' organisations and the progressive bourgeoisie. At the same time, the new strategy implied that social revolution would be abandoned as an immediate objective.[17]

As these popular-front policies were being formulated, republicans and workers on the Spanish left, made increasingly anxious by the Republican Government's right-wing policies and the advance of the extreme right, sought ways to escape the threat of totalitarian reaction. Even as the PSOE was radicalising, there was a strong sense that the entire left needed to join together if they hoped to confront the Republic's reactionary tendencies. However, while there were revived attempts to unify the left after October 1934, there were still significant political and tactical differences: in particular, important sectors of the workers' movement argued that the only way to stop fascism was through revolution. Joaquín Maurín had written as much in 1935 in *Hacia la segunda Revolución* (*Toward the Second Revolution*).[18] Maurín argued that, if the proclamation of the Republic and the reformist politics of the first two years, *el bienio reformista*, represented the 'first revolution', then now, with the reformist road proving unviable, the republican project exhausted and the fascist counterrevolution a growing threat, the workers needed to consolidate the as of yet incomplete democratic revolution and begin the immediate construction of the socialist, or 'second' revolution. According to Maurín, after October 1934 Spain found itself facing a 'democratic-socialist' revolution.

When, after October 1935, the great financial scandals of Alejandro Lerroux's Radical CEDA government – the Straperlo scandal being the most famous, but also the Nombela scandal over supplies for Spain's African army[19] – came to

---

17. [TN] Paul LeBlanc's brief explanation of the distinction between 'popular fronts' and 'united fronts' explains why the strategy of popular frontism meant that worker revolution was being abandoned: 'The popular front is not simply a tactical alternative to the united front; it represents a completely different strategy for effecting social change. Instead of being designed to bring the working class to power, it is designed to mobilise working-class support for far-reaching coalitions with liberal capitalist parties and reform-minded but explicitly pro-capitalist governments' (LeBlanc 2009).

18. Maurín 1935.

19. [TN] Alejandro Lerroux was the long-time leader of the Republican Radical Party (in most literature about the period they are known as the 'Radicals'), which, despite

light, the President of the Republic, Niceto Alcalá Zamora, dissolved parliament (*las Cortes*) and called for new elections.[20] These elections were the most tense and polarised of the republican period. The left established important goals for the elections: amnesty for political prisoners, the re-establishment of republican normality, and regaining the initiative for reforms that had been abandoned since the victory of the right in the November 1933 elections. Left-wing workers and republicans also decided to form a single front that would include all the organisations of the broad left, from the 'left republicans' (moderates), to the most radical of the workers' organisations. The Popular Front pact, signed on 15 January 1936, formalised the alliance for the Republic's Spanish territories, and a few weeks later, on 4 February, the same arrangement was made in Catalonia and called the *Front d'Esquerres* (Left Front). In the Spanish territories, the electoral coalition was formed by Manuel Azaña and Marcelino Domingo's Left Republicans (*Izquierda Republicana*), Martínez Barrio and Fernando Giner de los Ríos's Republican Union Party (*Unión Republicana*), the PSOE, the UGT, the Young Socialists (*Juventudes Socialistas*), the Spanish Communist Party (PCE), Ángel Pestaña's Syndicalist Party (*Partido Sindicalista*), and the Workers' Party of Marxist Unification (*Partido Obrero de Unificación Marxista*, POUM). In Catalonia, various left-wing republican parties signed the pact: the *Esquerra*, the Left Republican Nationalist Party (*Partit Nacionalista Republicà d'Esquerra*, PNRE), the Republican Catalan Action Party (*Acció Catalana Republicana*, ACR), the Left Republican Party (*Partit Republicá d'Esquerra*, PRE), the Catalan Socialist Union Party (*Unió Socialista de Catalunya*, USC), the Rabassaires Union Party (*Unió de Rabassaires*, the most important Catalan peasant union), the Catalan Proletarian Party (*Partit Catalá Proletari*, PCP), the Catalan Communist Party (*Partit Comunista Catalunya*, PCC), and the POUM.

---

the party's name, by the 1930s occupied an important position on the Spanish Right. He was named Prime Minister after the 1933 elections by the President of the Republic even though his party did not gain the most votes. Lerroux's Radicals formed a coalition with the larger CEDA party of José María Gil Robles (see next footnote). Gil Robles and the other deputies of his party were not given cabinet positions so as not to provoke the Spanish left, who considered Gil Robles a fascist and vowed to strike if CEDA members were appointed to the cabinet. The general strike of October 1934 was itself called due to the appointment of three CEDA ministers. Lerroux was famously corrupt, as the two scandals mentioned here suggest.

20. [TN] Alcalá Zamora's move to call for elections instead of simply appointing a new government (that is, forming a new cabinet) was a surprise and blow for the CEDA and their leader, José María Gil Robles. As leader of the largest party in the government, Gil Robles had expected to be named Prime Minister, justifying his strategy of regaining power for the Spanish right through parliamentary means. The nail in the coffin for Gil Robles came when the electoral front led by CEDA lost the February 1936 elections to the left-wing Popular Front coalition.

The Popular Front's programme was extremely simple: win back the Republic for the left, reinstate the reformist programme of the first biennium, free from prison those jailed in the aftermath of the October 1934 events, normalise civic life, and, in the case of the Catalan *Front d'Esquerres*, re-establish the Autonomy Statute and enforce again the *Llei de Contractes de Conreu*. But in no way did the programme ever propose to go beyond the politics of reform.

Although faced with a left organised into a single front, the Spanish right was unable to forge an alliance. Catalonia was the exception: the *Lliga* succeeded in organising the *Front d'Ordre*, which brought together Traditionalists (*tradicionalistas*), right-wing Lerrouxists of the Radical Republicans, the *Acción Popular Catalana* (the Catalan version of the CEDA), as well as regionalists.[21] But for many Catalans, the *Lliga* had lost its credibility because after 1934 it was associated with governments that did not support Catalan autonomy. As in 1917, this party of the Catalan bourgeoisie had placed its social and economic interests above its political and ideological nationalism.

The campaign leading up to the elections of 16 February 1936 was more tense and contentious than any other of the Second Republic. The Spanish right placed the 'Marxist threat' ahead of all other political concerns and repeatedly drew on three themes for political and ideological mobilisation, the same ones that they had invoked almost since the beginning of the Republic: religion, the agrarian question and the question of Catalan autonomy (which they attacked by playing on fears of a 'fragmented Spain'). In the most pure *il duce*-style fascism, they even presented the CEDA leader, José María Gil Robles, as *'el jefe'* (the chief or boss). The left rallied around the thirty thousand workers who had been in jail since October 1934. In Catalonia, the *Front d'Esquerres* added the goal of rescuing the Catalan government from jail and of restoring Catalan autonomy. Expectations were high, and everyone was conscious that these elections could determine the immediate future of the Republic. Significantly, in contrast to what had occurred in the November 1933 elections, the anarchists did not call for abstention – in 1933 their slogan had been *'frente a las urnas, revolución social'* ('social revolution instead of ballot boxes') – and electoral participation was higher than at any other time during the Republican period.

On 16 February, the Popular Front won by a narrow margin. In all of the Spanish territories, Popular Front candidates won in cities with more than 150,000 inhabitants, gaining a total of 4,654,116 votes. The right received 4,503,524 votes, although more than half of those were cast for what was actually a mixture

---

21. [TN] In the twentieth century, 'Traditionalist' is often used to refer to the Carlist movement (see p. 6, n. 2 above). During the years of the Second Republic before the military uprising, the Traditionalists were on the extreme right, concluding even before Franco that a violent overthrow of the Republican Government would be necessary.

of centrist and right candidates. On independent ballots, the centrists gained 400,901 votes and the Basque nationalists 125,714. Although the results were close, the electoral system in place since 1931 gave the Popular Front candidates an absolute majority in the *Cortes* (Parliament): 286 deputies for the Popular Front, 132 for the Right, 42 for the centrists, and 10 for the Basque nationalists.

In Catalonia the *Front d'Esquerres*, with a tally of 58.9 percent to 41 percent, won a more decisive victory over the *Front d'Ordre* than the popular front had won in the rest of the Republic; in fact, it gained a victory in all districts. In the city of Barcelona the *Front d'Esquerres* won with 62.66 percent, over the *Front d'Ordre's* 37.34 percent; in the province of Barcelona, the tally was 57.4 percent to 42.6 percent; in Tarragona it was 57.22 percent to 42.48 percent; in Lleida, 54 percent to 45 percent; and in Girona, 57.63 percent to 42.31 percent. As for the number of deputies in parliament, of the 54 representing Catalonia, 41 were elected from the *Front d'Esquerres* and 13 from the *Front d'Ordre*. Of the new Parliament's representatives, 21 belonged to the *Esquerra*, five to the ACR, three to the *Partit Republicá*, two to the PNRE, two to the *Rabassaires*, four to the USC and one each to the PCP, PCC, PSOE, and POUM. On the right, 12 deputies came from the *Lliga*, and one was a Traditionalist.

When the left regained control of the Republic, the dynamic that would end in civil war was set in motion. It is well known that on the very night of the elections, upon hearing the results, General Franco, still Chief of Staff of the armed forces, called on the government to annul the elections and declare martial law. Similar pressure was applied by the CEDA's Gil Robles, as well as by the monarchist leader and former minister of the Primo de Rivera dictatorship, José Calvo Sotelo. But the president, the conservative Manuel Portela Valladares, refused, choosing to maintain Republican legality. At the same time, the Spanish Military Union (*Unión Militar Española*), a clandestine organisation of right-wing military officers, began preparing for what they hoped would be an old-fashioned Spanish military *pronunciamiento*. This is also the moment when the conspirators began to seek negotiations with potential allies in the rest of Europe, particularly in Mussolini's Italy, in search of financial and military support for their plan.

Three days after the elections, Manuel Azaña formed a new government that, unlike the government of 1931–3, lacked Socialist (PSOE) ministers and was thus entirely made up of republican parties.[22] Azaña's government passed an

---

22. [TN] During the Spanish Second Republic (1931–9), the Prime Minister (the President of the *Government*) sat under the President of the *Republic*. The Prime Minister appointed the Cabinet (*Consejo de Ministros*), often making an attempt to represent all of the parties that made up the winning electoral alliance. The cabinet members (ministers), along with the Prime Minister, played the most important legislative roles. The legislative role of cabinet members would be even more pronounced during the war.

amnesty decree so that political prisoners from the October 1934 events could be released from jail, gave jobs back to workers who had been fired and pursued agrarian reform more zealously than during the biennium. In Catalonia, President Companys and the entire government were released from jail, and on Sunday, 1 March, they were greeted by crowds in Barcelona. From the balcony of the *Generalitat*, and before an impressive multitude, the Catalan president delivered the following historic words:

> Catalan people:
> You will understand that at this moment I must make a great effort in order to control my emotions in order to speak to you. This is my land, our land, this is our plaza and our balcony!...
> We must begin our task anew, after painful and bitter hours. Thanks to the will, sympathy and warmth of the sacred avalanche of people, we have returned.
> We are here as servants to our ideals. We bring our souls bursting with emotion: not shame, but instead a new spirit of justice and reparation. We bring with us the lessons of experience. We will suffer again. We will fight again. And we will win again! (Great applause)
> The task that awaits us is difficult, but I tell you that we are sure of our strength, a strength that will carry us forward for Catalonia and for the Republic.[23]

In Catalonia and everywhere else, the city governments that had been abolished after October 1934 were immediately re-established. In the fields, the *Llei de Contractes de Conreu* was again enforced.

Nevertheless, the spring of 1936 was extraordinarily turbulent. After the February elections, the political and social climate of Republican Spain became increasingly poisonous. Along with popular demands that the government put their promised reforms in motion, there were frequent strikes and a political radicalisation that turned unusually violent: confrontations, attacks and political assassinations perpetrated by right-wing extremists and Phalangist gunmen became commonplace, and they were answered in kind by the left. In the

---

Even though the Popular Front victory in 1936 depended on votes coming from the Socialists, the UGT, and the CNT, none of their parliamentary deputies were appointed to the cabinet. The rank and file of these workers' organisations was radicalising and did not want cabinet representation, and its leaders had agreed to refuse appointments. The PSOE and the UGT, in particular, saw the elections as merely one battle in their war against the fascists. Their abstention reflected a scepticism towards republican politics that they shared with the CNT, who traditionally eschewed electoral politics based on their opposition to the state in principle. Azaña, probably with some relief, was restricted to only appointing ministers that represented republican parties.

23. *La Vanguardia*, 3 March 1936.

famously contentious session of parliament on 16 June, Gil Robles stated that between 16 February and 15 June, 160 churches were burned, 269 assassinations perpetrated, 10 newspaper offices destroyed and 146 bombs exploded. In addition, there were 113 general strikes and 228 sectional strikes. What Gil Robles conveniently failed to mention – in his efforts to portray a Spain in chaos – was that a good number of the attacks and assassinations were committed by right-wing and extreme right-wing forces.[24]

In the spring of 1936, another event contributed to growing political tensions: Niceto Alcalá Zamora was replaced as President of the Republic, a position he had held since the formation of the Republic in 1931. Profoundly conservative, Alcalá Zamora had worked with the monarchists during the Restoration period, serving in several governments as a minister from the Liberal party. His conservatism might have helped stabilise the tense conditions in the spring of 1936, but instead he was dismissed and replaced by Manuel Azaña. The appointment only made things worse.[25]

Only Catalonia managed to avoid the heightened tensions experienced by the rest of the Republic. In what historians have called the 'Catalan oasis', the only assassinations for political motives were those of the Badía brothers, former police chiefs of the *Generalitat*. The brothers' assassination was attributed to anarchist militants who were 'settling accounts' for the Catalan police's repression of the anarcho-syndicalist movement during the early years of the Republic. In a move unthinkable among conservative forces in the rest of Spain, the *Lliga* initiated a *rapprochement* with the Catalan government in order to negotiate the details of implementing once again the *Llei de Contractes de Conreu*, the source of so much conflict earlier. Secret meetings were held between the *Lliga*'s leader, Francesc Cambó, and President Companys as they attempted to reach an agreement about how to improve the democratic system.[26] With the 26 May change of

---

24. Gil Robles's speech and a record of the entire parliamentary session can be found in the newspaper *La Vanguardia* from the following day (17 June 1936).

25. [TN] Alcalá Zamora was removed from the presidency of the Republic based on a constitutional provision that limited the number of times the President was permitted to call for elections in a single presidential term (six years). However, behind the move in parliament was the fact that he had lost the support of CEDA deputies. In effect, they were punishing him for calling the February elections that they had lost. They had hoped that, instead of calling elections, he would simply appoint Gil Robles as the new Prime Minister. Alcalá Zamora lacked support as well from the Left Republicans and the Socialists, especially after the government's repression in the aftermath of the October 1934 events. There were those who believed at the time, and many who still hold this position, that Manuel Azaña's ascension from Prime Minister to President of the Republic was a grave error and may have contributed to the circumstances that led to war, as the author suggests here.

26. This is the version of events offered by Marcel·lí Moreta, General Secretary of the *Lliga*'s Youth Organisation (Pagès and Pérez 2003, p. 58).

government in Catalonia, Dr. Manuel Corachán y García, a political independent considered by many to be a centrist, was named minister of health and social welfare.[27] According to some witnesses, the Catalan situation was so calm that people feeling unsafe in Madrid travelled to Barcelona, rented apartments, and established their homes there.

But the Catalan social climate was hardly the Arcadian peace that some have described. In the fields, social tensions still ran high, a response to the repression suffered after October 1934. After March, strikes – many of them spontaneous – became more frequent in the cities. The strike movement culminated in June with actions led by commercial workers as well as workers in the port of Barcelona. Also in the spring of 1936, a CNT conference in Zaragoza brought to an end the long-standing division in the CNT's ranks between the revolutionary workers of the anarchist union and the *Treintistas*, a more reformist tendency within the union.

Finally, many workers – not just political theorists like Joaquín Maurín – believed that the Republic's reformist strategies had been exhausted and that the Republicans could not stop the growing fascist threat. They believed, increasingly, that the only way to bring about social change and to defeat the fascists was to prepare for a workers' revolution. In fact, the Republican government found itself increasingly overwhelmed by a situation where it could not control forces either to its right or to its left. The military insurrection of 17 July began during this period of social tension and governmental crisis, dragging the Republic into the most brutal civil war of modern Spanish history.

---

27. [TN] As the Foreword explains, throughout this book, the term 'government', in 'change in government', 'government crisis', or 'forming a new government' usually refers to the cabinet. Particularly during the war of 1936–9, political struggles between parties that made up the governing coalition played out as competition for ministerial appointments. Hence, the author pays special attention to the circumstances behind appointing new ministers throughout the period and offers the details of their political affiliations.

Chapter Two
The Military Uprising and the Failure of the Rebellion

When Spanish troops began to mobilise on 17 July 1936 in colonial Africa, no one expected that a full-scale civil war was about to be unleashed. Even the officers involved in the conspiracy were convinced that their well-prepared and organised attack would overwhelm the enemy as soon as they took control of the Republican capital, Madrid. Besides, their intent was not to question the legitimacy of the Republican system, but instead merely to topple the sitting government. Beyond that, their political objectives were not well defined. Although the military's preparations for the insurrection had been an open secret for a long time, the government of Prime Minister Casares Quiroga, while having been repeatedly informed of the preparations, proved incapable of thwarting the insurrection. Meanwhile, most of the trade unions and political parties associated with the workers' movement were actively preparing for the possibility of a confrontation. On 18 July, Franco in the Canary Islands, Queipo de Llano in Seville, and the leaders of other military fortifications in Andalucía joined the rebellion. On the evening of 19 July, Casares Quiroga resigned his position as prime minister, and on the next day the rebellion spread to most of the garrisons on the peninsula. Although Diego Martínez Barrios, the government's new leader, apparently met with General Emilio Mola to ask the officers to reconsider their plan, in the end the Republican government could not reach a political solution to the crisis.

In Catalonia, the revolt had also been planned far in advance. As early as February 1936, Captain Luis López Valera of the Catalan section of the right-wing Spanish Military Union (*Unión Militar Española*, or UME), had begun preparations for the insurgency. In a few short months, the UME succeeded in branching out to all the Catalan military garrisons. Victory was not certain, however: although the anti-Republican officers were very active, many officers still supported the Republic. In fact, like high-ranking officers in other Republican territories, the Catalan general Francisco Llano de la Encomienda opposed the *coup* preparations. Consequently, the conspirators turned to General Manuel Goded, who, it was decided, would come to Catalonia to lead the rebellion once it had triumphed at his own garrison on the island of Mallorca. In the meantime, Álvaro Fernández Burriel, the Cavalry General, would lead the revolt along with a *junta* of fellow officers.

The officers' extensive preparations for victory can be seen in documents that were found in the home of Captain López Valera after the revolt's failure. These documents show that power would have been given primarily to military personnel in the new government:

Barcelona

Civil Governor: Emeterio Saz Álvarez, Colonel of the Infantry
Mayor: Francisco Isarre Bescós, retired Lieutenant Colonel
President of the City Council: Emilio Pujol Rodríguez, retired Quartermaster Colonel
Chief of Police: Luis López Varela, Captain of Artillery
Chief of Catalan Police (*Mossos d'Esquadra*): Fernando Lizcano de la Rosa, Captain of Infantry
Aerodome Chief: Rafael Botana Salgado, Aviation Commander
Postmaster General: Eduardo González Feijóo, retired Commander of Artillery
Head of Telegraph Administration: Andrés Martínez Uría, retired Commander of Infantry
Director of the Modelo Prison: Alfonso Rojas
Rector of the University: Gonzalo del Castillo Alonso
Head of the armed organisation Civic Union (*Unión Cívica*): Félix Negrete Rabella, retired Commander of Artillery

Girona

Civil Governor: Jesús Martínez Lage, Legal Captain
President of the City Council: Jaume Bartrina Mas, Lawyer
Military Commander: Rafael Sanz Gracia, Colonel of Infantry

Lleida

Mayor: Gabriel Alfambra Echeverría, retired Commander
President of the City Council: Andrés Pérez Pedriviejo, Forestry Corp
President of the Courts: José M. Olmedo, Judge
Chief of Police: Gregorio Villa Tolosa, Commander

Tarragona

Mayor: José Macián Pérez, Lawyer
President of the City Council: Manuel Guasch Fontoba
President of the Courts: José Bravo Mezquida, Judge
Chief of Police: Manuel Gómez, Policeman

The insurgents may have had elaborate plans for victory, but the *Generalitat* was not without friends. The Catalan president, Lluís Companys, had shored up support among the armed forces by appointing military officers to two high positions: Frederic Escofet, who had been sentenced to death and subsequently pardoned for his participation in the events of October 1934, was to be Companys's commissioner of public order, and Vicenç Guarner, a close ally of Escofet and the director of the anti-fascist Republican Military Union (*Unión Militar Republicana Antifascista*), the left-wing counterpart to the UME, was to be his police chief. Furthermore, the Assault and Civil Guards remained loyal. The Civil Guard (*guardia civil*), commanded by General Aranguren, answered directly to the Catalan interior minister (*Consejero de Gobernación*), Josep Maria Espanya. Due to both its traditional role in Spanish and Catalan society and Aranguren's affiliation with the UME, there were doubts about how the Civil Guard would react in the event of a military uprising, but Commissioner Escofet had made every attempt to guarantee Aranguren's loyalty to the Republic as soon as rumours of the revolt surfaced.

Not only was the Catalan military inconsistent in its support for the insurgency, but most of the civil forces also supported the left. The Catalan extreme right had always been insignificant in social terms: their largest contingent, the Traditionalists, could only offer the conspirators around seven hundred men in Barcelona and five thousand in all of Catalonia. Together, the CEDA youth organisation and the monarchists of *Renovación Española* (the party of Calvo Sotelo, who was assassinated just days before the insurrection began) could not muster even two hundred men willing to aid the insurgency. The Spanish fascists of the Phalange could only gather one hundred more.

Among the individuals involved in the conspiracy, some of the more notable were the businessmen Antonio Llopis, who had been president of the *Foment del Treball Nacional* (the Catalan equivalent of a chamber of commerce), and Emilio Juncadella. The conspirators also included Darius Romeu i Freixa, the Baron of Viver, whose estate in Argentona had sometimes served as a meeting place for the conspirators; the Phalangists Josep Maria Fontana Tarats and Josep Maria Poblador; and the Requetés leader, José Maria Cunill.[1] Of course, the *Lliga* did not participate in the military preparations. The military did not trust the *Lliga* because of their Catalan nationalism, which, for many officers, overshadowed the group's social and political conservatism. Most of the *Lliga*'s leaders were completely indifferent to the preparations being made, and they had installed their families in their summer residences, just as they did every year.

Facing this meagre force was a Catalan workers' movement that had spent weeks preparing for a potential military revolt against the Republic. The most powerful organisation among Catalan workers, the CNT, did not yet have the arms for a battle with the military, but it had thousands of combatants ready to fight and willing to take arms from anywhere they could find them. The rest of the organisations on the left, which had formed the *Front d'Esquerres* in February, were equally well prepared, although they did not have the numbers of the anarcho-syndicalists. The indisputable superiority of the civil Republican bloc would become even more evident when, at the moment of truth, far fewer conservative civilians than expected joined the rebellion.

In Catalonia, the failure or success of the insurrection would be decided by what happened in the capital city of Barcelona, the region's economic and political centre and the location of its most important military barracks. While the insurgency's success in Barcelona would predict success throughout Catalonia, the opposite was also true. Failure in Barcelona would doom the uprising in the rest of Catalonia. In the days leading up to the revolt, Captain Escofet tried to ensure the loyalty of the Assault Guard officers, arresting those directly involved in the rebellion and creating a defence strategy that could stop the military as soon as it took to the streets. Escofet's plan was ready by 18 July, when news of the *pronunciamiento*,[2] albeit confused and contradictory, began to spread.

---

1. [TN] The Requetés were a right-wing paramilitary organisation from Navarre, associated with the Carlists. In 1936 they supported the military uprising and joined Franco's Nationalist army *en masse*.

2. [TN] Military *coups* (*pronunciamientos*) in Spain followed a fairly traditional sequence of events from the middle of the nineteenth century until the insurrection of 1936. Even the *Tejerazo*, the Spanish military's last-ditch effort in 1981 to retake power after the transition to democracy, attempted to follow a familiar sequence of events. Barracks in Spain are placed in all of the principal cities, a reality that itself suggests that the modern Spanish military was more designed to police the Spanish population than to protect it from outside attack. In the event of a *pronunciamiento*, officers would lead their troops into the streets, arrest representatives of the government and announce the formation of a provisional (perhaps military) government that would usurp all existing civil powers. Success or failure of the *pronunciamiento* rested on the decision of

Just as it did in the Balearic Islands, Navarre, and Madrid, the military's insurrection in Catalonia began early in the morning on Sunday 19 July. In Barcelona, all regiments and barracks were involved except aviation and supplies (*intendencia*), but even in the rebelling barracks the insurrection was not always supported unanimously. In Tarragona and Manresa, military personnel did not rebel, but the barracks in Lleida, Seu d'Urgell, Girona, Figueres and Mataró all joined the insurgency. In Lleida, a provincial capital in western Catalonia, the army proclaimed martial law and occupied the most important points of the city, including the offices of the *Generalitat*, the Paería Palace (the town hall), the train station, and the radio station, and the Civil Guard closed political party and trade union offices, although they made no arrests.

The circumstances in Lleida allowed the CNT, the UGT and the Local Trade Union Alliance (*Unión Local de Sindicatos*), controlled by the POUM, to form a strike committee and declare a general strike for the next day, Monday, 20 July.[3] Girona, a provincial capital in northeast Catalonia, witnessed a similar sequence of events: after proclaiming martial law, the army occupied the city, and citizens responded that same morning by organising armed groups into an anti-fascist front to confront the military.

In Figueres, a small town between Girona and the French border, the San Fernando Castle barracks revolted, and just up the coast from Barcelona, in Mataró, Colonel Julio Dufoo of the Heavy Artillery Regiment declared war. In Seu d'Urgell, in the Catalan Pyrenees, Colonel Joaquín Blanco Valdés of Mountain Battalion 5 also declared war. While there were also officers involved in the conspiracy in Tarragona, Colonel Ángel Martínez Peñalver refused to rebel.[4]

In Barcelona, the army did what Colonel Escofet had expected: it left the barracks in the outlying areas of the capital and advanced on the city and its centres of power. It looked as if the officers hoped to follow the same plan and repeat their successes of 6 October 1934, when the *Generalitat* surrendered as soon as the first soldiers hit the streets. But conditions were very different in July 1936: in addition to Escofet's forces, the anarcho-syndicalists of Barcelona were ready for anything. They had already formed a Confederated Defence Committee (*Comitè de Defensa Confederal de Barcelona*) with the idea that it would take control

---

individual officers to lead their troops out of the barracks in cities across the country, and for their soldiers to follow. Since failure could mean summary execution, officers had to be confident of the *pronunciamiento*'s overall success before they would be willing to risk the action. Several factors would determine victory or defeat: the number of officers who refused to participate; the number of officers who would actually use their troops to defend the sitting government; or, as was the case in July 1936, these forces joined by the trade unions and left-wing political parties who led their ranks to arm themselves and fight against the insurrection.

3. Barrull i Pelegrí 1986.
4. For Tarragona, see Piqué i Padró 1998.

of working-class resistance in the event of any military actions. Men like Buenaventura Durruti, Juan (Joan) García Oliver, Francesc Ascaso, Gregorio Jover, and Gonzalo Sanz were on this committee, and they would be ready, after only the slightest deployment of troops, to call the anarcho-syndicalists into action.[5] During the night of 18 July, after hearing of the Spanish troop movements in Morocco and in garrisons all over Spain, many worker militants did not return home but instead spent the night closely watching army garrisons or sleeping at party or trade union headquarters. It was no secret that at any moment what was happening all across Spain could happen in Barcelona. President Companys repeatedly refused to arm working-class militants in spite of their pleas throughout the day and night of 18 July.

Nevertheless, many workers were able to use weapons they had kept hidden since the general strike of October 1934.[6] According to Carmel Rosa, a POUM militant, the POUM had hidden arms in a graveyard, while the anarchists had gathered arms tossed into the sewers by the militants of *Estat Català* after the failure of Companys's insurrection.[7] As a result, the insurgents had to confront not only the forces organised by Escofet, but also a significant number of armed militant workers. When more firearms became an absolute necessity, CNT

---

5. See Juan (Joan) García Oliver's memoirs *El eco de los pasos* (García Oliver 1978).
6. Here is the version of that evening's events offered by the daily publication issued by the *Generalitat*-president's office, the *Crònica diària*:
All night long the trade union and left-wing party buildings were filled with workers, and in every corner one could hear pistols being taken apart, cleaned, and greased while workers debated their efficacy. On the Ramblas, workers gathered under the night sky to await the latest news. Meanwhile, messengers hurried from one party building to the next, passing on *communiqués* and issuing warnings. The military garrisons were being watched by workers and by soldiers loyal to the government.
In spite of all their preparations, workers and their leaders knew that they did not have enough firearms, and so the Communists and Socialists sent a delegation to the government ministry offices around 3 a.m. on the morning of the nineteenth in order to request additional arms. Captain Meana intervened in order to show that there were no arms at the ministry. Meana was speaking the truth, since in the early hours of 19 July, official public forces had gone around to various armouries gathering arms. These were then deposited at the Ministry of Public Order (*Comisaría General de Orden Público*).
At 3:30 a.m. the petition was repeated, this time by CNT militants. The anarchist contingent was required to speak with Señor Espanya, and afterwards the anarchist leaders, among them García Oliver, spoke to their militants from the balcony of the ministry, where they instructed their members to occupy their respective positions on the barricades. After listening to their leaders, the anarchists departed in the same cars and trucks in which they had arrived. Later, the demand for arms was made by a group from *Estat Català*, who, like those before them, had to be convinced that no arms were being distributed because there were none at the ministry.
7. See Pagès and Pérez 2003, pp. 68–9.

militants stormed the city's armouries, especially the Beristain Armory on the Ramblas and those on various ships anchored in Barcelona's port. Early on Sunday, 19 July, as soon as the army began to take to the streets, sirens sounded on the boats in the port and in the factories. According to Juan García Oliver, one of the most well-known anarchist leaders, the insurgents' opponents had agreed that the sirens would be their signal to move into action.[8]

Activists positioned themselves behind barricades around the city and entered into skirmishes with the army. According to the version of events offered by the *Crónica diària*, a report published daily in Catalan by the office of the president of the *Generalitat*, the first troops to take to the streets were those of the Tenth Infantry, from the Bruc barracks in Pedralbes, and the Tenth Cavalry Regiment, from the Numancia barracks in Hostafrancs. Beginning around five o'clock in the morning, the remaining barracks in the city joined the uprising, including the Ninth Cavalry from the Girona barracks on Travessera and Comercio streets, the Seventh Light Artillery on *Sant Andreu* street, the Miner and Excavation Battalion from the Lepanto barracks on Corts-Catalanes-Hospitalet street, and the Atarazanas Arsenal and artillery barracks.[9]

The first confrontations occurred on the *Plaça de Catalunya* – Barcelona's main square – with soldiers who had come from the Pedralbes barracks. At *Cinc d'Oros Plaça*, where the *Paseo de Gracia* and Diagonal Avenue meet, Assault Guards and a fair number of civilians stopped three squadrons that had come from the Travesera barracks. This was also the first victory of the day: the battle lasted for nearly two hours until the soldiers were forced to retreat. Soon afterwards, fighting broke out on the *Plaça d'Espanya*, which had been occupied by a group of soldiers from the Cavalry Regiment on Tarragona street. Another group of soldiers made their way down the major thoroughfare of Paralelo Avenue, but they were blocked by a contingent of anarchists at the *Brecha de San Pablo*. A third group of soldiers occupied the *Plaça de la Universitat*, where they were soon isolated. Fifty artillery soldiers who had made their way from the *Sant Andreu* barracks toward the *Plaça de Catalunya* were routed by Assault Guards and citizens at the intersection of Diagonal Avenue and Balmes.

On Icaria Avenue, near the port, mountain artillery soldiers with orders to take control of the government ministry on *Plaça Palau* and then move on to the *Generalitat* were confronted by groups of guards and workers, who themselves had built barricades in the streets to block the soldiers' progress. On these barricades, the soldiers suffered their first important defeat: after a few hours of battle, they succumbed to the militant workers and lost all of their military hardware.

---

8. García Oliver 1978, pp. 172–3.
9. *Crònica diària*, 19 July 1936.

In the Example, the city centre, the military's situation was getting worse. Some soldiers scattered, abandoning their firearms as they fled. Colonel Francisco Lacasa and his soldiers were forced to retreat into the *Carmelitas* Convent, where they resisted until the next day, and the army's losses in the *Plaça de Catalunya* were significant. General Llano de la Encomienda, who had not joined the uprising, continued giving orders and making telephone calls against the revolt, contributing to the lack of coordination among the insurgent troops. Initial air-attacks on army barracks coming from Prat Airport, ordered by the loyalist Colonel Felipe Díaz Sandino, further demoralised the insurgents.

Meanwhile, the anarchists were taking advantage of the rifles and machine-guns that had been abandoned by or taken from the soldiers they had defeated. Since President Companys – who on Escofet's advice had taken refuge in the police station – had repeatedly denied arms to the anarchists, many of them had begun a siege of the *Maestranza de Sant Andreu* barracks, where a large number of arms were stashed. Beginning in the early hours of the morning, the anarcho-syndicalists had also laid siege to the Atarazanas barracks, where, thanks to sergeants Gordo and Manzana, they had succeeded in getting hold of more arms. Meanwhile, General Manuel Goded was making his way from Palma de Mallorca to take over command of the uprising as planned. When he arrived at military headquarters, Goded arrested Llano de la Encomienda and attempted to set things on the right track. But the battle was already nearly lost, and Goded's only hope was for the Civil Guard to join the insurgents. That hope was dashed, however, when at two o'clock in the afternoon a regiment of the Civil Guard, reinforced by soldiers from the quartermaster and led by Colonel Escobar, moved down *Via Laietana* Avenue towards the *Plaça de Catalunya* to defeat the rebellion once and for all.

From this point on, everything happened quickly. At the *Plaça de la Universitat* and the *Plaça de Catalunya*, the soldiers surrendered before mid-afternoon. Soon afterwards, Goded surrendered at the headquarters. *La Crònica* offers an account of the events:

> At around 5 o'clock in the afternoon, an attack on the General Command of the Fourth Organic Division was organised. Various groups of Republicans, workers, and citizens, under the command of Colonel Moreno, established the siege on Command Headquarters, which was bombarded by the same artillery that had been confiscated from the factious soldiers of the rebellion. Even though the battle lasted less than an hour, it was bloody and fierce. Seeing they had no way to resist the siege, and knowing that the rebellion had failed in the rest of the city, the factious soldiers raised the flag of surrender on the central balcony of the building at 6 o'clock in the afternoon. Loyal forces then entered Command Headquarters and took Goded prisoner, as well as the

other officials who accompanied him. Goded was transferred to the Palace of the *Generalitat*. When he was arrested, Goded was wearing his military uniform, covered with medals earned during the intrigue, and a sash around his waist. He was cynically smoking a cigarette when Moreno, Lieutenant Colonel of the Civil Guard, arrested him. It proved difficult to keep the soldiers from executing him right there. Meanwhile, General Aranguren, who had been loyal to the government from the beginning, took over Command Headquarters.[10]

When he arrived at the *Generalitat*, Goded was ordered by Companys, the Catalan President, to announce his surrender on the radio. His final message – intended for the troops that were under his command – had an immeasurable psychological effect: 'My luck has been adverse; if you wish to avoid the spilling of blood, you are released from your obligations to me as your commander'. Even though everything was virtually decided at this point, there was still some resistance at the Atarazanas barracks, the offices of military governance, and the Carmelite convent, all of which surrendered on the following day. The last violent combat took place during the first hours of the morning of 20 July, and it forced the surrender of the soldiers in the Atarazanas barracks:

> At around 8 o'clock in the morning, forces of the rebellion that had been defeated at the end of the *Ramblas* and forced back into the Atarazanas barracks (*Maestranza de Artillería*) on the previous day began firing upon citizens and forces loyal to the government from inside the building. In response, these forces, joined by others from the police, returned their fire and organised a new attack on the *Maestranza*. After two hours of intense fighting, the soldiers under siege faked a surrender and then fired their machine guns on the loyalist fighters as they moved closer to the building. The casualties included a captain of the Assault Guard, four Civil Guards, and various citizens, among them a representative of the Catalan Parliament, Amadeu Colldeforns, and his father; the CNT syndicalist leader Francesc Ascaso; an elector for President of the Republic; Enric Fontbernat, brother of the city representative Josep; and a high-ranking employee of the Department of Labour, Jové Brufau.
>
> Outrage at the soldiers' trickery and the resulting bloodshed led the loyal forces to attack the rebels all the harder until they completely defeated them around midday. This final attack was perhaps the bloodiest of the entire fight. It was necessary to use both artillery and aviation in order to defeat the insurgents, and their casualties were numerous, with many soldiers and almost all the officers dying. In the middle of everything it was necessary to confront a

---

10. *Crònica diària*, 19 July 1936.

group of factious soldiers who were shooting loyalists with machine guns from the cupola of the monument to Christopher Columbus.[11]

This final battle was particularly tragic, but the insurgents' defeat in Barcelona was decisive in driving the rest of Catalonia's rebel troops back into their barracks. News of the military's defeat in Barcelona even served to undermine the morale of soldiers involved in the uprising beyond Catalonia.

According to some historians, deaths from the two days of fighting numbered around four hundred and fifty, with approximately two thousand injured.[12] Newspapers from 5 August and including casualties from 2 August, however, indicate that in Barcelona alone there were 511 deaths from the events of 19 and 20 July. Of those, 193 still had not been identified. Among the victims, civilians suffered the worst casualties, with nearly three hundred members of the different workers' organisations killed.[13] In addition to the casualties at the Atarazanas barracks, leaders killed during the fighting included Germinal Vidal, secretary of the Iberian Communist Youth (*Juventud Comunista Ibérica*), the youth organisation of the POUM, who died in fighting at the *Plaça de la Universitat*; and Enrique Obregón Blanco, secretary of the Local Barcelona Federation of Anarchist Groups (*Federación Local de Grupos Anarquistas de Barcelona*), who died while fighting at the telephone exchange building (the *Telefónica*).

But 19 July was not just important because of the victory over the military: it also represented the critical moment when power was transferred to the streets – in other words, when the popular movement took effective control of Barcelona. More than that of any other group, the anarchists' contribution to the fighting had been decisive, and their final assault on the *Sant Andreu Maestranza* barracks put an end to the army's plot and brought them political and military hegemony. Although some commentators have claimed that the Civil Guard and other security forces were the decisive players in the army's defeat, it was the citizens and their popular organisations that played the most important role in the victory over the army. At the beginning of the fight, the weakness of the security forces was apparent. As Chief of Police Vicenç Guarner wrote, 'In our inferiority, the "iron will of our armed squads" was nothing more than modest metal shavings... The attitude of the Civil Guard was uncertain, and the local squads were militarily poorly trained... The outlook could not have been more distressing'.[14] Meanwhile, the worker's political parties and trade unions, above

---

11. *Crònica diària*, 20 July 1936.
12. *Crònica diària*, 20 July 1936.
13. *La Vanguardia*, 5 August 1936.
14. Vicenç Guarner 1980, pp. 66–7.

all the CNT, offered up thousands of men ready for whatever was necessary to defeat the uprising. In the end, and often paying with their own lives, they succeeded.

For their efforts, the workers' organisations, especially the CNT, capitalised on a victory that created such an imbalance in favour of popular power that nobody dared challenge them. The almost complete disappearance of the army – which became definitive after the Republican Government made the controversial decision to discharge all soldiers fulfilling their obligations as conscripts[15] – and the fraternisation that had occurred between Civil Guards and the workers during the day's fighting contributed to the victory of the popular forces. Similarly, the new military hegemony of the workers' movement was duplicated in a matter of hours on the social, political and economic terrain, creating the circumstances for one of the most profound social revolutions in modern history.

By 19 and 20 July, it was already possible to assess the successes and failures of the military insurrection. Just as they had in Catalonia, the military failed in Madrid, Santander, Vizcaya, Guipúzcoa, New Castile, the Mancha and Badajoz – with the exception of small nuclei in Toledo and the city of Albacete. The military also suffered defeat in Murcia, eastern Andalucía, and Menorca. In the region of Valencia, the outcome was not decided until the end of July, when it favoured the Republic. The military was victorious without resistance, however, in most of the cities of Old Castille, Burgos, Soria, Segovia and Ávila, the islands of Mallorca and Ibiza, the provinces of León, the Carlist-dominated Navarre and Álava, the three capital cities of Aragón, and Galicia. In Asturias, the military only triumphed in the capital city itself, Oviedo. In Extremadura, it was victorious in the province of Cáceres, and in Andalucía, in the provincial capitals of Sevilla, Granada, Córdoba, Huelva, and Cádiz.

The balance sheet of the insurrection saw Spain divided into two unequal zones, sharply separated both militarily and socially: the large areas of primarily rural and agrarian Spain, now under the control of the insurgent military, and the zones still controlled by Republican Spain, including many of the larger industrial cities of the country. Significantly, the Republicans had only maintained

---

15. On 18 July, the government made the following decree: 'All soldiers whose companies have participated in the uprising against the legally constituted republican government are hereby discharged of their duties'. This decree had a negative effect, especially among the troops in companies that had remained faithful to the Republic. Other actions adopted by the government on 18 July in response to the military insurrection included the decree declaring 'the annulment of martial law (*estado de guerra*) on the Peninsula, Morocco, the Balearic Islands, and the Canary Islands, all the places where it had previously been declared' and dissolving 'all the army units that take part in the insurrection'. See the *Diario Oficial del Ministro de la Guerra*, 19 July 1936.

control over their zone through popular opposition and the determined resistance of workers. In the end, between these two Spains the insurrection had sparked a full-scale civil war, a military struggle that was also social, political, and ideological, and that would prove almost immediately to be of international significance. And yet, from the perspective of July 1936, the duration of the war was still hard to predict.

Chapter Three
Political Transformations: the Crisis of the *Generalitat* and the Formation of the Militia Committees

The most important consequence of the 19 July movement in Catalonia was the sudden rise of the armed masses, and with this transfer of power to the streets came a socio-political disintegration that took any real authority or strength from the Republic's official institutions. By 20 July, everything had changed, and it was patently clear that Catalonia was facing civil war. But many workers and peasants also saw that they were facing a great opportunity – that of carrying out the social revolution they had longed for. Paradoxically, the military officers leading the uprising on 19 and 20 July had claimed that their actions were necessary in order to prevent social revolution, and yet their actions created the very conditions for such a revolution to begin. And it was the CNT that benefitted most, since in just a few short hours they had replaced the moderate *Esquerra* party to become the region's new dominant political force.

Although the ruling *Esquerra* had been greatly weakened by the aftermath of the general strike of 6 October 1934, it regained some of its former strength in the February 1936 elections. Both during July's military uprising and throughout the early period of the revolution, however, the *Esquerra* proved unable to control events. The radicalisation of land and urban workers had gradually stripped the *Esquerra* of its influence over two of its recent allies: the *Rabassaires*, the most important organisation in the Catalan fields, founded in 1922 by Lluís Companys, and the Catalan Socialist Union (*Unió Socialista de Catalunya*), comprising social democrats that were both socialist and Catalan nationalists. Both organisations were radicalising on the eve of the Civil War, with the Catalan Socialists in particular forging alliances with the Catalan Marxists. The radicalisation of the Catalan workers and their organisations explains why the moderate *Esquerra* was losing its influence and thus the ability to respond effectively during Catalonia's July days.

Catalonia's political panorama was complicated even further by this third political force: Marxism. Catalan Marxism had done everything in its power during the years of the Second Republic to win the CNT away from the influence of anarchism, but the Marxists themselves were anything but homogeneous. In fact, there were numerous organisations, in addition to the Catalan Socialist Union, that considered themselves to be Marxist organisations: the Workers and Peasants' Bloc (*Bloc Obrer i Camperol*, or BOC), the Catalan Federation of the PSOE, the Catalan Communist Party (*Partit Comunista de Catalunya*), the Communist Left (*Izquierda Comunista*), and the Catalan Proletarian Party (*Partit Català Proletari*), a small organisation that had come out of the Catalan independence-movement. After October 1934, however, the Marxists took seriously the need to unify into a single party. The moderate success of the Workers' Alliance (*Alianza Obrera*) throughout 1934 had created the circumstances for *rapprochement*, and, conscious of the new historical circumstances, all of the Marxist organisations believed in the profound importance of winning the Catalan working class away from the control of the Iberian Anarchist Federation (*Federación Anarquista Ibérica*, or FAI).[1]

The Catalan Marxist organisations began unity discussions in January 1935, but only the BOC and the *Izquierda Comunista* agreed to join forces. Since its creation in 1930, the BOC had been led by Joaquín Maurín, and in many respects it embodied the Catalan Marxist movement. *Izquierda Comunista* was a small Trotskyist organisation led by Andreu Nin. On 29 September 1935, the BOC and *Izquierda Comunista* united to form the Workers' Party of Marxist Unification (*Partido Obrero de Unificación Marxista*, POUM). From that moment until war broke out in July 1936, the POUM was the largest and most influential Marxist party in Catalonia, and it was led by Spain's leading Marxist theoreticians, Andreu Nin and Joaquín Maurín, both of whom had significant international reputations. The newly formed POUM considered itself a revolutionary party

---

1. [TN] When Hitler took power in Germany in 1933, the BOC initiated an attempt to unify all the revolutionary worker and peasant organisations into a single alliance to fight the rise of fascism in Spain. Along with the BOC, several other socialist, communist, and anarchist organisations signed on to this *Alianza Obrera*, but not the CNT.

that was both Leninist and anti-Stalinist. Espousing a critical Marxism free from any obligations to international organisations, the POUM defended the need for democratic and socialist revolution as well as the need for organising throughout the entire Republican territory, not just in Catalonia.[2]

The other organisations that had initially discussed merging with the BOC and *Izquierda Comunista* – the Catalan Socialist Union (*Unió Socialista de Catalunya*), the Catalan Proletarian Party (*Partit Català Proletari*), the Catalan Communist Party (*Partit Comunista de Catalunya*), and the PSOE's Catalan Federation[3] – reconvened discussions among themselves, but on a slower path, only finally coming together as the Unified Socialist Party of Catalonia (*Partit Socialista Unificat de Catalunya*, or PSUC on 24 July 1936, after the war had already begun. The new organisation, a fruit of the Popular Front's electoral victory in February 1936, was strictly a Catalan formation, and it was controlled by Moscow and the Communist International. Its political programme was generically anti-fascist, following the International's popular-front strategies, and it championed democracy without prioritising socialist revolution.[4]

Of course, when the military rebellion was defeated in Catalonia on 20 July, the PSUC did not yet exist. In any case, neither the POUM nor the four organisations that would soon form the PSUC were strong enough to challenge the hegemony of the CNT. At the same time, they were not so weak that they could be entirely ignored. On 20 July, then, Catalan Governor Lluís Companys called in representatives of all the parties that had signed up to the Popular Front electoral alliance (in Catalonia, the *Front d'Esquerres*). Knowing that the *Generalitat* had practically no power, and that Spain was heading toward revolution, Companys called the meeting in order to find a way of governing an increasingly un-governable Catalonia. Because of the CNT's overwhelming strength, the ability to reach any agreement depended on the anarchists. The CNT's leaders would undoubtedly want recognition for the power they had gained through their role in defeating the military – especially for suppressing the revolt in the *Maestranza de Sant Andreu* barracks, which resulted in workers gaining access to arms. Their victory on the streets of Barcelona had fundamentally changed the balance of political power, and now it was the Catalan *Generalitat* whose legitimacy was being challenged.

---

2. There is a growing bibliography on the POUM and the two principal leaders of the party. On Nin, see Pagès 1975, Pagès 2011, Bonamusa 1977, and Solano 2006. On Maurín, see Rourera 1992, Bonsón 1994, and Riottot 2004. On the BOC, see Durgan 1996.

3. [TN] The PSOE's Catalan Federation was led by Joan Comorera, secretary of the *Unió Socialista*, which, as has already been mentioned, was breaking away from the influence of the *Esquerra*.

4. On the creation of the PSUC, see Martin 1977. There is only one history of the PSUC during the Civil War: by Josep Puigsech (Puigsech 2001).

By bringing together representatives of the workers' organisations, Companys hoped to make room for them in the *Generalitat*. For Companys, this union of forces would be the ideal solution to the political uncertainty caused by the military rebellion and the workers' response to it; furthermore, it had the advantage of being legal, a move made possible by the Republican constitution. But Companys was aware of the anarchists' customary refusal to participate in bourgeois governments due to their theoretical opposition to state power. He was also aware that his own negotiating position was weak, since it was actually the anarchists who controlled the situation. The meeting was held, in the end, with the participation of a delegation of anarchists including García Oliver, Durruti, Josep Asens, Aurelio Fernández and Diego Abad de Santillán. Although the various accounts of this meeting differ in details, all versions concur that Companys acknowledged that the anarcho-syndicalists were the true masters of the situation in Catalonia, that he took blame for past repression of the anarchists (which he had personally ordered on more than one occasion), and that he offered himself up to them to be used as they wished. He then proposed the creation of a new organ of power that would include all the anti-fascist forces of Catalonia and that would act as a true government.

The proposal must have surprised the anarchists. In his memoirs, García Oliver affirmed that 'at that time, Companys was considered the counterrevolution. We anarcho-syndicalists of the CNT were fighting for libertarian communism'.[5] Companys's proposal was taken to the CNT, whose local and district (*comarcal*) committees had been meeting since the evening of 20 July. The decision to collaborate with Companys and the rest of the anti-fascist forces seems to have been made by the CNT's regional committee on the night of July 20, at the insistence of Federica Montseny, Diego Abad de Santillán, and Mariano Rodríguez Vázquez (*'Marianet'*). In effect, the local and district committees simply ratified the decision made by the regional committee. Whatever the actual details of the decision process, the fact of the matter is that the CNT had made the momentous decision to renounce its own political hegemony and its plans for a new social organisation in order to collaborate in a new body, the Central Committee of Anti-fascist Militias of Catalonia (*Comitè Central de Milícies Antifeixistes de Catalunya*).

Years later, García Oliver, who had opposed the decision, gave this explanation for the CNT-FAI's decision:

> The CNT and the FAI opted for collaboration and [bourgeois] democracy and renounced revolutionary totality, a decision that would lead to the strangling of the anarchist, confederal revolution. They trusted the word of a democrat

---

5. García Oliver 1978, p. 178.

and helped keep Companys in power as president of the *Generalitat*. They accepted the Anti-fascist Militias Committee and the proportional representation of forces that made up the Committee, and, even though it was not fair, they gave the UGT and the Socialist Party, who represented a minority in Catalonia, the same number of seats as the victorious anarchists. This representational distribution was a sacrifice on the part of the anarchists, and it was designed to steer the revolutionary parties onto the path of loyal collaboration and to prevent disturbances based on suicidal competitiveness.[6]

On 21 July, the *Generalitat* provided the new Central Committee of Anti-fascist Militias of Catalonia with a veneer of legality by decreeing it in the Official Bulletin of the *Generalitat* (*Butlletí Oficial de la Generalitat*). The Anti-fascist Committee members were Asens, Durruti, and García Oliver from the CNT; Fernández and Abad de Santillán from the FAI; José del Barrio, Salvador González Albadalejo, and Antonio López Raimundo from the UGT; Artemi Aiguader, Jaume Miravitlles, and Joan Pons from the *Esquerra*; Josep Miret Musté for the *Unió Socialista de Catalunya*; Tomàs Fàbregues from the ACR, a small organisation that followed the *Esquerra*; Josep Torrents from the *Rabassaires*; and Josep Rovira from the POUM. On the same day, the Anti-fascist Committee, reflecting Catalonia's new revolutionary situation, passed its first resolutions:

1. Revolutionary order has been established, and all member organisations of the Anti-fascist Committee will defend it.
2. To maintain order and vigilance, the Committee has established teams to enforce rigorous compliance with its orders. The teams will carry credentials to establish their authority.
3. These teams will be the only ones that operate officially on behalf of the Committee. Anyone operating without the Committee's official sanction will be charged with aiding and abetting the uprising and will suffer whatever sanctions the Committee deems necessary.
4. Night teams will be especially rigorous against those attempting to challenge revolutionary order.
5. From one o'clock until five o'clock in the morning, movement in the streets will be restricted to the following:
    a. all those carrying proper credentials from one of the member organisations of the Anti-fascist Committee.
    b. anyone accompanied by someone with credentials that can vouch for his or her moral reliability.

---

6. Ibid.

c. those who can justify their movement as a response to *force majeure* or other unforeseeable circumstances.
6. In order to recruit to the anti-fascist militias, member organisations of the Committee are granted authorisation to open enlisting and training centres.
7. Given the need to create a revolutionary order for combating fascist cells, the Committee hopes that there will be no need to demand compliance or to resort to disciplinary measures.[7]

Meanwhile, the Anti-fascist Committee assigned duties as follows: Jaume Miravitlles was named Secretary General and was in charge of publicity (print and radio), but he was later replaced by Llorenç Perramon; Francesc Durán Rossell and Marcos Alcón were put in charge of transportation, replacing Durruti when he left for the front; García Oliver was in charge of the War Commission, which in turn had two sub-committees, one for supplies, headed by Torrents, and the other for health, headed by Aiguader. Rafael Vidiella and Fernández were put in charge of the Investigation Commission; patrols and public order was assigned to Asens, Fàbregues and González; militia organisation went to Josep Tarradellas and was divided into two sub-committees, one for Barcelona and one for the provinces. Tarradellas also served as the *Generalitat*'s representative on the Anti-fascist Committee.[8] Throughout the months that the Committee existed, the person who most dominated and imposed his own personality on it was undoubtedly García Oliver.

In creating the Anti-fascist Committee, all the anti-fascist organisations of Catalonia had essentially agreed to form a new centre of power able to respond to the demands of war and revolution. The Committee's organisational structure was intended to address the rather abrupt change in the balance of social and political power after the 'July days'. Many have described the resulting situation as one of 'dual power', with the Anti-fascist Committee exercising real power while the government of the *Generalitat* still existed in name. In fact, the Committee allowed the *Generalitat* to continue governing in some areas, like finances, though the Committee still exercised influence in this area. But in the most important and urgent areas, such as the war, the creation of the militias that were sent to the Aragon front, and the expedition sent from Catalonia to the island of Mallorca, the Anti-fascist Committee was in charge.

The creation of the Anti-fascist Committee in Barcelona was echoed in many of the largest towns of Catalonia, independent of their local governments. Hoping

---

7. *La Vanguardia*, 22 July 1936. This account in *La Vanguardia* coincides with that of the *Crònica diària* for 21 July 1936.
8. The organisational chart of the Committee was published in *La Publicitat* on 2 August 1936.

to guarantee the continuity of local governments, the *Generalitat* issued a decree on 22 July dismissing the city council representatives that had not been elected on the lists of the Popular Front. Since this effectively eliminated representatives from the right, local council control passed to the left, even when these councils were devoid of members from the CNT and the FAI. Decrees from the *Generalitat* could not keep up with the pace of events, however, and numerous local anti-fascist committees sprang up to assume power at the local level. In short, the political revolution advocated by the CNT-FAI was growing tremendously, moving beyond the *Generalitat*'s control.[9]

In Catalonia's provincial capitals, local committees were quickly taking power. On 6 August, the Anti-fascist Front Committee (*Comitè del Front Antifeixista*) was formed in Tarragona with three activists from the CNT, three from the UGT, and one each from the FAI, the *Esquerra*, and the POUM. In Girona, the *Comité Antifascista*, presided over by the anarchist Expedit Duran and the *Esquerra*'s Miquel Santaló, began functioning towards the end of July. In Lleida, a popular committee was formed and presided over by the POUM leader Sebastià Garsaball. This committee oversaw the police department, headed up by Josep Rodes of the POUM, as well as the *Generalitat*'s representative, Joaquim Vilà from the UGT. At the end of July and beginning of August, in Sabadell, Terrassa, Manresa, Badalona, Figueres, Tortosa, and practically all of Catalonia, similar bodies were formed and given names as diverse as 'Committee of Public Health', 'Revolutionary Committee', 'Popular Committee', and 'Revolutionary *Junta*', etc. Whatever their name, they always reflected the new social hegemony that had been created by the popular reaction to the military uprising. Though all anti-fascist organisations took part, the committees were dominated by the organisations of the working class.[10]

In order for the unfolding political revolution to consolidate its gains, it would be crucial to centralise the new political power being exercised by the myriad committees with a structure that could enable its spread into different prov-

---

9. [TN] Although the CNT did not campaign for abstention in the February elections as they had in the 1933 elections, and as had been their traditional approach to all elections, they did remain consistent in not providing candidates for the Popular Front lists. Effectively, the Republican *Generalitat*'s attempt to reconstitute city governments based on electoral lists left the anarchists without representation. This was not simply a way of eliminating the right-wing supporters of the military rebellion from city governments of the smaller towns and cities of Catalonia, but quite possibly a move to shore up support for Republicans *vis à vis* the revolutionary anarchists. Of course, as in Barcelona itself, these governments still had to contend with the power of the anarchists in the new local committees.

10. For Tarragona, see Piqué 1998. For Girona, see Cercle d'Estudis Històrics i Socials 1986. And for Lleida, see Sagués 2003. On all of the Catalan revolutionary committees, see Josep Antoni Pozo González's doctoral thesis, presented in June 2002 (Pozo González 2002).

inces. Therefore, on 2 August, the Anti-fascist Committee in Barcelona pushed for the creation of regional committees, the Regional Committees of Anti-fascist Militias (*Comitès Comarcals de Milícies Antifeixistes*). These committees would watch over the creation of local committees, solve problems that could be handled without the intervention of the Anti-fascist Committee in Barcelona, and help inform the central committee about recruitment and military organisation. To coordinate the regional committees, the Anti-fascist Committee created the Commission of Regional Militias (*Comissió de Milícies Comarcals*), which in the first few weeks of its existence proved extremely active: we know that it played a role in the creation of many local committees (some eight hundred different local committees were formed), it sent out delegations to verify that its decrees were being followed, and it centralised the recruitment of militia members in the provinces as much as possible. As Oriol Nel·lo has shown in his study of the local government in Girona during the first months of the war, the Anti-fascist Committee defined its organisational jurisdiction by using for the first time territorial divisions that had originally been elaborated in 1933, during the first reformist years of the Second Republic, which provided for thirty-seven regional, rather than provincial, divisions.[11]

In just a few short weeks after the beginning of the war, then, political power in Catalonia had experienced a substantial upheaval. The Anti-fascist Committee was acting like a genuine government, taking on responsibilities in all aspects of political, economic, and social life. Meanwhile, local committees were taking on all the functions of local administration. Paradoxically, the *Generalitat*, led by Companys, continued to exist, just as the local governments continued to exist. This explains why political power in Catalonia in the first months of the war is often described, as we saw earlier, as 'dual power', or power simultaneously exercised by two separate institutions. In practice, however, the two different governments did not exercise equal political weight. The *Generalitat* owed its legitimacy to the Republican political order prior to the outbreak of war, but it was the Anti-fascist Committee that controlled all the mechanisms of political, social, and economic life in Catalonia. The *Generalitat*, at least until the month of September, had become strictly decorative.

The committees' power would soon cause problems. According to the CNT-FAI, the committees' existence would ensure the success of the revolution. In their view, the outbreak of war had sparked a revolution that nobody could stop and from which there was no possible return. The POUM, even though it had its own interpretation of the character of the revolution and the role of political power, agreed with the CNT that the revolution had to further the conquests it

---

11. See Nel·lo 1986.

had already made. The moderates, however, never supported the proliferation of committees, much less the acceleration of the revolutionary process. Instead, they were dragged along by circumstances, forced to accept the conditions set by the anarchists, while envisioning a social programme that did not go beyond what today we would call social democracy. Francesc Macià, an *Esquerra* member who had been the Prime Minister of the *Generalitat* until he died on Christmas in 1933, defined what he saw as the social ideal for the Catalan people with his famous phrase '*la caseta i l'hortet*' (a little house and a garden). But given the political pressures of the revolution in Catalonia in July and August 1936, the *Esquerra* had little choice but to follow along. Hence, they would adopt the strategy of doing whatever they could to mitigate the revolution's excesses and moderate its ultimate aims.

The *Esquerra* was joined in its project of curbing the revolution by another republican party, the small Catalan Republican Action (*Acció Catalana Republicana*, or ACR), and they were both soon aided by the recently founded PSUC. In contrast to the CNT-FAI and the POUM, the PSUC believed it was necessary to channel the revolution into more moderate, strictly bourgeois-democratic aims, with the goal of defending republican institutions for the war effort. This was the political line coming from Moscow *via* the Communist International. But at the end of July 1936, the PSUC was still a small organisation. Even though it controlled the Catalan section of the UGT – which was about to experience spectacular growth – and had begun to influence some peasant sectors thanks to its relationship with the *Rabassaires*, it could not come close to challenging the strength of the CNT.

Although the circumstances were far from ideal, the *Esquerra*, ACR, and PSUC soon began to work against the committees and for the full establishment of republican institutions. This was the goal of the *Generalitat*'s new government, which was established on 31 July with Joan Casanovas as Prime Minister (*conseller primer*). The PSUC was given three ministries: Joan Comorera was appointed Economic Minister, Rafael Vidiella (who had been a member of the CNT and who would later join the Catalan Federation of the PSOE) became Communications Minister, and Estanislau Ruiz Ponseti (a former member, like Comorera, of the *Unió Socialista*) became Minister of Supplies. President Companys hoped to expand the social base of the *Generalitat* and to gradually encroach upon the power of the Anti-fascist Committee. The formation of this government, however, was blocked by the CNT-FAI, which was still the dominant political force in Catalonia and which threatened to leave the Anti-fascist Committee if representatives of the PSUC were appointed to the *Generalitat*. In fact, the new government had not even met when on 6 August a new government was formed that excluded the PSUC. This government comprised strictly republican parties.

Still presided over by Joan Casanovas, it had Martí Esteve i Guau (from the ACR) as Finance Minister, Josep Calvet i Mora (from the *Rabassaires*) as Minister of Agriculture and Supplies, Lieutenant Colonel Felip Díaz Sandino as Defence Minister, and the following positions all filled by members of *Esquerra*: Josep Quero Molares as Minister of Justice, Josep M. Espanya i Sirat as Minister of the Interior, Ventura Gassol i Rovira as the Minister of Culture, Pere Mestres i Albet as Public Works Minister, Lluís Prunés i Sató as Labour Minister, Josep Tarradellas i Joan as Economic and Public Services Minister, Martí Rouret i Callol as Health Minister, and Joan Puig i Ferreter as Minister of Social Services.

As in other areas of the Republic, power was deeply fragmented in Catalonia during July and August, and the question of state power became a primary concern for all the Catalan political forces. Meanwhile, different understandings of the war and revolution further divided these forces. The CNT-FAI and the POUM saw the revolution as the way to win the war: in other words, the revolution was of paramount importance. The POUM differed from the CNT-FAI in that they considered it necessary to crown the revolution with the creation of a workers' government, one that would reflect the new social relations and that would be genuinely socialist and democratic. Andreu Nin, the most important leader of the POUM once Joaquín Maurín had been trapped and ultimately jailed in a zone controlled by the insurgents, gave the following statement about the POUM's position at a meeting in Barcelona:

> A strong government will be necessary: this is the general sense of Spain's masses. We need a strong government, but, of course, not a strong government in the sense given to these words by the bourgeois forces of the previous period. We need a strong government, one given the maximum authority necessary to give confidence to the working masses and one prepared to take the fight to the furthest consequences... For that reason, we hold that, in the current situation, the only government that can respond to this situation is a government without bourgeois ministers – in other words, a workers' government.[12]

The PSUC and the *Esquerra*, in contrast, defined the war as one between fascism and republican democracy. It would be necessary, from their perspective, to put an end to the 'detestable pseudo-revolution' (*sarampión seudorrevolucionario*) that only offered chaos and confusion. More explicitly than the *Esquerra*, the PSUC maintained that the problem of state power was one of authority:

---

12. These words were expressed in a meeting in Barcelona's *Gran Price* on 6 September 1936, and they were published in a pamphlet called *El POUM ante la revolución española* ['The POUM and the Spanish Revolution'] in 1936. See POUM 1936.

the existence of the committees implied, according to their newspaper *Treball*, 'barricaded highways' and 'cars with armed people who, under the pretext of protecting the revolution, foment terror in whatever regions or towns they pass through'.[13] Hence, the PSUC maintained that dual power must be ended and the authority of the *Generalitat* reimposed. In order for the *Generalitat* to govern, though, its cabinet needed to represent the forces in the street: legitimacy could only be gained with the participation of the CNT-FAI.

This problem of representation was shared by all the Republican zones not already controlled by the insurgents. Towards the end of the summer, when the war was looking like it would go on for a long time, it was evident that victory would be impossible without centralised power. In Madrid, the problem of representation arose in the first days of the war, with the government of Casares Quiroga, and it was passed onto the successive governments of Martínez Barrios and José Giral. Giral's government was still restricted to the representation of Republican parties. On 4 September, Giral resigned, like Martínez Barrios and Casares Quiroga before him. He offered the following explanation: 'Because of the grave circumstances being experienced in the country and the likelihood of civil war lasting for a long time, the current government desires and advises the replacement of this government with another that represents all the political parties, workers, and trade union organisations of recognised influence among the popular Spanish masses, from whom political power always originates'.[14]

A new government, formed by Francisco Largo Caballero, a leader of the left-wing socialists, included workers' parties and organisations for the first time since the war began. In this government, Largo Caballero was President and War Minister; Julio Álvarez del Vayo Minister of Foreign Affairs; Indalecio Prieto, Minister of the Navy and Air Force; Angel Galarza, Interior Minister; Juan Negrín, Treasurer; Vicente Uribe, Minister of Agriculture; Jesús Hernández, Minister of Education; José Antonio Aguirre, Minister of Public Works; Mariano Ruiz Funes, Minister of Justice; Anastasio de Gracia, Minister of Industry and Commerce; Bernardo Giner de los Ríos, Minister of Communications; Josep Tomàs i Piera, Minister of Labour; and José Giral Pereira as a minister without portfolio. In all, there were six socialist ministers, three left republicans, one Basque nationalist and one from the *Esquerra*. Significantly, there were two Communists, Uribe and Hernández, while the CNT continued its tradition of remaining outside of government. The POUM was unrepresented as well, because outside of Catalonia it had little political weight and few members.

The constitution of Largo Caballero's government shows that, as the days passed, no one, not even in Catalonia, continued to doubt the importance of cen-

---

13. *Treball*, 8 September 1936.
14. *La Vanguardia*, 5 September 1936.

tralising the government. Two critical questions remained, of course: what position would the CNT-FAI adopt, and what would be the nature of the new, single power? Once the new Popular Front government was established in Madrid, it was easier to do something similar in Catalonia. Josep Tarradellas, who had represented the *Generalitat* on the Anti-fascist Committee since August, would be the architect of this plan. The CNT-FAI, in support of the Republican war-effort and the idea of anti-fascist unity, essentially renounced the power they had gained and the organisations created by the revolution. The POUM, too, ended up contradicting its own revolutionary theory. On 26 September, three weeks after the formation of the new government in Madrid, the uncertainty over who would rule in Catalonia, the Anti-fascist Committee or the *Generalitat*, was settled in favour of the *Generalitat*, and a new Catalan government, presided over by Tarradellas, was formed to include all the anti-fascist forces.

Chapter Four
The Formation of the Popular Militias and the Aragon Front

At the beginning of the Civil War, it was still relatively easy for the diverse anti-fascist forces to agree: they had a common enemy in what was being called the military-fascist uprising, and the enemy had already triumphed in several areas of the Republic. For Catalonia, the closest threats, apart from the insurgents within the region itself, were in the neighbouring region of Aragon and on the island of Mallorca. The need to defend Catalonia and to liberate those territories was urgent, but it would not be easy: after all, the Catalan army had effectively disappeared after the defeat of the uprising. Moreover, there was scant possibility of rebuilding the military force, not only because the popular mobilisation had so effectively suppressed it, but also because the Republican government had discharged all the soldiers, freeing them from their duties (see Chapter Two). As a result, the army had practically ceased to exist in zones that remained loyal to the Republic. And even though many army officers had opposed the uprising, the Catalan working class was not inclined to trust them: Catalan workers were traditionally anti-military, and not many years had passed since the army had been systematically used to repress workers' strikes. The converse was also true: while many members of the military had remained loyal to the Republic, they did not trust the workers' revolution.

Given these circumstances, the only way to challenge the military rebellion was by creating a volunteer army, building from the ground up new military units suffused with a combative spirit and supplied with arms. Arms may not have been abundant, but this new army seemed to have enough to achieve their initial objective: an offensive on the three Aragon provincial capitals, where the rebellion was known to have succeeded, in order to prevent a fascist attack on Catalonia. There have been claims that the offensive, and the use of volunteers to accomplish it, was President Companys's own idea, but it in fact sprang spontaneously from the popular movement: the cry 'To Zaragoza!' could be heard in the streets of Barcelona soon after the rebellion was defeated.[1] Zaragoza, the largest city of Aragon and the regional capital, held special significance for many anarchists: not only was it considered Spain's second anarchist capital (after Barcelona itself), but it was also the birthplace of many anarchists then living in Barcelona.

As early as 21 July, some CNT militants, improvising as they went along, left Barcelona for Zaragoza, but they were stopped in the small Aragonese village of Pina de Ebro. In one of the first skirmishes against the fascists, Manuel Prieto, who had been one of the leaders of an anarchist insurrection in Fígols in 1932, was killed. On the following day, four airplanes, three Savoias and a Vickers, left Barcelona's Prat airport with the objective of bombing the Aragonese capital. Soon, however, the Militias Committee took charge of organising the offensive. Buenaventura Durruti, perhaps Spain's most famous anarchist, volunteered to lead the first column, and he was accompanied by two military advisors, Commander Pérez i Farràs and Sergeant José Manzana, and a Lieutenant of the Civil Guard, Pere Garrido. They intended to attack Zaragoza by surprise and occupy the city in less than a week.

The first call for volunteers met with a wave of enthusiasm so strong that not everyone who responded was able to enlist. On 23 July, the Durruti Column was ready, but some organisational problems delayed their departure until the following day. According to official sources, there were around four thousand men in the column as they waited on the large avenue *Paseo de Gracia*, between *Provenza* Street and the *Pi i Margall* monument. A source from the president's offices of the *Generalitat* described the Durruti Column:

> The column had ninety-six vehicles – around thirty cars and sixty trucks – filled with militia personnel. It had a variety of trucks provisioned with food, four CAMPSA (gasoline) tanker-trucks, an army tanker with drinking water, and around fifteen trucks with twelve artillery pieces and modern ammunition.

---

1. [TN] The common spelling in English for the Aragonese capital is Saragossa.

The column also included some fifteen military and Red Cross ambulances and a number of nurses. Commander Pérez i Farràs and Buenaventura Durruti's car led the procession. The expedition also had several armoured trucks that had been converted in the workshops of Hispano Suiza, and a truck that carried telegraph equipment to establish communications.[2]

The source goes on to state that the citizen militia was made up of rank-and-file members of the CNT, FAI, UGT, POUM, the Communist Party, the Catalan State Party (*Estat Català*), the Socialist Party, the *Esquerra*, former soldiers, Assault Guards, and a solid contingent of women, just as enthusiastic as the men, and many of whom wore overalls and carried rifles. Joining the ranks of volunteers were also some foreign athletes who had come to Barcelona to participate in the Popular Olympics, which had been cancelled because of the military insurrection.[3]

At 10:30 in the morning on 24 July, just before beginning the march, Durruti roused the troops with the following words:

> In Aragon our comrades and fellow workers are victims of the merciless fascist hordes. The always-alert Catalan proletariat, always in the vanguard of liberty in Spain, today more than ever must listen to us. But don't believe that we fight to defend individual interests, because this is about the whole Spanish proletariat, workers who can no longer live again 'the old way', the way we all know has made us live the most miserable of lives.[4]

Later on that same day, a second column departed, this one led by the cabinet-maker Antonio Ortiz and advised by Commander Salanova. It initially had about eight hundred soldiers, mostly CNT militants, and they were armed with around fifty machine guns and several mortars.

The liberation of Zaragoza turned out to be more ambitious than it had at first seemed. The Ortiz column, which had set out by train, had grown to around two thousand men, and they conquered Caspe on the very next day. Then, after occupying the entire area south of the Ebro River, they laid siege to Belchite. At 1 pm on 25 July, the *Generalitat* announced the occupation of Caspe in an official radio-broadcast: 'Forces of the Eighteenth Infantry Regiment, militia members (*milicianos*) from Lleida, and the artillery unit from Barcelona have occupied, after a brief bombardment, the city of Caspe with the cry of "Long live Liberty!"

---

2. *Crònica diària*, 24 July 1936.
3. Ibid. [TN] The 'Popular Olympics' was scheduled to begin on 19 July 1936, and had been organised by the Workers Organisation of Sport to protest the games that would begin in August in Nazi Germany.
4. *La Vanguardia*, 25 July 1936.

The people of Caspe welcomed the liberating column with their own cry of "Sister Catalonia!"'[5]

The Durruti Column, on the other hand, advanced much more slowly than expected. After stops in Cervera and Lleida, the column arrived in Bujaraloz, but an enemy air attack forced the troops to reorganise and thus lose critical time. Then, at the beginning of August, they set out again and took Pina and Osera. They did not, however, go onto Zaragoza: the insurgents had taken advantage of the delays to fortify their defences, and Colonel José Villalba, commander of the Barbastro garrison, advised Durruti against attacking for fear that the column might become isolated. In this way, the first Catalan fighters established themselves along what would become the Aragon front, about twenty kilometres from Zaragoza.

So began a generalised military mobilisation based on popular militias. The day after the first two columns left for Zaragoza, new columns set off for another of Aragon's provincial capitals, Huesca. An anarchist column commanded by Domingo Ascaso, Gregorio Jover and Cristóbal Aldabaldetrecu and advised by Captain Eduardo Medrano left for Barbastro, and after occupying Grañén and Vicién, established position outside Huesca. The newly created PSUC sent two thousand men under the command of José del Barrio, Angel Estivill, and Manuel Trueba and took up position in Tardienta, south of Huesca. The POUM organised two thousand *milicianos* in a regiment that set off for Aragon under the command of Jordi Arquer and Manuel Grossi. The POUM column conquered Leciñena and then sent part of the column on to Huesca. Joining forces with additional *milicianos* coming from Barcelona under the command of Josep Rovira, they occupied Tierz and Quicena just outside Huesca.

More columns left for Aragon in the next days and weeks. The anarchists sent out a thousand-member column they called the Falcons (*Aguiluchos*) in the middle of August, led by Joan García Oliver. In the middle of September, they sent out another column called the Black and Reds (*Roja y Negra*), advised by Captain Luis Jiménez Pajarero. The POUM sent out a second column of one thousand *milicianos* on 7 August under the command of Josep Oltra Picó and Sergi Balada, and they took up position in Alcubierre. The *Esquerra* formed the Macià-Companys column at the beginning of September, its fifteen hundred members led by Enric Cantauri and advised by Lieutenant Colonel Jesús Pérez Salas. Their target was the city of Montalbán.

The city of Tarragona also sent out militias. The first column, of two thousand Civil Guards, police, and militia volunteers, had already left on 24 July under the command of Ángel Martínez Peñalver. After setting off for Calaceite and

---

5. *La Vanguardia*, 26 July 1936.

passing through Falset and Gandesa, they positioned themselves in Alcañiz and Muniesa. Another column was led by Commander Amadeo Insa Arenal and another by Lieutenant Colonel Máximo Mena Burgos. Alpine militias operating in the High Pyrenees comprised fighters from both Aragon and Catalonia. In all, approximately thirty thousand people, all of them volunteers, took up arms in the first weeks of the war against the military insurgents occupying the Aragonese provincial capitals. The attacks on Huesca and Zaragoza were organised by Catalan militias, and the attack on the third capital, Teruel, was organised primarily by Valencian militias.[6]

In the end, the offensive failed for a number of reasons. First, the militias had more good intentions, enthusiasm, and optimism than actual military preparation. Their scant knowledge of military strategy and tactics, combined with a reliance on spontaneity, made them vulnerable in the face of professional troops who were well protected in established positions and well armed. The military objectives of the different columns were not coordinated, and the columns had a tendency to improvise. And troops occasionally lacked discipline: some volunteers who signed up for the militias in the first happy moments of victory abandoned the militias at the first sign of difficulty on the front. Thus, instead of the militias gaining a rapid victory, a front four to five hundred kilometres long emerged, extending into the Pyrenees and dividing Catalonia and parts of Aragon from the latter's provincial capitals.

Various bodies were formed to coordinate the militias. The highest command was the Aragon Front War Committee (*Comité de Guerra del Frente de Aragón*), formed by three leaders from the CNT column (Antonio Ruiz, Cristóbal Aldabaldetrecu, and Durruti), one from the UGT (José del Barrio), and one from the POUM (Jordi Arquer). In addition, the General Front Inspection (*Inspecció General del Front*) was created to supervise militia activities and to ensure communication between militia fighters and the defence department of the *Generalitat*. Finally, Colonel José Villalba was named operations commander for the Aragon Front. In practice, however, the militias maintained their autonomy – especially the anarchist militias, who refused to follow commands that would contradict their libertarian principles of self-management.

The creation of militias by the anti-fascist organisations was the result of popular initiative, but the *Generalitat* attempted to control them. The president of the *Generalitat* issued a decree on 21 July that both placed the 'citizen-militias' under the command of Enric Pérez i Farràs and formed a Defence Agency under Lluís Prunés i Sató that was meant to organise the popular militias. In the first months of the war, however, the militias did not answer to the *Generalitat* but instead

---

6. See the recent study by Judit Camps and Emili Olcina, based on the testimonies from dozens of volunteers (Camps and Olcina 2006).

followed the command of the Anti-fascist Militia Committee of Catalonia, which created structures to ensure that the new military formations were effective. In effect, the Anti-fascist Militia Committee had created a war sub-committee presided over by García Oliver, with Diego Abad de Santillán taking responsibility for the preparation of the militias. Also on this sub-committee were three army officers, the *Generalitat*'s defence minister, and representatives of the UGT, the *Esquerra*, and the POUM. Sub-committees in charge of health and provisions were formed to address the needs of both the militias and the civilian population, and they answered to the war sub-committee.

In September 1936, at the request of García Oliver, the People's War School was founded and began training officers for the new army. Directed by Lieutenant Colonel Plaza and housed in the building of the *Pías de Sarrià* school, it offered intensive courses preparing non-commissioned officers in thirty days, officers in forty days, centurion officers in sixty days, and artillery- and special-unit officers in sixty-five days. By the end of September, the school already had five hundred students and a waiting list of three hundred more. Vicenç Guarner, who had been a professor at the Infantry Academy in Toledo, was appointed the school's inspector general, and Captain Domingo Lara del Rosal was in charge of instruction. Lara del Rosal was also an instructor at the school and served on the Anti-fascist Military Committee with Lieutenant Silverio Gallego Salvador.

Catalonia's military reorganisation based on militias represented an authentic revolution that directly challenged military convention. In fact, the militias were conceived, especially by the anarcho-syndicalists, as a revolutionary army that would guarantee the revolution's triumph in the rearguard. The revolutionary army relied on the organic principles of self-management and self-organisation, rejecting all types of imposed discipline and hierarchical structure. As George Orwell wrote in amazement, the *milicianos* 'attempted to produce within the militias a sort of temporary working model of the classless society'.[7] Soldiers and officers in the new army had to have complete equality in salaries, provisions, and even military salutes. The only problem was the *milicianos*' characteristic mistrust of professional officers, and so García Oliver advocated the formation of worker and soldier councils to supervise the professional officers and keep them under control by means of committees and delegates that had the power to annul any of the officers' decisions.

Not all of the political forces in Catalonia shared the anarchist conception of what the new army should look like. The Esquerra, the PSUC, and the *Generalitat* favoured turning military control over to the *Generalitat*, and it was not long before this difference in perspective began to cause trouble. As early as 1 August,

---

7. Orwell 1952, p. 27.

when the *Generalitat*, following Madrid's example, ordered the mobilisation of reservists from the 1934, 1935, and 1936 draft classes in an attempt to reconstitute the army on a conventional basis, the order was not obeyed. In order to prevent further problems at the very moment of the Aragon offensive, the Militia Committee issued a decree on 3 August requiring the draft classes in question to report to their barracks and place themselves at the orders of the appropriate committees.[8] However, this solution was not without its own problems: the barracks they were to report to were already occupied by the different anti-fascist organisations: in Barcelona, the CNT occupied the Pedralbes barracks and four others; the *Esquerra*, the barracks of Montjuïc; the POUM, the Lepanto barracks; and the PSUC, the Parque barracks.

One more military expedition organised from Catalonia in August ended in failure and contributed to the political tensions in the region. The objective of this expedition was to conquer the Balearic island systems of Mallorca and Ibiza, in which all of the islands but Menorca had fallen to the army.[9] It seems that the idea of the expedition answered various needs of the Republican Government in Madrid, the Catalan *Generalitat*, and the Central Militia Committee. An enthusiastic organiser for the expedition was found in the head of the naval airbase in Barcelona, Captain Alberto Bayo, and he was joined by Manuel Uribarri, captain of the Valencian Civil Guard, who had apparently received requests for aid from Republicans on Ibiza.

Eight thousand volunteers from the CNT, the Catalan State Party, the PSUC, the POUM, and the Civil Guards joined the expedition, along with one hundred Mallorcans who had come to Barcelona for the Popular Olympics. On 5 August the volunteers boarded the *Almirante Cervera* and headed down the coast to pick up Uribarri and his troops in Valencia. On 7 August they occupied the island of Formentera with little trouble, and on the following day they attacked the island of Ibiza, which they occupied on 9 August after brief resistance from the army. The island of Cabrera had already been taken on 1 August by troops attacking from the island of Menorca. By the middle of August, then, all but the island of Mallorca itself had been retaken from the insurgents. At this point, however, Uribarri and Bayo argued, and Uribarri returned to Valencia with his troops. In a cablegram justifying his retreat to the government in Madrid, Uribarri accused Bayo of conquering Ibiza and placing it under Catalan control. The telegram ended, 'I see a tendency toward Catalan supremacism, a tendency that I sus-

---

8. 'The Central Committee of Anti-fascist Militias, in agreement with the *Generalitat*'s Defence Minister, orders all reservists of the 1934, 1935, and 1936 draft classes to report immediately to barracks and to put themselves at the orders of the Militia Committees created under the jurisdiction of the Central Committee' (*Crònica diària*, 3 August 1936).

9. [TN] Commonly known in English as Majorca and the Pine Islands.

pect of wanting to incorporate these islands under the Catalan Statute, and this would not be tolerated in Valencia'.

But that was not the end of the expedition's problems. After his victory in Ibiza, Bayo delayed his attack on Mallorca, believing it necessary to reinforce his troops first. The Militia Committee, which – according to a testimony given by García Oliver – had not been informed of the expedition's departure,[10] sent Bayo an ultimatum to attack immediately. The landing on Mallorca occurred on the night of 15 August, but instead of carrying out the attack directly on the principal city and port, Palma de Mallorca, in order to take advantage of the expedition's numerical superiority and the element of surprise, Bayo chose instead to attack the eastern side of the island between Portocristo and Punta Amer. With virtually no resistance, his troops took up position about twelve kilometres from the coast. On the same day, Bayo issued a *communiqué* that overflowed with optimism:

> I must state that this morning we made our landing with speed and decisiveness, forcing the small enemy groups, who were not keeping watch, to flee.
>
> We have gained the entire coast from Manacor Cove to Punta Amer. Our forces on the right flank, armed with machine guns and canons, are spread from Artá Bay to Cape Vermey.
>
> In Porto Cristo we encountered quite a lot of enemy fire, but the fascists fled in fear when faced with our attack and our airplanes.
>
> As in the previous days, Santa María, the principal hub for communications sent from Palma to our front, has been bombed intensely, and those communications have been destroyed. Consequently, the enemy will not be able to send help of any kind by rail or road, since these too have been cut off.
>
> So far we have had one corporal injured on the *Almirante Antequera* and fourteen injured and three fatalities among the *milicianos*, and these were taken immediately in a fuel truck to the Red Cross and onto the magnificently outfitted hospital ship, the *Marqués de Comillas*.
>
> I am absolutely confident in the success of the landing and the taking of the island, which has been well prepared up to the most minute details. The morale of the sailors and *milicianos* could not be better, and everyone hopes in two or three days to relieve Spain of the grief of the rebellious Balearic Islands.
>
> Many islanders have already joined our forces. We found a sailor and several children hiding in a well, scared to death. They said they raised a white flag so as not to fall victim to the fury of the fascist forces, which have committed unspeakable horrors.

---

10. García Oliver 1978, pp. 238–46.

> We are keeping watch over the island so no ships approach, and we hope that very soon the entire island will once again be in the power of the Republican Government. Long live the Republic.[11]

The expedition, however, was not the easy victory Bayo had expected. Even though the insurgents had fewer troops at the start, they responded quickly, and on 17 August, seventeen small units retook Porto Cristo and forced Bayo to retreat toward Son Servera. At this point the situation stagnated, leaving troops faced off on a fourteen-kilometre front. While Bayo waited for the surrender of the rebel troops and the Militias Committee became more and more convinced of the expedition's foolhardiness, insurgent Mallorcans waited patiently for the Italian military aid financed personally by Juan March.[12]

On 27 August, the first Italian airplanes arrived, and the counteroffensive led by Colonel Luis García Ruiz, Mallorca's military governor, began. On 3 September, the insurgents retook Son Corb. Bayo, abandoned by everyone, had to order his troops to re-embark that same night, and under less than ideal conditions: several hundred *milicianos* and injured were left behind, and a great deal of military hardware was left on the beaches. On 13 September the insurrectionists retook Cabrera, and then Ibiza and Formentera on 20 September. Meanwhile, in Barcelona, Bayo faced a court-martial that nearly condemned him to death.

In spite of the fiasco on the island of Mallorca, and no doubt in order to avoid recriminatory action from the Government of the Republic in Madrid, the *Generalitat* issued a statement on the mission that avoided any mention of the order to retreat and even congratulated Captain Bayo and the Catalan military:

> Now that the Catalan military units, following orders from the Government of the Republic, have returned from their mission to the Mallorcan front, the President of the Ministers of the *Generalitat* issues the following public statement:
>
> The heroic Catalan fighters have returned from Mallorca after a magnificent performance. Not a single man has suffered from the re-embarkation because Captain Bayo, with sound tactics making full use of our strong position, has been able to accomplish it thanks to the high morale and discipline of our undefeated troops. The order to retreat came directly from the Government of the Republic.[13]

---

11. In Catalán, see *Crònica diària*, 16 August 1936. For the version in Spanish, see *La Vanguardia*, 18 August 1936.
12. [TN] Juan March (1880–1962) was a Mallorcan trader, banker, and contrabandist with close ties to the insurgency and the Franco régime.
13. *Crònica diària*, 4 September 1936.

By asserting that the military operation was fundamental, the *Generalitat* clearly hoped to avoid reprisal from the Government of the Republic. Soon, however, the significance of the military defeat, beyond the immediate repercussions of Bayo's failure, would emerge: Mallorca became an aviation base for the Italian air force, administering supplies to the Spanish fascists throughout the war. In fact, fascist influence by way of Mallorca became so important that it provoked an international diplomatic conflict. The Italian presence on the island eventually decreased, largely due to British pressure, but Mallorca never stopped functioning as an immense aircraft carrier, and it soon began sending bombing-missions to the Catalan coast. Catalonia could offer little defence against this new front.[14]

At the end of the summer of 1936, Catalonia's military situation could not have been more alarming. Offensives in Mallorca and the Aragonese capitals had failed. The Aragon front had stagnated, with troops still holding positions that had been established in the first weeks of the war. Military engagement with the enemy was dwindling. A shortage of arms – the militias had little artillery and practically no air force – was causing tension among the different Catalan political forces, and there were mounting accusations that sixty thousand rifles had been hoarded in the rearguard. In December 1936 the anarchist leader Abad de Santillán and Colonel Jiménez de la Beraza, a member of the War Industry Commission, visited the front and saw firsthand the tensions created by the shortages. When, in a confrontational meeting, one of the anarchist leaders reported that his column had been forced to abandon certain positions because they lacked munitions, Jiménez de la Beraza responded harshly, detailing the difficulties of building the war industry in the Catalan rearguard. He insisted that 'all the arms that disappeared early on in the insurgency' be finally sent to the front, 'something that has not even come close to happening, in spite of repeated agreements to that effect by all of the political and trade union organisations'.[15] A similar confrontation occurred between Jiménez de la Beraza and José del Barrio, one of the leaders of the PSUC column, and the Colonel's final report emphasised the negative impression the visit made on him. Clearly, the military situation on the Aragon front had created a new source of tension and controversy in the Catalan anti-fascist camp.

---

14. For more about Bayo's landing on Mallorca and the Italian presence on the island, see the particularly interesting work of Josep Massot (Massot 1987a and 1988).

15. The development of this inspection of the front and the following meeting can be examined in more detail by looking at the document that was presented to the *Generalitat*'s War Industries Commission (*Acta de la Comisión de la Industria de Guerra de la Generalitat de Catalunya*, 12 December 1936, Montserrat Tarradellas Macià Archive, Poblet).

Chapter Five
Public Order and Political Repression in the Rearguard

The offensives in Aragon and Mallorca coincided with political repression and a wave of often indiscriminate assassinations in Catalonia as well as in other zones controlled by the Republic. While the dimensions of this violence were later exploited and greatly exaggerated by the Franco régime, the repression was in fact severe in the first months of the war, and it has provoked a great deal of heated debate in discussions of the war. This violence began the moment the military rebellion was defeated in Catalonia, when the masses held power in their own hands. A disruption of the value systems and norms of conduct that reign in a society during peacetime is not unusual in circumstances of deep social upheaval, of course, and that was the case here: the military uprising in Catalonia and the arriving news of the military's victory in other regions quickly led to a reaction of the common people that aspired not only to neutralise the enemy in the rearguard, but also to settle accounts. Republican security forces were not the only ones engaged in the repression: every anti-fascist party and organisation, as well as some groups that emerged during the revolution, took part in it. Violence was first directed towards the insurgents and those suspected of supporting them, but it was also soon aimed at the Church and anyone associated with religion, businessmen, landowners, and political bosses (*caciques*). Inevitably, there were occasions when the violence had little to do with politics and ideology, and was instead motivated by a desire for personal revenge.

It has often been asserted that most of the violence of those early days was the work of 'uncontrolled' groups (*incontrolados*). These groups acted outside of political or trade union control, taking justice into their own hands and claiming that their actions aided the revolution by eliminating right-wing suspects, people sympathetic to the insurgents and lifelong class enemies. As many historians have shown, the *incontrolados* and their famous night-time *paseos* (strolls) were fundamentally a product of the revolutionary situation experienced in Barcelona and its industrial periphery. All contemporary European revolutions have seen the appearance of actors with little political or social consciousness, actors formed by urban and industrial misery and marginalisation, who intuitively believe that a new society can only be built by destroying lives, churches, the homes of the rich, and all urban symbols that reminded them of the 'old world'.[1]

This violence occurred in response to a complex set of circumstances, and it is more important to make it comprehensible from a historical perspective than to simply condemn it for all of its arbitrary and bloody consequences. First of all, the initial outbreak of violence was caused by the war sparked by the insurgency, and the insurgents had already planned for the need to exterminate anyone who might oppose them. General Emilio Mola, who played a key role in the insurgency prior to July 1936, sent a confidential message on 25 May warning his co-conspirators that their actions 'must be extremely violent in order to defeat the enemy as quickly as possible'.[2] Franco, upon declaring war in the Canary Islands, insisted that 'with no excuses, all punishments should be exemplary in the seriousness with which they are imposed and the speed with which they are carried out, without hesitancy or vacillation'. General Queipo de Llano became famous for radio broadcasts like the one on 23 July, when he delivered the following gem to any village planning to challenge the Civil Guard: 'Morón, Utrera, Puente Genil, Castro del Río, prepare your graves!' He told his men, 'I authorise you, by my order, to kill like a dog anyone who dares challenge you' and, according to some testimonies, announced: 'Our brave legionnaires and regular soldiers have taught the reds what it is to be men, and on the way, they also taught the wives of the reds that now, finally, they have known true men, not castrated *milicianos*. Kicking and crying will not save them'.[3]

---

1. For a similar interpretation, cf. Solé and Villarroya 1989, particularly vol. 1, pp. 59–81.
2. J. Aróstegui 1996, p. 40. [TN] For more on General Emilio Mola and the use of terror, see Paul Preston's chapter 'Mola's Terror: The Purging of Navarre, Galicia, Castile and León' in Preston 2012, pp. 179–218.
3. See Queipo de Llano and Gibson 1986.

The idea of exterminating the adversary – and of 'sending all these lectures about human rights, humanitarianism, philanthropy, and other Masonic topics to hell', as Colonel Marcelino Gavilán Almuzara, the civil governor of Burgos after 19 July, put it – did not stop at mere threats, whether oral or written. Repression was ferocious and brutal wherever the insurgency was victorious, including in the Canary Islands, Ceuta, Melilla, Seville, Zaragoza, Galicia, and Zamora. In Vitoria, even priests accused of being Basque nationalists were executed.[4] More episodes occurred in the wake of the march of the 'Death Column' (*columna de muerte*) from Seville to Badajóz, which has been well documented by the historian Francisco Espinosa.[5] In all instances, violence against the insurgents' enemies was conveniently incited by Carlists, Phalangists, and other civil and military authorities who did not in the least concern themselves with the legal process when the violence was committed and who, in fact, encouraged it in every way possible.

Understandably, the first news of unrestrained violence committed by the insurgents angered many in areas where the rebellion had been defeated. Hence, in Catalonia, the first instances of violence were directed against soldiers who had played a leading role in the rebellion. The retaliation was sometimes *ad hoc*, taking place prior to the creation of a judicial system. This is what happened, for example, in the case of Colonel Francisco Lacasa, who had retreated with his men into the Carmelite convent on Barcelona's Diagonal Avenue on 19 July. The next day, upon his surrender, he was immediately executed, and the Civil Guards who accepted Lacasa's surrender were unable to prevent what was essentially a popular action. The insurgency's opponents also summarily executed many of the soldiers of the Atarazanas Barracks, after the soldiers' false surrender had caused several fatalities, including that of an anarchist leader, Francisco Ascaso.

Once the military revolt had been put down, however, insurgent officers were imprisoned and a system of justice was put into place to try them. As the historian Alberto Reig Tapia has pointed out, the Civil War was more military than civil.[6] On 2 August, there were 252 officers of different ranks imprisoned in the Montjuïc Fortress and on the Uruguay, a prison ship anchored in Barcelona's port. Among them were Generals Goded and Fernández Burriel, quartermaster general Francisco Giménez Arenas, seven colonels, two lieutenant colonels, and thirty commanders. The rest were captains, commissioned and

---

4. On the execution of Basque priests, see Raguer 2001, p. 136.
5. Espinosa 2003. Studies of Francoist repression are abundant, and the bibliography continues to grow. For a balanced, though still provisional, summary, see Casanova et al. 2002.
6. Reig Tapia 1986, p. 291.

non-commissioned officers.[7] By 30 July a special judge charged with conducting the investigation of the military revolt had already processed a court-martial against Goded and Fernández Burriel. The trial took place on 11 August, and the generals were sentenced to death and executed the next day.

The trial of Goded and Fernández Burriel began a series of hearings for officers involved in the insurrection. With the exception of the officers in Lleida, who were executed immediately following the insurrection, the rest were given trials. By February 1937, 228 officers had been tried, 120 of those had been given the death penalty, and 85 of those executions had been carried out. There were 76 officers sentenced to more than six years and 14 to fewer than six years. There were 18 acquittals.[8]

The violence that most typifies this period of repression was not directed against the military but rather against civilians, and it was perpetrated by popular organisations and by *incontrolados*. Certainly, the new revolutionary order, instituted immediately after the workers' victory in July, recognised the need for repressive organisations. On 9 August, intending to take charge of public order, the Militias Committee created Security Patrols (*patrullas de control*), which, in Barcelona, were made up of 700 men (325 from the CNT, 185 from the *Esquerra*, 145 from the UGT, and 45 from the POUM). At the same time, a new body, the Investigation Commission, was formed to take charge of searches, arrests and border control, and it was directed by the anarchist Aurelio Fernández. In practice, however, the Patrols ended up carrying out the same kinds of repressive actions as those carried out by the parties, trade unions and *incontrolados*.

The first weeks saw enormous disorder. In the larger cities, like Barcelona, the *incontrolados* became famous for their evening *paseos* and for the unidentified bodies found every morning on the Arrabassada road. There were searches, looting, pillaging, and uncontrolled violence. Not every act of violence committed in the first weeks of the war can be attributed to the *incontrolados*, however: all the political parties and trade unions were involved, and others besides the CNT and the FAI were responsible for assassinations. Militants from all the parties, from the *Esquerra* to the PSUC to the POUM, participated in repressive measures and helped terrorise the conservative and the wealthy. A letter written in September by Francesc Cambó, leader of the *Lliga Catalana*, to another *Lliga* leader, Ferran Valls i Taberner, conveys this sense of fear:

> One could say – though it may not be entirely true – that the assassinations, fires, and pillaging are done by people in Barcelona who are not Catalan. Outside Barcelona, unfortunately, Catalans are the ones who are setting fire to

---

7. *La Vanguardia*, 2 August 1936.
8. See Rubió i Tudurí 1937, p. 40.

things and killing.... They exterminate our political friends with visible satisfaction. Except for those who have been able to leave, we will see few alive when we return to Catalonia.[9]

Many were subjected to harsh repression: Phalangists, Carlists, militants from the Catalan CEDA, leaders of the free unions, men of the *Lliga*, conservatives, Catholics, and employers who had responded cruelly during previous periods of social strife. Explanations for the violence have often resorted to psychological or messianic notions, but it is not true that Catalan or Spanish workers are more cruel or destructive than workers in other countries, or that Iberian anarchism believed it necessary to completely destroy the past in order to create their ideal society. Rather, as the Anglo-Australian historian George Rudé has repeatedly shown, the dominant classes have used violence throughout history in order to hold onto their power, and the Catalan workers, once they gained power, no doubt remembered the historical repression they had suffered. Examples abound: the Montjuïc hearings from the last decade of the nineteenth century, the repression unleashed during the Tragic Week of 1909, the years of *pistolerismo* sponsored by the bosses between 1919 and 1923, the Primo de Rivera dictatorship between 1923 and 1930, and the repression during the two conservative years (1934–6, *el bienio negro*) of the Second Republic.

Whenever they wielded power, Catalan workers attempted, almost always impulsively, to settle accounts. Inevitably, they targeted employers, the political and ideological right wing, and anyone who in one moment or other acted against workers. It stands to reason, in fact, that the violence might have been even worse if many of the leaders of the *Lliga* had not been on vacation in their summer homes when the war broke out in July, allowing them to escape with little trouble and pass over to the Francoist side. Not surprisingly, even some leaders of the *Esquerra* disappeared and went into hiding for fear of being the targets of persecution or assassination. During social upheaval, some of the worst human instincts are unleashed, and the resulting violence can often have nothing to do with class conflict. This does not, of course, excuse the excesses and arbitrariness of much of the violence and bloodshed. Atrocities like the murder of the Carlist founder of the free unions, Ramón Sales Amenós – who was dismembered in front of the Barcelona offices of the CNT newspaper *Solidaridad Obrera* – cannot be justified. The anonymity of the large cities allowed excesses that, in the end, hurt the cause of both the Republic and the revolution.

In contrast to the heavily populated urban centres, Catalonia's small agrarian communities were characterised by social relations that were much more per-

---

9. This letter can be found in the original Catalan in the appendix of *Cataluña contemporánea: II (1900–1939)* (Balcells 1976, p. 148).

sonal: everyone knew everyone else's name and surname, friends and enemies, likes and dislikes. Landowners knew their tenants, tenants their landlords. They all knew how everyone else voted and whether or not they went to church on Sunday. Although these distinct social relations sometimes helped to prevent bloodshed, repression in the countryside was often, for the same reason, even more cruel than in the cities. Catalan rural areas had experienced enormous social tensions because of the *Llei de Contractes de Conreu*, and repression following the October 1934 revolution fell hardest on Catalonia's peasants. After the Popular Front victory in February 1936, peasants began to regain ground, and by late July they had nearly turned the tables completely. This history helps to explain much of the repression led by newly created local committees during the war's first days. The repressive agents were not always members of a particular community: sometimes they had been brought in from outside to organise the local committee, and sometimes another local committee was acting beyond its own jurisdiction.

In some cases, individuals with dubious moral character and a taste for vengeance gained political control and directed the repression; in others, local committees with a high degree of integrity managed to avoid excessive measures and even confronted patrols that came from outside the community. In other words, responses were inconsistent. In L'Alt Empordà, for example, different villages had radically different experiences: in Palau-savardera and Armentera, there was not one execution, while the committee in Orriols became notorious for its excesses.[10]

Anti-clerical violence was so severe that some historians contend that the Civil War was in part a war over religion. In the first weeks of the war, the Church and everything representing it suffered from persecution that was unprecedented in all of contemporary Catalan history: churches, convents, and monasteries were burned, religious symbols and objects were destroyed, and priests were executed. These events, common in both the countryside and the city, were the culmination of a popular anti-clericalism that had begun with the burning of monasteries in 1835 and that had appeared again during the Tragic Week.

In Barcelona, few churches or convents were spared, although the cathedral and the Pedralbes Monastery were protected by the *Generalitat*. In some convents, the bodies of nuns were exhumed, their skeletons and mummies exposed in the street for several days. Nothing like it had been seen during the years of the Republic, at least in Barcelona, and similar events took place in the rest of Catalonia, although the cathedrals in Girona and Tarragona and the Montserrat, Poblet, and Santes Creus monasteries were all saved. The new cathedral in

---

10. For more on the committee in Orriols, see Maymí 2001.

Lleida, which had been protected by the POUM, was burned down by Durruti's militia *en route* to Zaragoza. Some church buildings were used as warehouses or shelters, and all, whether used or unused, were closed to religious services during the war.

The *Generalitat* attempted to shield from anti-clerical violence members of the Catholic hierarchy as well as Catalonia's artistic treasures, which in many instances were in the hands of the Church. With this in mind, they ordered protection for the Bishops of Tortosa and Girona. They also offered protection to Barcelona's bishop, Manuel Irurita, although he refused it and, like the Bishop of Lleida, was later assassinated.[11] Cardinal Vidal i Barraquer was rescued by the *Generalitat*'s police after having been arrested by an anarchist patrol in the Poblet monastery. He left the country, as did the Abbot of Montserrat. By 20 July, the *Generalitat* had declared Barcelona's cathedral and many other churches and buildings state property in an attempt to preserve them. The government also put the parliamentary representative Soler Pla in charge of ensuring the protection of all the monuments in Catalonia's artistic centres. Soler Pla went to Montserrat, where he asked 160 monks and acolytes to abandon the monastery, seized and inventoried the library, and left government police (*Mossos d'Esquadra*) to stand guard. Pla also went to Vic, Ripoll, Santa Cecilia, and Sant Joan de les Abadesses, whose twelfth- and thirteenth-century archives were also seized by the *Generalitat*.[12] However, he arrived too late to avoid the destruction of some of Vic's artistic treasures.

This fierce repression of the Church has historical and structural causes that, while they do not justify the excesses or arbitrariness of much of the violence, can help to explain the anti-clericalism of the Catalan masses. Catalan anti-clericalism has a long tradition, beginning at least by the early nineteenth century and first manifesting itself in the attacks on monasteries in 1835. The working class saw a close connection between the Church and the wealthy, and in poor neighbourhoods, where the Church dominated the educational system, Catholic educators were seen as corruptors of conscience. For the urban poor, the church played an ideological role on behalf of the ruling classes. Not long after Tragic Week in 1909, the poet Joan Maragall, even though he had profound Catholic and conservative convictions, denounced the ties between the church and the rich in his article, '*L'església cremada*' ('The Church in Flames'), published in *La Veu de Catalunya* (*The Voice of Catalonia*).[13]

---

11. Bada, 2011.
12. For more on the measures taken by the *Generalitat*, see the *Crònica diària*, 20 and 23 July 1936.
13. Maragall 1978, pp. 199–205.

Another factor contributing to this anti-clericalism was the Church's anti-Republican attitude, adopted almost from the beginning of the new régime. The Republican government was similarly antagonistic: in 1931, the leaders adopted a constitution that established the separation of church and state and barred religious orders from the educational system, and they went on to secularise the cemeteries and prohibit the ringing of church bells. The antagonism between the Church and leftist Republicans was always visible and was the source of numerous conflicts throughout the Republic. The situation was only further inflamed when, on 19 July, a rumour spread that shots were being fired against Republican forces from churches and convents, including the Carmelite convent.[14] The Spanish Church soon baptised the Civil War as a religious crusade – a stance quickly adopted by the Vatican – and many priests directly collaborated with the rebel military officers in zones where the insurgency had triumphed. Speaking with Maurice Sollin from the Parisian daily *L'Oeuvre*, Lluís Companys declared:

> At the moment, the situation of the clergy is, and will continue to be, extremely critical. The clergy has sided too openly with the bloody rebellion, with holy-war mysticism, and with the enemies of the Republic... Such an attitude has provoked an unbridled hatred among the popular classes... and the whole religious programme is now seen in the light of this hatred... The Church's freedom to function in Spanish society, it seems to me, will be absolutely impossible for a very long time....[15]

Whatever the reasons for its intensity, anti-clerical persecution represents a significant percentage of the violence following the war's outbreak. Of the 6,844 priests and members of religious orders assassinated during the war in Republican zones, 2,437 were killed in Catalonia: 1,541 priests and 896 members of religious orders. That is to say, Catalonia's share of all the Republican religious assassinations is a relatively high 35.6 percent. Of the total number of 8,360 assassinations in Catalonia, those targeting representatives of the Church amounted to 29 percent.[16]

Commentators like the anarchist leader Federica Montseny, writing in *La Revista Blanca* of 31 July 1936, were already estimating that four or five thousand deaths in Catalonia had been caused by Republican repression. Today we know that, during the whole war, such repression took the lives of 5,923 civil victims and 2,437 clergy and members of religious orders. While the number is

---

14. It is still unclear whether this rumour was true.
15. Companys's statement can be found in Catalan in the *Crònica diària*, 26 August 1936.
16. On religious repression, see the classic study by Antonio Montero Moreno (Montero Moreno 1961). For the Catalan context, the book by Josep Massot i Muntaner is particularly interesting (Massot 1987b). Also, see Pagès 1993b.

unquestionably high, it is nowhere near the tens of thousands of victims claimed by Franco's propagandists for decades – nor can it be compared with the repression inflicted within the rebel zone.

Even though the violence continued to be intense until the end of the summer of 1936, the Catalan political class, from the *Generalitat* to most of the political parties and organisations, made every effort to end the bloodshed. The *Generalitat* succeeded in saving the lives of all the Catalan bishops except the bishop of Barcelona. Martí Barrera, the Catalan minister of labour, hid priests from Solsona in his flat in Barcelona for several days. Several priests and right-wing political leaders were able to leave for France or Italy thanks to passports issued by the Catalan government. In addition, Catalan politicians continually called for an end to repressive excesses. On 27 July, the *Generalitat* asked the Catalan people to 'stop the violence and spilling of blood' and stated that 'uncontrolled groups, whose insane fury compromises everyone and makes all citizens indignant, must be stopped and punished'.[17] On 30 July, the CNT declared its position with unmistakable clarity: 'Let not the revolution drown us all in blood! Just retribution, yes! Assassinations, never!'[18] And *Solidaridad Obrera*, the CNT's newspaper, published a warning that could leave no doubt about the organisation's intentions: 'WE WILL SHOOT ANYBODY found guilty of doing anything against people's rights, anybody who assumes, without authorisation, any of the powers granted by the federal organisation [the CNT], granted specifically to a committee made up of members of the anti-fascist front, choosing the most even-handed and responsible men'.[19] On 31 July, following the assassination of Desiderio Trilles, leader of the UGT, the Central Committee of Anti-fascist Militias bluntly stated:

> All those who loot or vandalise will be shot at the scene of their crime. All those who enter private homes or collectives without authorisation from the Anti-Fascist Committee will be executed in the same way, without full trial. All those who take justice into their own hands, whatever organisations they represent, will feel the weight of our justice.[20]

Similarly, *Avant*, the POUM's daily, stated in the 31 July edition: 'We must resort to extreme measures, without wavering, in order to put an end to acts that dis-

---

17. *Crònica diària*, 27 July 1936.
18. 'Que la revolución no nos ahogue a todos en sangre! Justicieros conscientes, sí! Asesinos, nunca!' (Peirats 1971, vol. 1, p. 174).
19. 'PROCEDEREMOS A FUSILAR A TODO INDIVIDUO que se compruebe ha realizado actos contra el derecho de gentes, a todo individuo que se haya conferido por sí y ante sí atribuciones concedidas por la organización confederal y específica a una Comisión compuesta por elementos del frente de lucha antifascista, eligiendo a los hombres más ecuánimes y más serios'. (*Solidaridad Obrera*, 31 July 1936).
20. *Crònica diària*, 31 July 1936.

honour and hurt the revolution'.²¹ Similar calls were repeated in the following weeks, throughout August and September, including in a series of articles by the anarchist leader Joan Peiró, published in the Mataró edition of *Llibertat*.²² In Madrid, related ideas were being expressed by the socialists Indalecio Prieto and Julián Zugazagoitia.

Both sides in the Civil War engaged in repression, but, as the French historian Pierre Vilar noted, there is a fundamental difference between the repression of one side and that of the other. While in the Republican zone the terror of the first months was mostly haphazard, carried out by the *incontrolados*, in the insurgent zone the violence was systematic, as they were obeying orders coming from superiors.²³ While there were frequent calls in the Republican zone to end this kind of violence, the zones controlled by the insurgents saw few or no attempts to control it. In fact, the battle cry of General Millán Astray, Franco's comrade in the Foreign Legion, was 'Long live death!' (*'Viva la muerte!'*), and there were frequent calls throughout the zone to exterminate the 'enemies of Spain'. There is a crucial difference between, on one side, terror managed by leaders advocating a scorched-earth policy and, on the other, violence created during a revolutionary process and immediately condemned by that side's leaders. And this major difference must be taken into account by any rigorous analysis of the war.

---

21. *Avant*, 31 July 1936.
22. Later these famous articles would be published in a book entitled *Perill a la reraguarda* (*Danger in the Rearguard*) (Peiró 1987). In addition to his writing, Peiró distinguished himself for his attempts to save numerous lives of both civilians and clerics in Mataró, the capital of the Maresme region of the province of Barcelona.
23. Vilar 1986, pp. 151–8.

Chapter Six
The Republican Justice System: From Popular Tribunals to Special Tribunals[1]

The outbreak of war and the subsequent shifts in social hegemony directly affected the system of justice, which underwent enormous changes in its institutional structure and judicial powers. When the war began, justice was subordinated to the new revolutionary order, but ongoing political transformations continued to condition the judicial system's evolution.

Throughout the Republican zone, the first weeks of the war saw the implementation of what was called 'popular justice'. Although Catalonia acted independently from the rest of the Republic in the administration of justice – at least until April or May of 1937 – the Catalan process was nevertheless similar to that elsewhere. On 23 August 1936, the Minister of Justice in Madrid created the first popular tribunal to judge the 'crimes of rebellion and sedition and actions against national security, by whatever means committed'. It was decided that the tribunal would comprise three judges schooled in law and fourteen popular jurists appointed 'by the political parties and trade union organisations that make up the Popular Front, with two members from each party and organisation'. In each case, the procedure would be 'summary'. Two days later, tribunals with the same composition were created in the rest of the Republican zone.[2]

---

1. This chapter is an abbreviated version of my article 'La justícia revolucionària i popular a Catalunya (1936–1939)' (Pagès 2004b).
2. The decree was published in number 237 of the *Gaceta de la República*. I have consulted the version that was published in the *Diario Oficial del Ministerio de la Guerra*, 19 September 1936.

In Catalonia, the first court-martials of insurgents had already been carried out before 26 August, when popular juries were created to repress fascist activities. These juries were to operate within the principal courts of the province, and they assigned punishments determined by the Code of Military Justice. The juries were made up of three magistrates and twelve jury members elected from public associations, political parties, trade union organisations, and other non-mercantile associations. They had to act expeditiously: their indictments were to be completed within eight days.[3] On 28 August, the cabinet issued a new decree that amplified the popular juries' jurisdiction to include crimes of rebellion and sedition and crimes against national security.[4]

Almost immediately after the decree, courts were created in several cities: Barcelona on 28 August, Tarragona on 30 August, and Girona on 8 September. Only Lleida bucked the trend, since its popular tribunal had been created at the initiative of the local Committee of Public Health (*Comité de Salud Pública*), formed at the beginning of the war. Lleida's tribunal did not try military officers because the great majority had already been executed in the days after the rebellion.[5] The juries in the other cities, in contrast, primarily considered cases involving officers who had played important roles in the military rebellion. In Barcelona on 2 September, the jury began operating on the prison ship *Uruguay*, and it maintained rather intense activity until February 1937, with the majority of its death sentences issued in the last months of 1936. In Tarragona, two trials were held against officers of that city on 12 September and 2 November 1936. Six death sentences were issued and carried out. In Girona, trials were held on 7 and 12 October, and seven officers were condemned to death, although only three were executed. In Figueres, trials were held on 28 and 30 September, with no death penalties issued.[6]

A full popular justice system – one that could deal with civil as well as military cases – was not established until somewhat later. In fact, it was not until the first Unity Government, presided over by Josep Tarradellas, was formed on 26 September that the idea arose for creating popular tribunals to judge political crimes committed by civilians. The formation of popular tribunals was seen as a necessary measure, one that could put the brakes on the summer's excessive repression. The initiative came from Andreu Nin, the new minister of justice and law in the *Generalitat* and the POUM's political secretary. Nin created the popular

---

3. The decree that created these juries can be found in *Diari Oficial de la Generalitat de Catalunya*, 26 August 1936.
4. *Diari Oficial de la Generalitat de Catalunya*, 28 August 1936.
5. For more on the situation in Lleida, see Barrull i Pelegrí 1995 and Sagués San José 2003.
6. More on the repression in Tarragona can be found in Piqué i Padró 1998. For more information on the judgements against the two garrisons in Girona, see Clara i Resplandis 1990, pp. 141–53.

tribunals by decree (the decree of 13 October) in order to 'guarantee the integrity of the proletarian conquests [of the revolution] and contribute to victory in the war'. They would 'consider all acts that contributed, directly or indirectly, to the military rebellion or the fascist movement of 19 July 1936, and impose the appropriate sanctions, in agreement with public conscience, on those responsible'.[7]

The extensive provisions of the decree established not only the kinds of crimes the tribunals would hear – especially those crimes considered counter-revolutionary – but also the judicial procedure to be followed from the moment of accusation to the final sentencing, the procedural safeguards on behalf of the accused, and the functions of the prosecutor. The decree created four popular tribunals in Barcelona and one each in Girona, Lleida and Tarragona. Finally, it established the composition of each tribunal, the procedure for the election of tribunal members, and the characteristics required of each member. The tribunal would be composed of a president and eight members, one from each of the eight organisations that formed the Catalan anti-fascist block. A series of provisions added later named the tribunal presidents and prosecutors, established the kinds of crimes assigned to each tribunal, and determined the salaries of presidents, prosecutors, and tribunal members.[8]

Finally, on 24 October 1936, a new decree regulated the procedures for commuting death penalties, an extremely controversial subject that, given the context of civil war, had tremendous significance both nationally and internationally. In order to oversee the death penalty, a commission was created to examine all the death sentences issued by the popular tribunals. The commission was to send a report to the *Generalitat*'s minister of justice, who was then to report to the *Generalitat* so that the government could decide on an appropriate action.[9]

The tribunals began to function at the end of October, and in the first weeks they primarily heard the cases of civilians accused of collaborating with the July military rebellion. Because these courts have not been studied as a group, we cannot draw any definitive conclusions about their actions; however, fragmentary information about them is revealing. Without doubt, the most active popular tribunals were the four in Barcelona Between November 1936 and February 1937, forty people given death sentences by these courts were executed. Analysis of more than three hundred sentences issued by Barcelona's tribunals to people who at some point served time in the city's main prison, the Modelo, shows that there were 48 death sentences, 21 sentences of 30 years, two sentences of

---

7. *Diari Oficial de la Generalitat de Catalunya*, 15 October 1936.
8. I have written about the organisation of these tribunals in Pagès 1990a, pp. 47–63; Pagès 1993a; and in 'Andreu Nin, conseller de Justícia de la Generalitat de Catalunya', a talk given at the Andreu Nin Conference (*Jornadas de estudio sobre Andreu Nin* [1892–1937]) on 25 March, 1993. It can be found in Alba et al. 1998, pp. 79–94.
9. *Diari Oficial de la Generalitat de Catalunya*, 5 November 1936.

25 years, 12 sentences of 20 years, five sentences of 15 years, 16 sentences of ten years, and 41 sentences of fewer than eight years. One hundred and sixty-one prisoners were freed.[10] The most numerous decisions were, then, the two extremes: death sentences and decisions granting liberty. Many of the death sentences, once they were commuted, were converted into life sentences, which, according to the legislation in effect, amounted to 30 years in prison. There is no doubt that the tribunals mostly heard crimes classified as 'fascist' or 'fascist activities', 'counterrevolutionary', and 'military rebellion'.

In Girona, the popular tribunal commenced activity on 5 November 1936. We only have information about the first months of this tribunal's activity, or until the end of 1936. Cases were heard for 67 civilians, most of whom were accused of collaborating with the military uprising in July, although some were militia-members accused of committing violent acts of retaliation after the rebellion failed. Of those accused, 20 were condemned to capital punishment; of those, four were executed, 12 absolved, and the rest imprisoned.[11]

In his exhaustive study of the Tarragona tribunal, Jordi Piqué shows that between 21 December 1936 and 15 February 1937, the tribunal, presided over by Andreu Massó, processed 102 people and issued 29 death penalties. Twenty-six of those penalties were commuted, and only two were executed. Six of the remaining defendants were given terms of life in prison; three were given 30 years, two were given 15 years; 13 were given ten years, one was given eight years, three were given five years, one was given 18 months and one day, four were exiled, and one was given an economic sanction. Twenty-six had their charges dismissed, and six were absolved.[12]

The tribunal in Lleida, which extended its territorial domain to numerous towns in the Huesca province of Aragon, proved to be the most active – and the most severe – in Catalonia. The first tribunal in Lleida after the war began operated under the auspices and authority of the local Committee of Public Health, at a time when most of the city's military leaders involved in the July uprising had already been executed. The tribunal functioned for just one month, from 22 August until late September, and in this period 145 people were condemned to death.[13]

When the popular tribunal was created in Lleida at the end of October 1936 – in compliance with the *Generalitat*'s decree of 13 October – it was no less severe

---

10. See Pagès 1996, pp. 281–2.
11. See Clara 1986.
12. Piqué i Padró 1998, p. 276.
13. See Solé i Sabaté and Villarroya 1989, vol. I, pp. 130–6. Lleida's popular tribunal was later studied by Jaume Barrull i Pelegrí, who indicates that only 128 were condemned to death. After October, the tribunal no longer held trials, but it remained active (Barrull i Pelegrí 1995, pp. 47–73).

than its predecessor. Records indicate that 90 death sentences were issued, 11 of which were commuted between November 1936 and 10 January 1937. Sixteen death sentences were commuted between 11 January and April 1937.[14] The available information on sentences issued by Lleida's popular tribunal and served, at least in part, in the Modelo prison, shows that five of the prisoners had been condemned to death; 42 were given sentences of 30 years; 11, of 20 years; three, of 15 years; 21, of ten years; four, of eight years; one, of six years; 16, of five years; two, of three years; six, of one year; and one was sent to a reformatory.[15]

Compared to those of other Catalan popular tribunals, the sentences issued by the Lleida tribunal are harsher. Even so, the general trend in all the tribunals was to rule with severity, particularly early on, when civil war, political reprisals, and severe repression in the insurrectionary zone would have heightened the emotions of the tribunals' deliberations. Such emotional intensity also helps to explain why, on occasion, the tribunals issued sentences for 'the moral conviction that the accused were acting as fascists', a ruling that appears more than once in the records.

Although the tribunals' sentences could be severe, the body organised for commuting death sentences moved into action very quickly. In fact, even before the commission overseeing death sentences had been created, the first pardon had been proposed by Andreu Nin and granted on 8 October 1936. The day after the decree establishing the commission was published in the *Diari Oficial de la Generalitat de Catalunya*, six more death sentences were commuted. The commission seems to have functioned from October 1936 until March 1937, and it interceded on at least 90 death sentences issued by the popular tribunals. According to statistics published in the *Diari Oficial*, the commission commuted four death sentences in October, 15 in November, 29 in December, 33 in January, four in February, and six in March.

In October 1936 the Republican Government created two additional tribunals: emergency juries (*jurados de urgencia*), established by decree on 10 October, and guard juries (*jurados de guardia*), established on 17 October. The emergency juries were to examine 'acts of disaffection against the [Republican] régime not provided for or sanctioned under the Common Penal Code or in the special penal laws'. They could impose fines and loss of liberty. The guard juries were to consider crimes of factionalism discovered *flagrante delicto*, as defined by the edicts of the Ministry of Interior, and they issued sentences based on the Code of Military Justice.

The new tribunals began operating in Catalonia in late April and early May 1937, when Joan Comorera from the PSUC was Minister of Justice in the *Generalitat*.

---

14. Barrull i Pelegrí 1995, pp. 80 and 93.
15. Pagès 1996, p. 283.

At this time, the popular tribunals were also undergoing a transformation: on 23 February 1937, Joan García Oliver, now the Republican Government's minister of justice, had converted them into 'special' popular tribunals, expanding their jurisdiction to include common crimes as well as political crimes and also non-military crimes committed by citizens.

The presence of these new tribunals in Catalonia represented a clear standardisation of the Catalan and Spanish Republican judicial systems, contrasting with the pronounced independence of Catalonia's judiciary earlier in the war. Catalonia's gradual loss of judicial autonomy paralleled the loss of independence in other spheres of Catalan political life.

The formula used to constitute the new tribunals, published in the *Generalitat*'s daily newspaper, was based on several decrees from the Republican Government's Ministry of Justice (those of 28 August, 10 October, and 13 and 23 February).[16] All three courts, then – both the two new tribunals and the modified popular tribunals – came out of Republican Government legislation. From June until December 1937, these were the only tribunals addressing cases of political repression in the Republican territory, and in Catalonia, the sentences issued became more temperate. The records of the new 'special' popular tribunals, which functioned until January 1939, offer the clearest example of such attenuation: in Barcelona, of the 485 verdicts issued by tribunal number one, 431 (or 88.7 percent) were found not guilty, and of the 379 verdicts issued by tribunal number two, 338 (91.3 percent) were found not guilty.

The guard juries and emergency juries were also more lenient. The highest volume of cases heard by these tribunals was during the summer of 1937, especially in July. The cases concerned prisoners charged with crimes against the government who had not yet been processed, many of whom who had already spent several months in prison. The emergency juries reviewed sentences issued earlier by the popular tribunals, and in every case they considerably reduced the initial sentences. Sometimes, they freed prisoners already sentenced to prison terms of various lengths.

Even though the Republican Government was responsible for the reorganisation of the justice system in Catalonia, it harshly criticised the actions of the new tribunals and obliged the president of Barcelona's High Courts (*Audiencia Territorial*), Josep Andreu i Abelló, to explain their behaviour. Andreu filed his brief with the *Generalitat*'s Minister of Justice on 7 December 1937.[17] His arguments clearly reflect the procedures used in the tribunals, and he attributes the mild sentences to the following factors:

---

16. See the *Diari Oficial de la Generalitat de Catalunya*, 1 May 1937.
17. The brief can be consulted in the Archivo Nacional de Cataluña, Fondo Bosch Gimpera (document B.G., 6,2,1).

> Until recently, the police statements, if they actually existed, were insufficient. Most of the time the accused were placed automatically at the disposition of the judicial authority for having already passed their 30 days behind bars, or they were placed in the hands of the Guard Jury by the Government Authority, with statements so laconic they only said: 'We put at the disposition of the judicial authority the fascists enumerated on the reverse of this brief'. Then, on the day of the trial held by the emergency jury, the police would offer no evidence or explanations that would permit the tribunal to form an opinion. In spite of everything, most of the time, the sentences issued are those permitted by the penal codes of the emergency juries.

Andreu also questioned whether the tribunals had actually been made up of popular juries constituted with representation from the trade unions and political parties. This was the cause, in his mind, for the absolution of all the crimes for 'holding firearms illicitly' and the fact that 'in the trials after the May uprising, the first two that were held, in spite of having proved with certainty the intervention of the accused in the events that resulted in victims, the jury issued a "not guilty" verdict.[18] This verdict motivated the prosecuting Attorney to ask for the suspension of all other trials in order to gather a prosecutorial panel on behalf of the Republic to decide whether or not to take all the remaining indicted after the May events before a Tribunal of Espionage'.[19]

Political events, tensions among Catalan anti-fascist forces and the conflict in the Catalan rearguard in May 1937 all clearly affected the Republican judicial system. The political changes that provoked the events of May 1937 transformed both judicial actions as well as the exercise of repressive measures. Once the new government of Juan Negrín was named, 'popular justice' was replaced by 'special justice' (*justicia especial*), a kind of justice that proved more cerebral and cold. It was directed from the state, centralised, and, in many ways, harsher than the justice seen during the first months of the war. The progressive loss of the war and the growth in 'fifth-column' activities were other factors that played a role in the new exercise of justice. The biggest change in the justice system of this period concerned who was being accused and tried: it was no longer just rebellious military officers and their supporters – Phalangists, monarchists, Carlists, and those suspected of giving aid to the military insurrection – who were brought before the courts, but also militants of radical left-wing organisations like the POUM and certain sectors of the CNT.

---

18. [TN] The May Events are described in Chapter 10.
19. Archivo Nacional de Cataluña-Fondo Bosch Gimpera (Andreu i Abelló).

This was not the first time that 'special courts' had been created during the Civil War: they had, in fact, proliferated since the beginning of the conflict.[20] But 'special' justice took on much greater significance in the last months of the war through the Court of Espionage and High Treason (*Tribunal de Espionaje y Alta Traición*) and the Special Guard Tribunals (*Tribunales Especiales de Guardia*).[21] These courts presided over the judicial life of the Republican zone during the last months of the war, and they worked alongside the Military Investigation Service (*Servicio de Investigación Militar*, or SIM), created by Republican government decree in August 1937.

The Court of Espionage and High Treason, created by the government in June 1937, was to deal with 'acts of espionage, high treason, defeatism, and all aggressions, however covert, against the Régime, in these times when public bodies should act most effectively'. In Catalonia, the court was established by a Decree-Law on 22 August 1937, and even though its formation was clearly defined as the right of the Spanish Republican government, the Catalan government was granted some voice in appointing members to the tribunal.

The civil members of the Catalan Espionage Tribunal were named at the end of September: the president, nominated by the Spanish government, was Alfonso Rodríguez Dranguet; the two members nominated by the Catalan government were the judges Pelai Sala and Pascual Galbe; Santiago Sentís and Carles Gerhard were appointed as alternates. Gerhard, however, would dedicate a good part of his time to the Espionage Tribunal after February 1938. The tribunal's two military members would be named soon afterwards by the Defence Ministry. Fernando Martín López, Manuel García Padrón, Manuel Armentia Juste and Rafael Bonmatí Valero were also members.

The Court of Espionage and High Treason was also headquartered in Barcelona, and from the moment the Negrín government moved to the city in the autumn of 1937, it delivered highly emblematic judgments, including the one issued against the POUM directors in October 1938. The Catalan tribunal began proceedings in December 1937, and it had processed 1,386 people before 31 July

---

20. For instance, in Catalonia, Alfonso Rodriguez Dranguet was named special judge in the investigation of the July 1936 military rebellion; then, in January, he was appointed to the preliminary inquiry into Fatarella's armed conflicts. He acted again as judge in the proceedings over the May 1937 events. In June 1937, Judge Josep M. Bertran de Quintana was named special judge in the preliminary investigations into the clandestine morgues and cemeteries that had been opened in order to determine responsibilities for the repressive excesses of the first months of the war.

21. [TN] The formation of the Special Guard Tribunals (*Tribunales Especiales de Guardia*) was decreed by President Negrín in November 1937 and should not be confused with the guard juries (*jurados de guardia*) or the emergency juries (*jurados de urgencia*) created in October 1936 and mentioned earlier in this chapter.

1938. Of those, it brought 758 to trial. During the course of the long year in which it existed, at least 2,147 prisoners in the Modelo were processed by the court. Of the 1,409 sentences it pronounced, 70 were for the death penalty, 147 were for 30 years in jail, 30 for 20 years, 20 for 10 years, 80 for six years and one day, and 978 were let go. The death sentences were inexorably carried out, and the prison sentences nearly always specified that they were for work camps.

The Court of Espionage and High Treason was much less severe than the Special Guard Tribunals, which were created by the Republican Government on 29 November 1937, 'to repress crimes discovered *flagrante delicto* of espionage, high treason, and defeatism'. In March 1938, the tribunal's jurisdiction was expanded to include crimes related to supplies, and at the beginning of May it was expanded further to intervene in all crimes of espionage, high treason, defeatism, and supplies violations, regardless of whether or not they were *flagrante delicto*. The tribunal's omnipresence in Catalan judicial life, above all with regards to political crimes, was indisputable. Its power was only mitigated by the fact that all death sentences had to be reviewed and confirmed by the Court of Espionage and High Treason.

For numerous reasons, the conduct of both of these 'special' courts was controversial: firstly, they reported directly to the S.I.M., the new counter-espionage organisation that had created a profound feeling of insecurity and even terror for many Catalans. Secondly, they operated entirely outside the control of the *Generalitat*, which had been marginalised and snubbed by the Republican Government. Thirdly, after May 1938 rumours circulated about their militarisation, spurring the *Generalitat*'s Minister of Justice to begin working to prevent it. And finally, the court's severe punishments were often accompanied by obvious irregularities in procedure.

In Catalonia, these courts began functioning in May 1938. There were six of them: three in Barcelona and one each in Girona, Tarragona, and Lleida. The three Barcelona tribunals were active from March 1938 to January 1939, during which time they sent more than a thousand prisoners to the Modelo. Their sentences were harsh: 211 defendants were sentenced to death, 219 to 30 years, 95 to 20 years, 71 to 10 years, 160 to six years and one day, 88 to fifteen days, and only 28 were given their liberty. Usually, the heaviest sentences were issued for the crimes of high treason and defeatism, while the lightest were for crimes related to supplies, like hoarding, price-gouging, etc.[22] In Tarragona, the tribunal presided over by Benjamí Jané Jané was also particularly severe: between May and December of 1938 it processed 621 people, of whom 339 (54.6 percent) were

---

22. Pagès 1996, pp. 289–90.

found guilty, 142 (23 percent) were absolved, and 94 (15 percent) saw their cases dismissed. Tarragona issued 11 death sentences.

Because of these judgments, the proceedings of the special tribunals came to be a genuine obsession for the *Generalitat*'s Ministry of Justice. On 22 July 1938, a report signed by Jordi Olivar Daidí, an alternate parliamentary representative for Catalonia, and written at the request of Bosch Gimpera, made several accusations, including the following:

> It is emphatically true that the authorities, whether or not they are agents of the S.I.M., have only rarely reaffirmed their diligence before the trial court. The tribunal pronounces the sentence with nothing more than the interrogation of the accused, weighing as evidence only the police report and, in some cases, documents or testimonies offered by the defence. It always ignores any questioning from the accused.
>
> ... during the trial the accused are always questioned about the actions that motivated the investigation.
>
> In some cases, the defendant has maintained that his statement to the police was coerced and has gone on to give details about the coercion. A statement of this kind is almost never put on record, nor are investigations ever ordered into the charges.
>
> The dominant feeling in the Ministry of Justice is constant, intense fear, *felt by everyone* [emphasis in the original].[23]

These 'special' courts that inspired such great fear at the end of the war were fundamentally different from the courts of 'popular justice' that were active at its beginning. They remained highly active up until Barcelona fell to Franco. One sentence was issued as late as 16 January 1939, just 10 days before Franco occupied Barcelona and after much of Catalonia had already fallen to his army.

---

23. Olivar Daidí, 22 July 1938, document 5.10, Archivo Nacional de Cataluña-Fondo Bosch Gimpera.

Chapter Seven
Social and Economic Transformations

The outbreak of war profoundly transformed Catalonia's social and economic life and affected both public and private spheres. Previous chapters have discussed political and military upheavals, but even more significant in a discussion of revolution are the economic changes, particularly changes in property relations. Along with these transformations, subtle changes could be seen in urban areas, especially in industrial centres. Urban Catalonia – with Barcelona in the lead – dressed in proletarian garb. The cities were adorned with the red flags of revolution and the red and black flags of the anarchists. In the wave of seizures during the first days of the revolution, working-class parties and trade unions took over spacious, central localities, and they decorated the buildings' facades with their organisations' names and symbols. Motor vehicles were covered with the names of parties and trade unions.

The revolution was not plotted in advance by communists and other 'enemies of Spain', as was claimed then and for many years afterwards by the insurgent military officers and the Franco régime. The 'Marxist threat', although invoked to help justify the military action, was practically nil on the eve of the Civil War. Some organisations, like the CNT-FAI and the POUM, had the realisation of a social revolution as an aim, but there were many others, like republicans of various kinds, the socialists of the PSOE (excluding their most radical members), the PCE at the national level, and the PSUC in Catalonia, whose aspirations went no further than the reformist programme of the Popular Front.[1] Moreover, no one, not even the anarchist revolutionaries in the FAI, had a precise strategy for initiating a revolutionary movement.

The revolution that the officers of the insurrection claimed they wanted to prevent was a direct result of their own actions to thwart it: it was the insurgency itself that provoked the inversion of powers and the general collapse of Republican institutions, thus creating the conditions for a revolution. As surprising as it might seem, revolution on 19 July was not the conscious decision of any political party or trade union committee. Even after 19 July, the course was not adopted by the leaders of any organisation. For instance, the Central Committee of the POUM, a revolutionary Marxist organisation, published on 24 July a platform of demands in which the most radical points were the 'control of production by factory, shop, or mine committees' and the 'distribution of lands from large estates to poor peasants', along with other points demanding a thirty-six hour working week, pay for days lost to strikes, and the progressive revision of the statute on Catalan autonomy.[2] The demands of the POUM leaders were not keeping pace with the revolutionary momentum created by the Catalan proletariat. Neither the FAI nor the CNT found themselves better able to lead the masses, particularly when, after the meeting on 20 July, they refused to proclaim libertarian communism.[3]

The revolution was, instead, a spontaneous action of the empowered Catalan proletariat, who believed that revolution was a historical necessity, an obligation and a right. That this movement was spontaneous is shown by the development of events. After the military uprising had sparked a few days of general strikes, Catalan factory workers returned to work and found that many of their employers, bosses, and foremen had fled or gone into hiding, some for political or ideological reasons, others fearing retaliation or reprisals. Given that workers had achieved power after decades of intense class conflict, it is not surprising that many Catalan factory owners were afraid. Workers took over factories, then, out of a need to restart production, and they initiated in this way what came to be called 'collectivisation'. As Josep Maria Bricall has shown, the process of collectivisation implied that economic power within the factories and shops had

---

1. [TN] As we have seen elsewhere, the PSUC was not formed until after the beginning of the war. However, many writers today refer to the pre-war *Unió Socialista de Catalunya* by the name of the organisation its members would ultimately lead.

2. See the POUM daily newspaper *Avant*, 24 July 1936.

3. [TN] 'Libertarian communism' is the name used by the anarchists themselves to describe their revolutionary objectives. As Chapter Three explains, the CNT and FAI, unwilling to assume centralised power at the moment that they were most powerful, implicitly gave centralised command back to Companys, who proceeded to capitalise on it.

passed into the hands of the workers. The workers instituted a system of self-management (*autogestión*), in which they essentially became the new owners.[4]

Collectivisation of the factories spread rapidly. In the first few days, the process was spontaneous, but it quickly came to be instigated by the trade unions, especially by the CNT. In just a few weeks, companies in diverse fields – metallurgy, textiles, chemical production, the service sector, entertainment, etc. – had all collectivised. In just a few days the Catalan economy experienced the most important transformation of its history with respect to property relations. But the process was occurring in circumstances of confusion: the collectivisations were enormously individualised, and the mixed Catalan economy made it difficult to organise economic resources for the war. Worker leaders quickly realised that they needed a structure that could bring order to the Catalan economy, regulate the collectivisations, and confront the problems created by the war. And so, on 11 August, the Catalan Economic Advisory Council (*Consell d'Economia de Catalunya*) was created 'to appropriately structure and normalise the Catalan economy and solve the grave economic problems that have arisen'. Advocated by the *Generalitat* and approved by the parties and trade unions, the new institution would have jurisdiction in all of Catalonia and would 'bring order to Catalan economic life'.[5] The Advisory Council would make decisions in the economic sphere, and it would generate the regulations and agreements to be executed by the *Generalitat*.

The composition of the Catalan Economic Advisory Council, established by the same decree that created it, became a precedent for the constitution of the Unity Government in September. Josep Tarradellas, minister of economy and public services for the *Generalitat*, would preside over the new Advisory Council and would be joined by Martí Barrera, Vicenç Bernades and Joan B. Soler from the *Esquerra*; Ramon Peipoch from the ACR; Eusebi C. Carbó, Joan P. Fàbregas, and Cosme Rofes from the CNT; Antoni García Birlán and Diego Abad de Santillán from the FAI; Joan Fronjosà, Joan Grijalbo i Serres, and Joaquim Puig i Pidemunt from the UGT; Estanislau Ruiz i Ponsetí from the PSUC; Joaquim Pou i Mas from the *Unió de Rabassaires*; and Andreu Nin from the POUM. The make-up of this committee, similar to that of the Central Committee of Antifascist Militias, showed the hegemony of the workers' organisations while at the same time creating an opening for republican organisations representing the petit-bourgeoisie.[6]

---

4. Bricall 1970, see especially pp. 186–9.
5. *Butlletí Oficial de la Generalitat de Catalunya*, 14 August 1936.
6. For recent work on the Catalan Economic Advisory Council, see Cendra i Bertran 2006.

The Catalan Economic Advisory Council first set about defining its objectives and philosophy in a declaration of principles known as the 'National Plan for Socialist Transformation' (*Pla de transformació socialista del país*), elaborated by Nin, Peypoch, Fàbregas, Ruiz i Ponsetí, and Pou. Nin – the only member of the committee with practical experience in the revolutionary process, having lived for nine years in the Soviet Union – seems to have played an essential role in writing the document. On 17 August, the Advisory Council approved the plan, which announced the intention to establish control over companies that still maintained private-property relations and to promote the collectivisation of large rural estates as well as medium- and large-scale industry. The plan's eleven resolutions accounted for virtually all aspects of the Catalonian economy:

1. Regulate production based on consumer needs, sacrificing superfluous industries or production and energetically stimulating the creation of new industries that, due to the changing value of the *peseta*, should be established.
2. Monopolise foreign trade in order to avoid attacks on the new economic order from outside.
3. Collectivise large rural estates for use by peasant syndicates aided by the *Generalitat*, and require the unionisation of agricultural workers on small- and medium-sized rural estates.
4. Partially devalue urban properties by means of rent reduction and by establishing equivalent rates when it is not considered appropriate to benefit the renters.
5. Collectivise large industry, public-service establishments and public transport.
6. Seize and collectivise establishments abandoned by owners.
7. Expand the system of distribution co-operatives and the use of the co-operative system for large distribution enterprises.
8. Establish workers' control over banking businesses and eventually nationalise the banking system.
9. Establish trade union control over all industries that continue to employ the system of private property.
10. Reabsorb unemployed workers into agriculture and industry in order to stimulate the revaluation of agricultural products, the return of workers when possible to the fields (facilitated by the new agricultural system), the creation of large industries to supply manufactured goods that will be difficult to import, and the electrification of Catalonia, mainly for railways, etc.
11. Quickly abolish separate taxes in order to implement a single-tax system.[7]

---

7. This is translation of the Spanish version of these resolutions, which appeared in the *Crònica diària* 18 August 1936.

It was an ambitious plan. In practice it would mean the complete overhaul of the Catalan economy. It was so ambitious that, as Albert Pérez Baró points out, two and a half years later many of the initiatives had not been implemented, and others had not even been discussed.[8]

The plan, however, formed the basis for a minimum programme that all the social and political forces in the Catalan government had agreed upon. The next step was the elaboration of the Collectivisation and Workers' Control Decree (*Decret de Col·lectivitzacions i Control Obrer*), which would work to legalise the revolutionary transformations and establish collectivisation norms. However, problems arose within the Advisory Council during the decree's elaboration, especially over how to determine the limits of small- and medium-sized enterprises. The CNT-FAI and the POUM favoured the collectivisation of all enterprises larger than 50 workers as of 30 June 1936. The *Esquerra* and the PSUC favoured collectivisation for enterprises larger than 250 workers. After heated debate, the decree issued on 24 October set the number of workers for small- and medium-sized enterprises at 100.[9]

This complex decree was, without doubt, the most important one passed during the war. It identified those enterprises that would be collectivised and those that would remain in private hands, although the latter would still be supervised by the Workers' Control Committee; it created groups of collectivised enterprises all operating within a particular productive sector; it divided the economy into 14 different sectors in order to aid these groups; it created General-Industry Advisory Committees designed to formulate work plans for industry sectors, orient the Enterprise Advisory Committees, and co-ordinate industrial tasks in the larger sphere; and finally, it laid plans for an Industrial and Commercial Credit Union that would collect 50 percent of all the profits from collectivised enterprises, invest them following the guidelines of the Catalan Economic Advisory Council and the General Industry Advisory Committee, and facilitate credit to those collectivisations that needed it.[10]

Once the Collectivisation and Workers' Control Decree had established the legal framework, a long series of decrees and orders followed that regulated the collectivisations, a process unprecedented in Catalan history. Although the total number of enterprises affected by the collectivisation process is difficult to determine, the most recent estimates have calculated that there were four thousand five hundred commercial and industrial firms with workers' control

---

8. Pérez Baró 1970.
9. For more on these debates, see the minutes of the commission in Cendra i Bertran 2006, pp. 47–61.
10. The entire *Decret de Colectivitzacions i Control Obrer* can be found in Pérez Baró 1970, pp. 187–99.

committees and nearly two thousand collectivised enterprises. There were five thousand to six thousand more in the approximately 600 Industrial Groupings.[11] The Industrial and Mercantile Incorporation Commission, which was created by the Franco régime after the war ended, notes that 6,712 collectivised enterprises were either breaking up or already dissolved by September 1939.[12]

It has often been asserted that the collectivisation process was catastrophic for the Catalan economy in that it created a kind of chaos (*descontrol absoluto*) in which each worker considered himself to be the owner of the enterprise and disciplined work was remarkable for its absence. A decline in production seen at the beginning of the war and eventually reaching an alarming rate seems to support this notion. This interpretation, however, is flawed not only for its blatant anti-collective tendentiousness, but also because it ignores the historical circumstances in which the revolutionary process occurred. It is true that the collectivisations were no 'arcadia' of equality and progress, and that on more than one occasion there were outbreaks of labour indiscipline. It is also true that, on many occasions, the former owners, some of whom had not fled, joined the factory committees hoping the tide would eventually turn back in their favour. The anarchist leader Joan Peiró pointed out publicly the excessive salaries that some enterprises were paying workers.[13] However, the thirty months that the process lasted are not sufficient for drawing adequate conclusions, especially if we take into account the permanent boycott that the Spanish Republican Government decreed against the collectivisations, completely isolating them. Furthermore, the process occurred in the context of civil war. Catalan industry traditionally imported many of its raw materials from abroad and exported manufactured goods to the rest of the Spanish market. When the war began, importing raw materials became difficult, and the Spanish market shrank appreciably. The problems of collectivised industries began to worsen when stocks of raw materials ran out and the important question of financial credits arose. One of the collectivisation problems arose because the anarchists had not taken control of finances: the *Generalitat* controlled all of the banks, and so, on more than one occasion, workers had to go to the Salary Payment Office (*Oficina Reguladora de Pagament de Salaris*), an office created by the *Generalitat* after 19 July, in order to collect salaries that had been lost during the July Days.

In contrast with the Catalan industrial sector, the Catalan fields were not significantly affected by the tide of collectivisations. In contrast to other parts of Spain, where large estates were predominant, farming in Catalonia was dominated by small- and medium-sized properties and the tenant-farming of

---

11. See Pujol 1986, p. 7 and Castells i Duran 1993 and 1996.
12. Aracil 1999, p. 40.
13. Peiró 1937, pp. 17–24.

small- and medium-sized fields. Furthermore, in the agricultural sector, the largest union organisation was the *Unió de Rabassaires*, whose principal slogan had always been 'the land for he who works it' (*la terra per al qui la treballa*). The CNT, by contrast, had only a small presence in the Catalan fields. Although the Plan for Socialist Transformation called for the collectivisation of the large estates, in practice neither the Economic Advisory Council nor the *Generalitat* adopted significant measures regarding Catalan agriculture. On 27 August 1936, a decree created the Agricultural Syndicate Federation of Catalonia (*Federació de Sindicats Agrícoles de Catalunya*) and on 1 January 1937, a new decree liberated all tenant farmers (*masovers*), vineyard tenant farmers (*rabassaires*), and share-croppers (*parcers*) from their obligations. But no special measures were adopted to regulate collectivisation.

Collectivisation did, however, take place in some areas, like Empordá, Baix Llobregat, Baix Ebre, and certain parts of Lleida. Some writers have realistically estimated four hundred collectivisations.[14] The process caused some conflicts, particularly between the collectivisations, pushed by the anarchists, and traditional peasant individualism. The *Generalitat*'s Ministry of Agriculture was forced to denounce the pressure from certain groups to force peasants to collectivise their lands. The Ministry reminded Catalans that only confiscated estates could be collectivised, and it warned them that 'authors of all [other] attempts to collectivise must be denounced as saboteurs of the revolutionary order'.[15] Still, conflicts and confrontations continued.

In nearby Aragon and in territory that had been liberated by Catalan militias, however, collectivisation was a powerful force. Many historians have noted that militias coming from Catalonia greatly influenced the spread of agricultural collectives in Aragon and that collectivisation went farthest in this region. There, some four hundred and fifty agrarian collectivisations were carried out in spite of the fact that Aragonese anarchism, like Catalan anarchism, was strongest in urban and industrial centres. Because of the strength of Aragonese anarchism, the region formed an institution of autonomous libertarian power: at the end of September 1936 the CNT's regional committee called an assembly, in Bujaraloz, of urban and village committees as well as leaders of anarchist militia columns, including Durruti and others. This assembly, composed exclusively of anarchists, created a Regional Defence Council. Presided over by Joaquín Ascaso, the Council established its capital in Fraga, but it did not receive official recognition from the Republican Government until 23 December 1936, when members of the

---

14. There is not an extensive bibliography on the collectivisations in Catalonia. Besides the collective efforts published in *Col·lectivitzacions al Baix Llobregat (1936–1939)* (Adín, et al. 1989), see Cárdaba 2002.

15. *Crònica diària*, 12 October 1936.

Spanish Communist Party, the Left Republicans, the UGT, and the Syndicalist Party were included on the council.[16]

Catalonia's economic revolution affected many other aspects of social life as well. Since most city dwellers were renters, one such transformation, concerning urban property and housing, was particularly important. The National Plan for Socialist Transformation called for a partial devaluation of urban properties, and so the Economic Advisory Council faced, from the moment it was created, a controversy that different organisations hoped to address in contradictory ways. The CNT favoured the syndication of urban properties, while the UGT and the POUM favoured municipalisation. The intensity of the controversy explains the delay in adopting a policy, although a 12 August decree from the *Generalitat* did reduce housing rent in all of Catalonia. It was not until 1 February 1937 that the Joint Commission for the Administration and Control of Urban Property was created, and not until 11 June 1937 that the decree ordering the municipalisation of urban property, the UGT's plan, was approved.[17] The decree's objective was the conversion of all properties that produced rent for their owners into municipal property. As Francesc Roca points out, this was the first time ever that a measure was passed to collectivise all urban property. In a city like Barcelona, that entailed the administration of around three hundred thousand dwellings.

Like the revolution in the economic, political, and military spheres, the social revolution brought about profound changes, even if they may have been limited by the difficulties of war. Roca has underscored the task of putting into effect a 'new urban economy' that, with the intervention of trade unions, workers' political parties, and official government offices and municipalities, proposed modifying the cities structurally, rationalising urban life, and ending the implicit irrationality and marginalisation of the city under capitalism. At the same time, the revolution created for the first time a network of services accessible to all citizens.[18]

Among these transformations were those effected by the Council of the New Unified School (*Consell de l'Escola Nova Unificada*, or CENU). The CENU was created on 27 July 1936 with the aim of overcoming deficiencies in education, especially in industrial areas. Presided over by the rationalist teacher Joan Puig Elias, the council was to elaborate an educational plan for each child from birth until university. It hoped to build the New Unified School based on 'the principles of rationalism and human fraternity', and the teaching philosophy would be based on 'the universal sentiment of solidarity' and support 'the concerns

---

16. Casanova 1985.
17. Roca 1983, pp. 73–110, and Cendra i Bertran 2006, pp. 81–98.
18. Roca 1983, pp. 73–110.

of human society and the suppression of all types of privileges'.[19] At the end of October 1936, the CENU announced the opening of seventy school clusters with a capacity for thirty thousand children in Barcelona.[20] Despite the enormous difficulties of the task, no child was to be without a school. In the end, unfortunately, the experience was too brief, and the war sent so many refugee children to Catalonia that by December 1948 the number had risen to four hundred and forty-seven thousand.

But initiatives in education did not stop there. In addition to a fresh impetus for the libertarian and popular educational clubs (*ateneus*) so traditional in Catalonia, the collectivisations often set up schools based on rationalist principals. The Student Federation for Freedom of Conscience (*Federació Estudiantil de Consciències Lliures*) started workers' institutes, a sort of popular university that would function parallel to the already existing university. Educational initiatives for women included the groundbreaking Institute for Women's Professional Adaptation (*Institut d'Adaptació Professional de la Dona*). Created by the *Generalitat*, the institute was designed to give women technical and professional training at a time when they were playing an important role in replacing men in the workplace.[21]

Another revolutionary reform was put into place in public health and public assistance. On 28 August 1936, the General Health Council (*Consell General de la Sanitat*) was formed by the *Esquerra*, the workers' parties, the trade unions, and a representative from Barcelona's city government. The Health Council divided Catalonia into twenty regional health centres, each with its own regional health council.[22] The councils' campaign to eradicate prostitution by way of so-called *alliberadors de prostitució* and their 25 December decree on artificial pregnancy interruption were conquests that, while they may not have always achieved the results they had hoped for, show that they were attempting to bring about significant changes in social morality.[23]

---

19. See the decree in Consell de l'Escola Nova Unificada 1936.
20. *Crònica diària*, 27 October 1936.
21. For the role women played during the civil war, see Nash 1999.
22. Roca 1983, pp. 59–62.
23. Nash 1999. pp. 230–3. [TN] *Alliberadors de prostitució* were centres created by the anarchists whose goal was to put an end to prostitution. According to the anarchist women's organisation Mujeres Libres, in *liberatorios de prostitución* (the name in Castilian): 'the following plan would be followed: 1-Medical and psychiatric study. 2-Psychological and ethical treatment to promote a sense of repsonsibility in participants. 3-Professional preparation and direction. 4-Moral and material aid whenever necessary, even after work with the *liberatorios* has been completed. We hope that all workers' organisations, women's groups, and political parties as well as all politically conscious women and men will collaborate in this work. For its part, *Mujeres Libres* will contribute with the greatest constructive and emancipatory enthusiasm' (*Mujeres Libres*, Number 3, July 1936).

One of the social transformations that most influenced wartime propaganda was the new social image of women. Propaganda commonly showed women *milicianas* with rifles on their backs, ready to fight fascism at the front. Though the image became an important symbol during the war, women fighting at the front were more the exception than the rule. Women did move into the workforce in droves, and they often moved into jobs traditionally held by men. An atmosphere of social equality for women had been prepared in the previous years, and after the outbreak of war, all of the political and trade union organisations created women's sections, including Free Women (*Mujeres Libres*), already created in April 1936 by the CNT; the Women's Secretariat (*Secretariado Femenino*), created in September 1936 by the POUM; and the Catalan Women's Union (*Unió de Dones de Catalunya*), associated with the PSUC. The creation of the Working Women's Centre (*Casal de la Dona Treballadora*), directed by the Aragonese anarchist Amparo Poch, was also a significant achievement of this time.[24]

These transformations and others that occurred at the beginning of the war pose numerous interpretive challenges for historians. The first challenge is to consider the historical viability of the changes and their effects. Like the collectivisations, these transformations must be examined within their historical conjuncture, keeping in mind not only the difficulties that had to be overcome – and the difficulties that could not be overcome – but also the opposition of Catalan political sectors that did not want to see the revolution go too far and that did whatever they could to block its development. Given what was accomplished and the philosophy that inspired it, even in the often hostile environment in which it was achieved, the experience was undeniably positive. The achievements were a product of workers' determined self-management, and they represented the culmination of a long series of demands made and victories won, over many years, by the Catalan workers' movement.

Historians must also interpret the meaning of the transformations. For anarchist historians, following the lead of José Peirats, there is no doubt about their revolutionary character.[25] Bricall and Roca argue that, as a consequence of the revolutionary process, Catalonia was moving towards socialism during the war – a socialism that combined a new model of workers' self-management with planning.[26] This socialism was, at least in the first few months, plural and anti-authoritarian, and it seemed to many who experienced it that the utopian dream of socialism was transforming into an egalitarian reality.

---

24. See Rodrigo 2002.
25. Peirats 1971. [TN] These three volumes have now been translated into English by Chris Ealham and Paul Sharkey (Peirats 2001–).
26. Bricall 1970 and Roca 1983.

Chapter Eight
The War Economy and the War Industries

Upon creating the Defence Council and the Catalan Anti-fascist Militia Committee, we were immediately confronted with the enormous difficulty of providing war materials for the expeditionary forces and for those who needed to organise the rearguard without delay.

On their own initiative, factories and shops began to produce war materials. Everyone had ideas and made enthusiastic offers. But it was all disjointed, inefficient, sterile. It would be necessary to channel efforts, organise the enthusiasm, and give unity to everyone's work. And the government of the *Generalitat* hastened to rectify the difficult and even chaotic situation.

The war fronts grew. The war multiplied our demands. Munitions ran out. It would be necessary to organise an army, but it would also be necessary to improvise factories to build war-materials. For this supremely urgent task there would be no other solution than that of converting peacetime industry into a war industry that would begin to function immediately...[1]

These words, written by Josep Tarradellas, reveal the situation in Catalonia when war first broke out. Catalonia's all-important industrial sector was based on a peacetime economy, and there had never been any

---

1. [Josep Tarradellas] *L'Obra de la Comissió de la Indústria de Guerra. Generalitat de Catalunya*. These words come from an undated, typed document that though without a signatory, was written by Josep Tarradellas, president of the Commission. It is in the [archives] Archivo Montserrat Tarradellas i Macià.

initiative to develop an arms industry. Spanish arms were manufactured in other regions: Toledo, Sevilla, and Oviedo, to name just a few. The outbreak of war created a new demand and drove the Catalans to use their ingenuity in converting peacetime industry. Initially the efforts were spontaneous and intuitive, but in time, with a little planning, a substantial war industry was created out of nothing but the pre-existing Catalan industrial infrastructure. The initiative came first from the trade unions. In his memoirs, Joan García Oliver explains that it was he, in a conversation with Artillery Colonel Ricardo Giménez de la Beraza, who made the decision to create a war industry.[2] The key person chosen by the CNT to mobilise trade union members for this task was Eugenio Vallejo, from the metallurgy union. García Oliver states that he gave the following instructions to Vallejo to get the project underway:

> I will name you as representative of this Committee [the Catalan Anti-fascist Militia Committee] before the union and the workers. The union will make you its representative to work on behalf of the workers. Then I will put you into contact with Prunés from the *Generalitat* so that you, the union, and he can resolve the question of financing. With Colonel Giménez de la Beraza, you will form the Technical Committee for Industry and Production, whose mission will be to determine and produce the war supplies most needed: specifically, machinery and raw materials. With the union organisation, this should all be institutionalised through a process of socialisation, syndicalisation, or collectivisation.[3]

In the end, the *Generalitat* did not appoint Lluís Prunés i Sató, who at the time was minister of labour, but rather Josep Tarradellas. Tarradellas was named Minister of Public Services at the end of July, when Casanovas was president. That title was changed to Minister of Economy and Public Services on 6 August, during Casanovas's second term. At the beginning of August, Tarradellas was also the *Esquerra*'s representative on the Militia Committee, and from 26 September 1936 until the crisis of May 1937, he was prime minister and headed up the Office of Finance for the *Generalitat*. Tarradellas took his responsibilities so seriously that many years later he bluntly stated, 'I created Catalonia's war industry'.[4]

Indeed, from the Catalan war industry's beginning until its end, Tarradellas played a key role. From his position in the *Generalitat* he did everything possible to make the war industry a reality. Tarradellas proposed the creation of the War Industry Commission to direct and regulate the industry, and he presided over

---

2. García Oliver 1978, pp. 205–6.
3. García Oliver 1978, p. 206.
4. This comes from an interview with the journalist Tristán La Rosa in *La Vanguardia Española*, 8 September 1976.

it from its formation on 7 August 1936, defending it against every challenge. The brief decree establishing the commission stated in its first article that the new body 'would be in charge of production, distribution of acquisitions, inspection, and trials of all aspects of the industrial mobilisation'. The commission would take control of 'all factories, shops, laboratories, and centres of industrial mobilisation and arms trials and production seized by the *Generalitat* for these purposes'. The second article established that the commission 'would act under the authority of the Minister of Economy and Public Services and would comprise three representatives from the Defence Ministry, three from the Ministry of Economy and Public Services, one from the Finance Ministry, and one more from the Ministry of the Interior'. Finally, in article three, the decree stated that the new body would control the production of all war material in Catalonia: 'All industrial establishments retooled to produce war materials will not produce such material without the express authorisation of the War Industry Commission, which will take control of all such production'.[5]

On the same day that this first decree was issued, the *Generalitat* issued a second decree in order to 'seize, requisition, or occupy, according to need and in agreement with the Workers' Control Committee' a long list of enterprises: *S.A. Cros, Fabricación Nacional de Colorantes y Explosivos, Sociedad Electroquímica de Flix, Unión Española de Explosivos, Maquinista Terrestre y Marítima S.A., Hispano Suiza S.A., Material para Ferrocarriles y Construcciones S.A., Productos Pirelli S.A., Rivière S.A., Elizalde S.A., Metales y Platería Ribera S.A., Francisco Lacambra*, and *G. De Andreis Metalgraf Española*. The objective of the seizure was to 'employ all useful productive facilities for the manufacture of war materials'. At the same time, the *Generalitat* maintained the right to name a delegate to each of the industries and authorised an advisor from the Ministry of Economy and Public Services to seize, occupy, or requisition, whenever necessary, any other industry that might be of use in the war effort.[6]

Over the next few days two more orders were approved to regulate arms manufacturing in Catalonia. On 11 August, a decree was passed that strictly prohibited 'the manufacture of arms and all other war materials without the express authorisation of the War Industry Commission' and 'maximum sanctions' were set for 'industrialists or private producers who manufacture or attempt to manufacture such materials without obtaining the above-mentioned authority'.[7] Another order on 2 September announced that all industrialists, producers, and traders dealing with iron, steel, copper, brass, lead, tin or other metals were required to refrain from trading or moving these materials without express authorisation

---

5. *Butlletí Oficial de la Generalitat de Catalunya* 225, 12 August 1936, p. 1025.
6. *Butlletí Oficial de la Generalitat de Catalunya*, 225, 12 August 1936, pp. 1025–6.
7. *Butlletí Oficial de la Generalitat de Catalunya*, 227, 14 August 1936, p. 1050.

from the War Industries Commission. These industrialists, producers, and traders were given 48 hours to provide a detailed account for the War Industries Commission of their warehouse stocks of metals or alloys.[8]

In addition to these orders, on 12 August 1936 the Cabinet of the *Generalitat* (*Consell Executiu de la Generalitat*) named Tarradellas, Vallejo and Jiménez to the War Industries Commission, along with Lluís Arinzón i Mejías, Francesc Salses i Serra, Marià Martín Izquierdo, Manuel Martí Pallarés, Joan Deulofeu i Arquer, Alfred Sanjuán i Colomer, Miquel Ramírez de Cartagena and Josep Quero Molares.[9] All of the members represented the different ministries involved in the production of arms.

From this moment on, the development of arms manufacturing proceeded quickly, and a month later a basic war industry structure was functioning, with the first industries involved in arms production coming out with their first materials. On 9 August, Tarradellas and Vallejo made their first inspection of factories, including, according to the newspaper *La Humanitat, Hispano Suiza, Maquinista Terrestre y Marítima*, and *Material para Ferrocarriles y Construcciones*.[10] On 13 August, just one day after the appointment of the War Industries Commission, President Companys showed journalists assigned to the Palace of the *Generalitat* a twelve-kilogram aviation bomb that had been manufactured in Catalonia and that Tarradellas had sent that morning.[11]

Once created, the War Industries Commission had to organise itself in order to accomplish the tasks with which it was charged. For the specific task of manufacturing arms, the Commission divided its activities into three sections: chemical industries (detonators, explosives, etc.), metallurgical industries (arms, munitions, fuses, etc.), and aviation industries.[12] A month after the Commission's formation, twenty-four factories in Catalonia had begun to manufacture war material, and in October 1937 roughly five hundred factories and shops were under the control of the Commission. In all, more than fifty thousand workers received their weekly payslips from the Commission, totalling around three and a half million pesetas. Roughly thirty thousand more workers laboured in enterprises producing ancillary materials for the war.

The Commission was also in charge of initiating the construction of new factories: by the time the Commission's term was over, the *Generalitat* owned fifteen factories in different parts of Catalonia. At the same time, the Commission

---

8. *Diari Oficial de la Generalitat de Catalunya*, 5 September 1936, p. 1350.
9. *Crònica diària*, 12 August 1936.
10. *La Humanitat*, 9 August 1936. Also, *La Publicitat*, 10 August 1936 and *El Diluvio*, 11 August 1936.
11. *Crònica diària*, 13 August 1936. A photograph of Companys showing the bomb to journalists appears in *La Humanitat* of 15 August 1936.
12. *L'Obra de la Comissió de la Indústria de Guerra*, pp. 21–4.

took on other tasks, like supplying arms for the front, buying and distributing raw materials and handling petitions for funds from factories needing to buy raw materials or industrial equipment abroad. In addition, the Commission took charge of other areas like the inventions office and efforts to control or stop the production of clandestine arms, just to name a couple.

The first and most important goal was to produce arms and materials like gunpowder for the front. In addition to the *Generalitat*'s enterprises, the Commission was in charge of getting new factories up and running. There was a particular need for factories equipped for chemical production: before the war, Catalan chemical industries had been dedicated almost exclusively to the production of dyes, fertiliser, mineral acids, synthetic ammonia, bleach, soda, or mining explosives. After a detailed study of the existing chemical factories in Catalonia, only one was found to be suitable for producing explosives: all others would have to be built.

The Commission assigned a number from 1 to 15 to each of the new factories under construction. Number 1 produced lead tetraethyl for the ethylation of gasoline, which makes gasoline stronger and longer-lasting for use in aviation. Until June 1937, tetraethylide was produced in the Commission's laboratories, but after 1 July 1937 a factory designated specifically for the production of lead tetraethylide, ethyl-chloride and octanol was set up in Badalona. The same factory transformed lead tetraethylide purchased abroad into ethyl fluid. With 21 workers, it was the only such factory in Spain and only the second commercial factory of its kind in Europe.

Factory number 2, the Cellulose and Celluloide Co-operative, produced gunpowder made from esparto grass that had been transformed into cellulose. Number 2 began operating in November 1936 in Barcelona's Bordeta neighbourhood, producing four thousand kilograms of natamita, an explosive made of potash-chlorate and naphthalene that has the same effects as dynamite. In September 1937, total production reached thirty-eight thousand kilograms. In addition to natamita, number 2 manufactured shot of sizes 7½ and 7, and after July 1937, it produced gunpowder for rifles and cannons along with both common and special wicks for explosives. Toward the end of 1937, there were 397 workers in the factory.

Factory number 3 was the National Dye and Explosive Factory, a dye factory that, after August 1936, produced trinitrotoluene, an explosive. At first, it produced eleven thousand kilograms per month, but after September production grew to thirty-seven thousand kilograms per month. Number 3 produced other explosives as well.

In October 1937, factories 4, 5, 6, 10 and 13 had not yet begun production, despite the War Industries Commission's expectations. Number 4, in La Canya, a village near Olot, was supposed to produce cellulose from esparto grass. In

October, preparation for the factory had gone far, but it never actually began production. In August 1938, when the factory passed into the hands of the Republican Government, production still had not begun, in spite of the official announcement that 'production is about to begin and that test runs have been entirely satisfactory'.[13]

Factory number 5 in Queralps was to produce dyes and organic materials, although their uses were never clear. On 12 August 1938, at the last meeting of the War Industries Commission, Tarradellas stated: 'The manufacture of the planned products cannot be completed because the Government of the Republic is not interested at the moment, and so the factory will concentrate on producing ethyl acetate, sulphur chloride, bromide and others we are testing now'.[14]

Little is known about factory number 6. Nothing is mentioned in the War Industries Commission's *Informe de resultats* (performance report) or in the final assessment offered by Tarradellas in August 1938. The record only shows that in February 1937, the Commission awarded number 6 a site for the production of 'dyes and synthetic products', but the factory was probably never built.[15]

Factory number 10, also a chemical products plant, was being built in Cardona for the production of potassium chlorate, and it had another site in Suria where bromine would be produced. At both sites, production began before construction was complete. In Cardona, a provisional plant was producing two hundred and fifty kilograms per day of 98 percent pure potassium chlorate. When construction was complete, the factory was expected to produce one thousand two hundred kilograms per day. In August 1938, Tarradellas expected the factories to be completed in only three months.[16] The Suria factory produced bromine from unused bleach, and it seems that this was the first time bromine was made in Spain. During August, twelve kilograms of bromine were being produced per day, even though output was expected to increase to thirty kilograms per day.

Finally, the last factory under construction in August 1938, number 13, was expected to produce explosives. The Commission saw this factory, located in Gualba, as particularly important, but it experienced endless setbacks. On 12 August 1938, the factory was still unfinished in spite of the fact that there were five hundred construction workers and the stone used for the installation

---

13. Minutes from the War Industries Commission of the *Generalitat*, 12 August 1938 (*Comisión de la Industria de Guerra*).
14. Ibid.
15. Minutes from the War Industries Commission of the *Generalitat*, 25 February 1937 (*Comisión de la Industria de Guerra*).
16. Minutes from the War Industries Commission of the *Generalitat*, 12 August 1938 (*Comisión de la Industria de Guerra*).

had already exceeded twenty thousand tonnes. Meanwhile, some of the factory's departments were expected to begin production soon: for instance, the department of nitration was supposed to be up and running on 31 August.[17]

The rest of the factories passed through their own respective ups and downs. Factories 7 and 12 were supposed to produce Mauser cartridge rolls to replace the ones used up in the first days of the war: they would be sent to the armoury and barracks around Catalonia. From the beginning, the Commission pushed for the conversion of those factories that could most easily be adapted to cartridge production, but on 27 December 1936 it decided to create the first factory designed specifically for cartridge production: Factory number 7, on Denia Street in Barcelona.[18] At about the same time, another factory was set up in Girona to produce cartridge rolls, but it did not come under the control of the Commission until March 1937. In October 1937, 580 workers were employed in these two factories.

Factory 8, called 'Dawn' (*Amanecer*), began production in September 1936, manufacturing illumination rockets and other pyrotechnical devices.[19] After June 1937, production expanded to bombs and then, in October, lit signal-rockets. Later, a provisional workshop was set up in the same factory to manufacture black gunpowder as well as transport and signal rockets. The plan was for this provisional arrangement to end when factory 13 was up and running in Gualba.[20]

Factory 9, on Llull Street in Barcelona, employed 142 people to install charges in different types of hand grenades. This was extremely dangerous, and, at first, there were serious accidents due to the workers' lack of experience with the procedure. The construction of the bombs required assembling 23 different parts, including the casing, the safety clip and ring, the bracket, and the fuse.

Factory 11 in Gramanet del Besós (Santa Coloma de Gramanet) produced explosive materials like fuses and detonators. The factory produced, moreover, mercury fulminate, lead nitride, and other highly explosive powders. Capsules and mouldings were manufactured, capsules for Mauser cartridges were filled, and fuses and detonators were activated. Number 11 had 13 departments, and all the machines, instruments, and tools in the factory had been produced in Catalonia. In October 1937, there were 513 workers in the factory.

Initially, factory 14 repaired rifles and Mauser muskets. However, since the barrels for the rifles both in service and those stored in the armoury were often

---

17. Ibid.
18. Minutes from the War Industries Commission of the *Generalitat*, 27 September 1936 (*Comisión de la Industria de Guerra*).
19. Ibid.
20. Minutes from the War Industries Commission of the *Generalitat*, 12 August 1938 (*Comisión de la Industria de Guerra*).

not calibrated, there was an urgent need to produce new barrels. The special machines needed to drill and file the barrels could not come from abroad, due to the non-intervention pact among Western powers, and so they were built in Catalonia in buildings confiscated from the Salesian Mission in Barcelona. The machines were set up in one of the mission buildings that had been converted into factory space. On 1 March 1937, the Commission decided to use the warehouse of the Salesians to assemble rifles, and so number 14 became the factory where parts of the rifle produced all over Catalonia were assembled into the final product.

Number 15, in Olot, was the last factory that the Commission set up. This factory produced 'Fontbernat' machine guns, thanks to the collaboration of all the small shops in the city of Olot and to the production of all the necessary machines and implements in these same shops.

The autonomy enjoyed by the War Industries Commission and its capacity for initiative raised numerous suspicions on the part of the Republican Government in Madrid, anxious over the development of such a strategic industrial sector that was outside its control. For this reason, Madrid acted quickly to impede the Commission's work, particularly with regard to finances and the acquisition of raw materials, two areas in which Madrid's support was critical. After the May events in 1937, when Juan Negrín was presiding over the new Republican Government in Valencia and Indalecio Prieto was the new war minister, this lack of support became even more visible. On 6 June, Indalecio Prieto appointed Angel Pastor Velasco to the newly created position of Under Secretary of Arms and put him in charge of the war industries.[21] In June 1937, complaints had already been made against the government in Valencia: according to the Catalans, the Republican Government's under secretary of arms was doing all he could to obstruct the work of the Catalan Commission.[22] On 23 September 1937, the Republican Government decreed the creation of its own, identically named, 'Catalan War Industries Commission' (*Comisión de Industrias de Guerra de Cataluña*), with the aim of 'unifying the efforts of the state and those of the Catalan *Generalitat* with regards to war industries in the autonomous region'.[23] In practice, however, the new commission was under the direct control of the Republican Government's Ministry of Defence. The objective in creating this body was none other than to

---

21. *Diario Oficial del Ministerio de Defensa Nacional* 138, 9 June 1937. [TN] The 'May events' are those following the attempted takeover of the anarchist-held telephone company (*Telefónica*) in May 1937. See chapter 10.
22. See the minutes from the War Industries Commission of the Generalitat, 22 and 26 June 1937 (*Comisión de la Industria de Guerra*).
23. *Diario Ofical del Ministerio de Defensa Nacional*, 24 September 1937. (TN) As this was a Spanish Republican Government creation, the name of the commission is in Castillian Spanish.

eliminate the *Generalitat*'s role in arms production. As was happening in other spheres after the May Events of 1937, the Republican Government was reclaiming control of the powers it had lost in July 1936. As a result, the War Industries Commission of the *Generalitat* lost control of all factories other than those it had built.

After the power shuffle following the May events, the Catalan war industries never recovered. It was clear that the Republican Government had decided to buy war material on the European market and had no interest in producing arms for itself. The industries were neglected, and even the factories dependent on the *Generalitat*'s Commission had a difficult time surviving. On 16 August 1938, the Republican Government – which now resided in Barcelona – took over the factories that were still in the hands of the *Generalitat* and that had been created by the *Generalitat*'s Commission. The decree, published three days later, stated in no uncertain terms: 'All factories and shops producing arms, munitions, powders, explosives, and war implements that have not yet been placed under the direction of the under secretary of arms, no matter whether they belong at present to central bodies or those of the autonomous region, or if they have been initiated by independently functioning military units, will fall under the authority of the under secretary, such that either the under secretary or whomever that person delegates will be in charge of the aforementioned shops and factories.'[24]

The revealing part of the decree was the reference to the need for a unitary command in all spheres of the Republic's military efforts. Just as single command of all the armies had been achieved, it was seen as critical that this same unity be extended to all spheres, and particularly to the war industries.

The idea of a single command was not new, and it seems obvious that if the Republican Government had not effected this plan until now, it was because of its own impotence. At this point in the war, however, there had already been many changes in the Republican rearguard, and the *Generalitat* was a shadow of its former self. As Companys protested in a long letter to Negrín in April 1938, the Republican Government completely eclipsed the *Generalitat* when it moved to Barcelona. Perhaps what is most surprising is that the Republican Government waited until August 1938 before completely liquidating the Catalan war-industries. When the Catalan War Industries Commission was finally left with no factories under its control, it would be scarcely six months before Catalonia was occupied by Franco's armies and the Republic suffered its final defeat.

---

24. *Diario Oficial del Ministerio de Defensa Nacional*, 19 August 1938.

Chapter Nine
Forming the Unity Government and the First Political Disagreements

By the end of the summer of 1936, the war was not going well for the Republic: it had failed to gain even a single substantial victory over the rebelling military, while the rebels themselves had managed to link the army in Africa with that of the North in order to 'liberate' the Alcázar in Toledo (in the process creating an important myth for Franco), to establish positions on the Peninsula, and to halt or defeat every Republican military offensive. In the face of a war that looked as though it would drag on, the need for a unified command was obvious. At the beginning of September, Prime Minister José Giral announced his resignation, and on 4 September a new cabinet was formed, presided over by new Prime Minster Francisco Largo Caballero, a left socialist, with a collection of ministers representing political parties and trade union organisations. In a note made public on 4 September, Giral's government explained in no uncertain terms the intentions behind their resignation: 'The grave circumstances the nation is experiencing and the duration of the civil war we are enduring, which it appears will be long, leads the present government to desire and advise that a replacement government be created that will represent each and every one of the political parties and worker and trade union organisations of recognised influence among the Spanish people, from whom power always originates'.[1]

---

1. *La Vanguardia*, 5 September 1936.

The new government was formed by Largo Caballero (President and War Minister), Julio Alvarez del Vayo (State Minister), Indalecio Prieto (Sea and Air), Angel Galarza (Interior), Juan Negrín (Treasury), Vicente Uribe (Agriculture), Jesús Hernández (Education), José Antonio Aguirre (Public Works), Mariano Ruiz Funes (Justice), Anastasio de Gracia (Industry and Commerce), Bernardo Giner de los Ríos (Communications), Josep Tomàs i Piera (Labour), and José Giral Pereira (minister without portfolio). In all, there were six socialist ministers, three left republicans, one Basque nationalist, and one *Esquerra* member. The big news was the presence of two Communist Party members – Uribe and Hernández. Meanwhile, for the moment, the anarchists of the CNT continued their traditional apoliticism, choosing not to participate.

The formation of Largo Caballero's government in Madrid made it easier to form a new government in Catalonia. There, the CNT did break with tradition when they joined the new Unity Government, created on 26 September, presided over by Josep Tarradellas. Tarradellas was Minister of Finance as well as Prime Minister, and he was joined by Felipe Díaz Sandino (Defence); Andreu Nin from the POUM (Justice); the Esquerra's Ventura Gassol (Culture); Artemi Aiguader, also from the Esquerra (Internal Security); three CNT members: Joan P. Fàbregas (Economy), Josep Joan i Domènech (Supplies), and Antoni García i Birlán (Health and Social Assistance); two from the PSUC, Joan Comorera (Public Services) and Miquel Valdés (Labour and Public Works); *Rabassaires* member Josep Calvet (Agriculture); and Rafael Closas from the ACR as a minister without portfolio.

The formation of Catalonia's new government brought an end to the governments controlled exclusively by the *Esquerra* since the beginning of the war. It had two significant new features: first, it brought under one unified government the full plurality of anti-fascist organisations and parties, and second, as has been mentioned, it gained the participation of anarchist leaders, who were departing radically from their usual rejection of political power.[2] But the demands and exigencies of the moment made participation in government more opportune since, as the manifesto of the new cabinet explained, the new basic objectives were to identify strategies to better wage the war, to establish new economic norms, and, above all, to resolve the problems caused by lack of discipline and control. Among other things, the manifesto declared:

> Fascism has raised arms against the Republic and mired the country in the horrors of civil war. Hoping to save the privileges of the traditional castes and of big capitalism, fascism has destroyed them and added to the anguish of war

---

2. There is a sizable debate among anarchist ranks about their participation in government. See Lorenzo 1969.

the inevitable difficulties of reconstructing the economy on a new basis. The cabinet of the *Generalitat* proposes to confront with determination the reality imposed upon us by criminal fascism, to win rapidly and decisively the war, and to build immediately, on the ruins of the régime that fascism sank on 19 July, a more just economy whose general lines advance the way things ought to be on the day after victory.[3]

Finally, on 5 November, four anarcho-syndicalists from Catalonia joined Largo Caballero's government: Joan Peiró (appointed Minister of Industry), Joan García Oliver (Justice), Juan López (Commerce), and Federica Montseny (Health). On the same day the National Committee of the CNT publicly justified their entry into the Government of the Republic by referring to wartime demands and, above all, to the assault of Franco's army on Madrid: 'A supremely important factor in this decision is the difficult situation on certain war fronts, and especially the central front where the enemy stands at the doors of Madrid. For this reason, in these moments of such profound historical responsibility, conscious of the hopes that people in general have to carry out this task, and sure that this responsibility will guarantee that the fight against fascism will take us down the path of victory, we do not hesitate to make this sacrifice for the working class (*el pueblo trabajador*), to whom we owe everything and for whose cause we fight'.[4]

For both the Catalan government and the government of the Republic, which had moved from Madrid to Valencia as of 6 November to avoid Franco's siege, the challenge was to use their newly regained stature – brought by the participation of the anarchists – to bring order to the rearguard, regulate new institutions, put an end to illegal actions, bring legality to the social revolution and, above all, win the war. The task was enormous. By participating in the government, the revolutionary forces implicitly recognised and legitimised Republican institutions in Catalonia and renounced the bodies that, since the July Days, had challenged the authority of those institutions. Hence, the Militias Committee dissolved itself by decree on 1 October, and a decree issued on 9 October by the Interior Security Council, along with a 12 October order, dissolved all local committees with instructions that they were to be replaced by new city governments. The new norm stated that the city governments (*ajuntaments*) would be formed before a popular judge of the locality and that they would respect the same representative proportionality as the newly formed Cabinet.[5]

---

3. *La Vanguardia*, 27 September 1936.
4. *La Vanguardia*, 6 November 1936. [TN] From 1881 to 2011, this publication was in Castillian Spanish, hence 'el pueblo trabajador'.
5. *Diari Oficial de la Generalitat de Catalunya*, 11 October 1936. The decrees appeared in Spanish in the *Vanguardia* on the same day. The decree dissolving the local committees stated:

Putting the new orders into effect did not take long: throughout October many new city governments appeared in Catalonia. In Barcelona, for example, the new government was formed on 21 October, with nine representatives from the *Esquerra* and the CNT, six from the PSUC – who added to their growing strength by providing representation for the UGT – and three each from the POUM, the ACR and the *Rabassaires*. Carles Pi i Sunyer from the *Esquerra* continued as mayor. In Lleida, the new government formed on 23 October. Félix Lorenzo from the CNT became mayor only after overcoming strong resistance from POUM militants: as the dominant workers' organisation in the city, the POUM was severely disadvantaged by the new representational distribution mandated by the *Generalitat*. In Girona, however, both the *Esquerra* and the PSUC refused to participate, and so the city government only had representatives from the CNT and the POUM, with 14 and six councillors respectively.[6]

The obligation to duplicate the political proportionality of the *Generalitat* posed yet another problem, since not all organisations maintained an active presence in all of Catalonia's municipalities. This led both to the creation of artificial parties that had not previously existed in many cities and to dual militancy, where parties and organisations with extra members ceded them to other organisations so that the decrees coming from the *Generalitat* could be followed. In practice, at the beginning of October 1936, the only organisations that could boast of an effective presence in the whole of Catalonia were the *Esquerra* and the CNT. With the new decree in effect, the political panorama in Catalonia diversified and became more complicated, and in the long run, the only organisation that benefitted from the *Generalitat*'s degree was the PSUC, which had only recently formed and was experiencing spectacular growth.

The new Unity Government played a significant role in gradually re-establishing republican normalcy, although there is some debate about the value of such changes. Barcelona's mayor, Carles Pi i Sunyer, wrote in his memoirs that 'the new government's programme consisted in re-establishing, as much as possible, civil discipline, channelling the revolutionary fever toward goals appropriate for

---

'First article: All local committees in Catalonia, whatever they are called, shall be dissolved, and so shall all local bodies of a cultural, economic, or other nature that may have arisen as a result of the subversive movement.

Second article: Refusal to dissolve will be considered a factious act and anyone involved will be turned over to the Popular Justice Tribunals'.
Barcelona, 9 October 1936, First Councillor José Tarradellas.

6. In his memoirs, Carles Pi i Sunyer writes about the inclusion of CNT militants in Barcelona's city government (Pi i Sunyer 1975, p. 416). *La Vanguardia* of 22 October 1936 gives significant coverage to the formation of the Barcelona government. For Tarragona, see Piqué i Padró 1998, pp. 49–50. For Girona, see Cornellà 1986, pp. 135–87. And for Lleida, see Sagués San José 2003, pp. 91–4.

the moment, and doing something reasonable and positive for the war effort'.[7] There was a little of everything in this new government: by means of the Collectivisation and Workers' Control Decree and other measures, it began the process of legalising the revolution begun by the masses. Yet, as Pi i Sunyer points out, while the government was legalising revolutionary changes, they were also channelling them and limiting them – in other words, applying the brakes to the revolution. This strategy of the *Generalitat* was an old trick that the Government of the Republic would also use: legalise revolutionary gains in order to block the revolutionary process. And in Catalonia, with their participation in the *Generalitat* and the city *ajuntaments*, this strategy had the effective consent of the CNT, the FAI, and the POUM.

The normalisation process included regaining public order and bringing political repression under control. To accomplish this task, the Government of the Republic created the Rearguard Vigilance Militias on 16 September 1936, and it placed them under the auspices of the General Security Office. On 9 October, regulations were established for making arrests. In Catalonia, new measures were also adopted to regulate repression. In the courts, the Justice Department's Andreu Nin dissolved the Legal Office that had been created in the first weeks of the war, directed in succession by Ángel Semblancat and Eduardo Barriobero: the office had never succeeded in defining a new juridical system and had instead resorted to a seemingly infinite number of irregular procedures.[8] To its credit, the Legal Office had created the popular tribunals discussed here in Chapter Six, which helped to bring the political repression seen at the outbreak of war under legal and institutional control.

In another action, the different vigilance and defence services that had been created in the first period of the war – the security controls, border controls, information services, etc. – were placed under the direction of an Interior Security Committee linked to the Interior Security Council and formed with the same representative proportionality as the *Generalitat*'s cabinet. The anarchist Aurelio Fernández was appointed as the committee's general secretary, and Dionís Eroles, also an anarchist, was named commander of the security patrols. The testimonies all agree that these changes effected a significant decrease in repressive action compared with the first months of war, as those accused of collaborating with fascism were generally tried by the popular tribunals.

Naturally, the biggest challenge for the new governments was the war itself. As prime minister and minister of war of the Republican Government, Largo Caballero moved quickly, adopting measures on 29 September 1936 to 'militarise' the militias, a first step in creating a new army that would soon be known as the

---

7. Pi i Sunyer 1975, p. 415.
8. See Pagès 1990a and 1998.

Popular Army (*Ejército Popular*) and that would bring back military hierarchy and centralised command.⁹

In Catalonia the process was slower. On 3 October, after dissolving the Militias Committee, the Defence Council of the *Generalitat*, overseen by Felipe Díaz Sandino, took over the military responsibilities of the committee, although he named the anarchist García Oliver Secretary General of the Council. Then, on 27 October, following the lead of what was happening in the rest of the country, the *Generalitat* militarised the militias, re-imposing the army's traditional hierarchies. After 1 November, all Catalan militias on the Aragon front were to obey the Code of Military Justice that was in effect before the outbreak of war:

> Article One: As of 1 November, all anti-fascist militias recruited up until now will be subject to the regulations of the Code of Military Justice established by the cabinet of the *Generalitat*, as well as those being written at this time. All measures deemed appropriate, whether punitive or compensatory, will be effected and given legal force by the popular tribunals appointed for this purpose as well as by the Executive Committee.
>
> Article Two: While the new Code of Military Justice awaits approval, discipline will be effected according to the Code of Military Justice currently in effect.
>
> Article Three: Persons enlisted in the current anti-fascist militias whose age does not correspond to the legal age for active duty determined in the new regulations and who do not wish to place themselves under the new code will indicate their request to the leaders of their respective units within the timeframe indicated in the first article. The respective leaders will pass on such requests to their sector commanders and these in turn will communicate to the Defence Council the requests of those unwilling to serve and proceed to grant their resignations.
>
> Article Four: All mobilised personnel assigned to health services, war industries and rearguard services, with the exception of nurses and women, will also be subject to the preceding articles.
>
> Article Five: Each sector leader will propose to the Defence Council within a term of ten days a plan for organising their militias and columns into

---

9. See *Diario Oficial del Ministerio de la Guerra*, 30 September 1936. Article 1 of the decree states clearly:
   As of 10 October, militia volunteers of the Central Army and, after 20 October, all other militia volunteers will take on the military's features and regulations, with all its classes and ranks, for as long as the current circumstances last. When the aforementioned dates have passed, all members will be held to the laws of the Code of Military Justice, other military regulations, and the rewards, punishments and other procedures currently in place and applicable to the permanent military forces of the Loyal Army of the Nation.

battalions, companies, and sections, in agreement with the provided staffing plans, and for distributing among their units, with no distinctions made on the basis of party affiliations, the machine guns, mortars, infantry cannons, communications supplies, and other war materials available in the sector, making sure to provide the supplies necessary for a number of complete units. Sector leaders will also propose leaders for each group of three battalions and their respective staff officers.

Article Six: The general commander of the militia artillery will propose an analogous plan for the artillery organisation of the entire front.[10]

These measures, which would have been unthinkable at the beginning of the war, were adopted largely because of the favourable predisposition of the anarchist leaders, who little by little were abandoning their anarchist principles. Even García Oliver, before accepting his appointment as a minister, had been on the High War Council (*Consejo Superior de Guerra*), a body created by the Government of the Republic to reorganise the Republican military forces and work towards creating the Popular Army. Around the time when the anarchists were beginning to participate in government, a phrase circulated, attributed to Durruti, that revealed the new attitude of the CNT and FAI: 'We renounce everything except victory' ('*Renunciamos a todo menos a la victoria*'). Nonetheless, Durruti's immediate reaction to the militarisation decrees was far from positive. Durruti had been on the front since the first days of the war, and on the radio on 5 November he stated forcefully, 'If this militarisation decreed by the *Generalitat* is intended to scare us and impose iron discipline, they are mistaken. We welcome those who have cooked up the decree to come to the front to see our morale and our discipline, and then we will go and compare what they find in our ranks with the morale and discipline in the rearguard'.[11]

The militarisation of the Catalan militias, in any case, proceeded slowly, and in practice it met with the opposition of anarcho-syndicalist militants unwilling to renounce their ideas of self-management (*autogestión*). In fact, it was not until the beginning of 1937 that the transformation of the militias into the regular Popular Army began. The anarcho-syndicalist militias active on the Aragon Front became the 25th, 26th, and 28th Divisions; the Lenin Division of the POUM became the 29th Division; and the PSUC militia became the 27th Division. The Macià-Companys column was converted into the 30th Division. Colonel Vicenç Guarner was appointed head (*jefe supremo*) of all the forces, and the Catalan Army was renamed the Eastern Army. Leaders coming from the militias were able to rise no further than the rank of Commander. Until the summer of 1937,

---

10. *Diari Oficial de la Generalitat de Catalunya*, 28 October 1936. The same decree was published in Spanish in *La Vanguardia* the next day.
11. *La Vanguardia*, 6 November 1936.

however, the military reorganisation was still more theoretical than real: the newly named divisions did not change their composition in any substantial way, their leaders were the same, and the government had neither the opportunity nor sufficient authority to intervene in the appointment of militia leaders.

While some measures adopted by the Unity Government were carried out, others were never thoroughly normalised, particularly after a number of other factors, both internal and external, began to negatively affect Catalan society. The war continued to go badly for the Republic: in addition to the defeats suffered against Franco's African army, the rebel offensive in the Basque Country first conquered Irún and then, soon afterward, San Sebastián. After 20 October, Franco decided to make a general assault on Madrid, with the hope of rapidly occupying the Republican capital. In response to the offensive, the Republican government moved to Valencia on 6 November. The President of the Republic, Manuel Azaña, had already taken up residence in Barcelona's Parliament Palace (*Palau del Parlament*) on 19 October.

Apart from the negative effects on the morale of the combatants, the first Republican defeats spurred a flood of refugees to Catalonia that would not stop throughout the rest of the war and that would compound the difficulties of providing food and housing for the region. The 6 November 1936 editorial in *La Vanguardia* speaks to the massive arrival of refugees, initially coming from Extremadura and Andalucía, and the urgent need to find solutions to the problems presented by their arrival. Among other things, the editorial states:

> The refugees create in Barcelona, a city already overwhelmed with needs, a new problem. It is extremely difficult to interrupt these new immigrant waves, waves caused by the drama we are all living. While there are thousands of war refugees who look for help among us, there are more, many more, that are still roaming, sleepwalking among the smoking mines of homes that will probably never be reconstructed and through desolate fields where they were once able to eke out a meagre existence.[12]

At the beginning of autumn, the food problem was becoming acute, especially in Barcelona. On 13 October, a family ration card was established, and on 8 December, a war menu was implemented in public establishments. A decrease in industrial production, beginning in November, and the increase in food prices led to a rise in unemployment. As inflation hit, private hoarding and the consequent disappearance of silver coins from circulation posed the first problems of fractional currencies, forcing the *Generalitat* to issue after 1 December the first paper bills of 2.50, 5, and 10 pesetas.

---

12. *La Vanguardia*, 6 November 1936.

There were soon even more problems. The Aragon front was inactive, and the different Catalan anti-fascist forces began to exchange accusations. On 17 November, the war reached Catalonia proper when the rebel cruiser *Canarias* bombed Rosas Bay. Political problems also emerged. The question of how to maintain public order was still unresolved and was an enduring source of tension. On 27 October, for example, Minister of Culture Ventura Gassol fled to France, fearing an anarchist attempt on his life. On 20 November – the same day Durruti was killed on the Madrid front – the FAI responded to accusations against them by asserting their opposition to what they said were 'various groups of individuals going from village to village committing all sorts of villainous misdeeds'. On 24 November, Andreu Revertés, the *Generalitat*'s police commissioner and a man linked with *Estat Català*,[13] was removed from office and executed after being accused of organising a separatist movement and seizing a shipment of gold and silver ingots that the Madrid Government had sent 'by error' to Barcelona.[14]

Into this tense atmosphere was added controversy between the PSUC, an orthodox communist party increasingly tied to Stalin, and the POUM, an oppositionist communist party critical of Stalin. The origins of the controversy were numerous and complex. First, there was a substantial difference in the politics that each party advocated: while the PSUC supported a return to 'republican normality', the POUM advocated a radical politics that would deepen the revolution. Furthermore, the POUM had been extremely critical of Stalin when in August 1936 the first trials of the old-guard Bolsheviks began in Moscow and culminated with the execution of, among others, Lev Borisovich Kamenev and Grigory Zinoviev.[15] The POUM was also critical of the Soviet Union's politics of neutrality and its faithful adherence to the international Non-Intervention Pact that, until October 1936, Stalin maintained toward the war in Spain.[16] Moreover,

---

13. [TN] *Estat Català* (Catalan State Party) was a Catalan independentist party formed by Francesc Macià in 1922 that, according to Albert Balcells, supported complete separation from, and insurrection against, the Spanish state (Balcells 1991, p. 81). The party did not participate in the Unity Government.

14. In *La Vanguardia*, 26 November 1936, the Interior Security Minister, Artemi Aiguader, stated that he could not make public the reasons for Revertés's dismissal. A meeting of the *Generalitat* ratified the dismissal and named Martí Rauret as his replacement. The same newspaper, on 27 November, announced that a new police commissioner was taking over and, in the only public reference to the case of Revertés's dismissal, reported Aiguader as saying that 'it is better not to talk at this time about what has happened in the offices of the Police Commissioner, and that he, from his position, was prepared to be unyielding with anybody not acting within the law'.

15. See 'Resolución del Comité Ejecutivo del POUM sobre el proceso y el fusilamiento, en Moscú, de 16 bolcheviques de la Revolución de octubre', (Resolution of the Executive Committee of the POUM on the trial and execution in Moscow of sixteen Bolsheviks of the October Revolution) in *La Batalla*, 28 August 1936 (Comité Ejecutivo del POUM 1936).

16. *La Batalla*, 13 September 1936.

the PSUC and the POUM were attempting to occupy the same political space. This incompatibility was exhibited clearly in September 1936 when the POUM tried to negotiate with the leaders of the Catalan UGT, which was controlled by the PSUC, over the entry of the unions of the Workers' Federation of Trade Union Unity (*Federación Obrera de Unidad Sindical*, or FOUS), which were affiliated with the POUM, into the UGT's trade union federation. The FOUS did finally join the UGT in September 1936, but without the PSUC and the POUM arriving at an agreement prior to the reorganisation.[17]

The conflict between the two communist parties would only grow worse. At the time, the PSUC was experiencing spectacular growth, going from six thousand members in July 1936, when it was created, to sixty thousand by April 1937. The POUM, meanwhile, claimed to have thirty thousand members in December 1936.[18] The PSUC's growth, according to sources close to the organisation, was linked to the political project the party defended: popular frontism and moderation.[19] A propaganda campaign, begun in October 1936, contributed to the spectacular growth of the PSUC as well as, on the national level, to that of the PCE (Spanish Communist Party).

The 14 October arrival in Barcelona of the Soviet ship *Zyrianin*, loaded with three thousand tons of provisions, provided occasion for a plethora of public tributes to the Russian people.[20] At the celebration of the anniversary of the Russian Revolution, on 8 November, the Soviet Consul in Barcelona, the ex-Trotskyist Vladimir Antonov Ovssenko, addressed the Catalan people in one of the most enthusiastic popular gatherings of the first part of the war:

> You are our class brothers with the same dreams that we have, and therefore, our sympathies are with you.
>
> We want to help you in the fight against fascism that has sold your country to foreigners and has mobilised Moors and bandits to assassinate workers and to impose their desire to exploit you.

---

17. *La Batalla*, 2 September 1936, published a recommendation from the Executive Committee of the POUM that all the affiliates of the FOUS join the UGT. The POUM leader, Andreu Nin, explained the recommendation in the party newspaper at the end of the month in the article '¿Por qué los sindicatos de la FOUS ingresan en la UGT?' ('Why are the FOUS Affiliate Unions Joining the UGT?') (*La Batalla*, 23 September 1936).
18. With regards to the PSUC, the statistics come officially from the party, according to Andreu Mayayo (1986). The statistics for the POUM were given in a meeting of the Augmented Central Committee celebrated in Barcelona in December 1936. See Pagès 1986.
19. See, among other things, Mayayo et al. 1986.
20. The 15 October 1936 edition of *La Vanguardia* had this dramatic headline: 'In Barcelona's port. The arrival of the Soviet steamer *Zyrianine* has awakened great enthusiasm. Enormous crowds at the docks. Show of sympathy for the USSR and its representative in our capital. Welcome speeches'. See also the information given in the *Crònica diària*, 14 October 1936.

We, all workers and all people with human conscience, cannot allow this. We will make every effort possible to prevent it from happening again.

It is from this square that your President Companys was the first to proclaim the Republic. It is he who expressed the sentiments of all his working people (*todo su pueblo de trabajadores*), and it is because of him that fascism will never be able to conquer or destroy the Republic. This magnificent people has united to defend the Republic and to forever destroy fascism. Fascism will be annihilated. Down with fascism! Long live Republican Spain! Long live the Catalan people fighting against fascism! Long live the noble hero of this magnificent struggle, President Companys![21]

Soon afterwards, the first confrontation between the POUM and the PSUC broke out. At the end of November, the POUM denounced the Soviet interferences that had prevented them from participating in the Madrid Defence Council (*Junta de Defensa de Madrid*), a body created after the government's move to Valencia.[22] On 28 November, the consul general of Barcelona published a *communiqué* in the pages of the PSUC newspaper, *Treball*, that accused the POUM newspaper, *La Batalla*, of forming a part of the international fascist press.[23] From this moment on, the PSUC waged a campaign to expel the POUM from the *Generalitat*.

The crisis of the Unity Government came into the open on 12 December. On 13 December, the Secretary General of PSUC, Joan Comorera, declared that 'the POUM has initiated a shameful campaign of attacks and slanders against the great proletarian country and friend, using exactly the same arguments as the fascist Germans and Italians'.[24] The CNT, in contrast, chose to view the crisis as a mere spat between the PSUC and the POUM and continued to advocate the Unity Government. In the words of one of the CNT's leaders, Joan P. Fàbregas: 'The CNT believes that it is essential to continue collaborating with all trade union and political sectors that until now have formed the cabinet, since in these dangerous moments we men of the CNT understand that creating divisions could damage the task we have in common'.[25]

The crisis lasted until 17 December, when a new 'syndical' government was formed. The POUM lost its representation, and PSUC members Rafael Vidiella, Joan Comorera, and Miquel Valdés joined as representatives of the UGT. In this way, the PSUC achieved the same representation as the *Esquerra* – which in this

---

21. Printed in *La Vanguardia*, 19 November 1936.
22. See 'El POUM y la junta de Defensa de Madrid', *La Batalla*, 27 November 1936.
23. See *Treball*, 28 November 1936. It was published in Spanish by *La Vanguardia* on the same day.
24. *Treball*, 13 December 1936.
25. *Crònica diària*, 15 December 1936.

government served to represent the petit-bourgeoisie – and just one ministry fewer than the CNT. The composition of the new government was as follows:

Treasury	Josep Tarradellas, Esquerra
Defence	Francesc Isgleas, CNT
Economy	Diego Abad de Santillán, CNT
Public Services	Josep Juan Doménech, CNT
Health and Social Assistance	Pedro Herrera, CNT
Provisions	Joan Comorera, UGT (PSUC)
Labour and Public Works	Miquel Valdés, UGT (PSUC)
Justice	Rafael Vidiella, UGT (PSUC)
Interior Security	Artemi Aiguader, Esquerra
Culture	Antoni M. Sbert, Esquerra
Agriculture	Josep Calvet, *Rabassaires*

José Peirats, one of the official historians of the anarcho-syndicalist movement, wrote that 'the CNT itself swallowed the bait', fooled by the apparent trade-union orientation of the cabinet.[26] At the time, Peirats and the anarchist leaders enthusiastically welcomed the 'trade-unionist' cabinet, and Peirats defended the new government in the CNT's newspaper:

> From now on, Catalonia can count on a government without political parties. The CNT will not tolerate any impositions, from wherever they might come, nor admit exclusions that might be interpreted as a desire to break the established proletarian unity. Whoever might aspire to do so has not succeeded in finding in us any grounds to satisfy their desire, and the parties without a trade union foundation that participated in the cabinet of the *Generalitat* have been relieved of those functions. It is not they who have been called to govern political life, but instead the trade unions, cornerstone of the new economy that is being born and that will achieve perfection through experience itself.[27]

In the end, the new government failed to resolve any of the problems. In fact, the problems grew worse, leading to a decisive confrontation: the May events of 1937.

---

26. Peirats 1971, volume 2, p. 102. [TN] Peirats does not explain here why he does not consider the *Esquerra* members on the cabinet to be representatives of a political party.

27. *Solidaridad Obrera*, 17 December 1936

Chapter Ten
The May Events of 1937

After the formation of the new 'trade union' government, Catalan society faced even more difficulties, and relations among those involved in the political process deteriorated further. The shortage of food was the most serious issue. The scarcity had been acute since the beginning of the war, especially in Barcelona, and it was so serious by the end of July 1936 that the Central Supplies Committee was urging Catalan farmers to inform their local governments of the livestock they had available for public consumption. The committee also asked farmers to continue bringing their goods to the Barcelona markets so that citizens in the capital would not be without provisions.[1]

At the beginning of October, with the war an undeniable reality, the Central Supplies Committee initiated a campaign to put an end to the daily food queues that were causing numerous confrontations.[2] A few weeks later, the Supplies Ministry began to distribute ration cards to households for access to scarce goods.[3] People were already making trips from Barcelona into Catalonia's agricultural areas, such as Maresme, Baix Llobregat, and Garraf, in search of food. These trips became so frequent that at the beginning of December the Supplies Ministry decided to confiscate packages with meat, eggs, and chickens at the city's entry points. The *Crònica diària* wrote that the Ministry considered the ability to leave the city in search of food 'an unfair

---

1. *Crònica diària*, 31 July 1936.
2. *Crònica diària*, 3 October 1936.
3. *Crònica diària*, 20 October 1936.

advantage for those who had the means to travel. Furthermore, it was well-proven that 90 percent of the goods that were brought into the city were then sold at exorbitant prices and were not, naturally, being purchased by workers'.[4]

Tensions increasingly mounted as people began to look for politicians to blame for the scarcity. Soon after the formation of the new government, the CNT and the FAI accused the new minister of supplies and the secretary general of the PSUC, Joan Comorera, of being responsible for the bread shortage in Barcelona. Meanwhile, the PSUC mobilised its members to organise a demonstration of support for Comorera and to blame instead the committees, particularly the 'supplies committees' controlled by the CNT, which were responsible for the distribution of food in Barcelona. There were thirteen such committees, one in each district, and each was charged with running the warehouse for its respective district. The committees were in charge of doing everything possible to provide food for the sick and milk for children, and they were to ensure that everything else was sold in the most rational way possible. It did not take long for tensions to escalate. On the same day that the Supplies Ministry called publicly for calm (*serenidad*) in the face of the bread shortage and stated that enough wheat and flour would be arriving to feed the rearguard and the front in just a few days, the first protest was organised by women in Barcelona demanding 'fewer committees, more bread, and just one government, the *Generalitat*'.[5] The day before, in the neighbouring city of Hospitalet de Llobregat, armed groups had stolen all the supplies and caused significant damage in an assault on two provisions co-operatives (*L'Avenç* and *Respeto Mutuo*).[6]

Protests by women against the food shortages continued into January and February 1937. There were two on 5 January. The first one took place in front of the Palace of the *Generalitat* and led to President Companys meeting with a commission of women who carried a banner saying: 'Anti-fascist women demand the abolition of the Control Committees. We want the government of the *Generalitat*. U.H.P'.[7] The second protest occurred in the early evening in front of the Supplies Ministry on *Paseo de Pi i Margall* street, and in this case women

---

4. *Crònica diària*, 9 December 1936.
5. *Crònica diària*, 26 December 1936 and *La Vanguardia*, 27 December 1936.
6. *La Vanguardia*, 27 December 1936.
7. [TN] The UHP, or *Unión de Hermanos Proletarios* (Proletarian Brothers' Union), was a broad alliance of labour organisations and parties that formed during the 1934 revolution in Asturias. The acronym became a popular battle cry on the Republican side during the Civil War. The UHP was seen as heroic among the Spanish and Catalan working class, and the PSUC women wanted, no doubt, to associate their activity with the revolutionary Asturian miners.

carried a banner that said: 'We demand more bread, fewer controls, and just one government'.[8] It was clear that neither demonstration was spontaneous.[9]

The conflict between the CNT and the Minister of Supplies continued. On 5 February 1937, the Ministry accused the CNT of having seized potatoes and wheat, an act denied by the CNT's *Solidaridad Obrera* newspaper. On 22 February, and in opposition to Comorera, the CNT's distribution, food, and transportation unions confiscated 15,000 sacks of flour from a warehouse on Provenza Street.[10] Comorera issued a decree on 27 February introducing bread rationing in all of Catalonia and establishing a maximum of 250 grams of bread daily per person.[11]

The CNT did not welcome Comorera's action. A second unresolved problem had to do with public order. The appointment of Eusebi Rodríguez Salas, aka *El Manco* (the one-handed), as the *Generalitat*'s new police commissioner in December 1936 demonstrated the influence of the PSUC over the minister of interior security, Artemi Aiguader of the *Esquerra*. Rodríguez Salas's history is revealing: he had begun his political life in the Tarragona Socialist Association at the beginning of the second decade of the century, and he later joined the CNT. A supporter of the Russian Revolution, during the 1920s he was one of the founders of the Communist Federation of Catalonia and the Balearic Islands, and

---

8. *Crònica diària*, 5 January 1937.

9. [TN] The slogans calling for 'one government' and the 'abolition of the Control Committees' reveals the not so 'spontaneous' designs of the PSUC when organising these protests. Both slogans reveal the political objectives of undermining the CNT's strength on the committees and other remnants of the revolution, and of transferring more control to the *Generalitat*, where the Catalan communists were rapidly gaining power and influence.

10. See Ucelay Da Cal 1982, p. 318.

11. *La Vanguardia*, 3 March 1937, published the Minister's decree without further commentary:
> Taking into consideration the need to distribute fairly among all the Catalan villages the production and stocks of wheat regulated by this Ministry, and taking into consideration also that there must be no stockpiling or the possibility of stockpiling any kind of food, especially wheat, if our economy is to function, and it being necessary to systematise forms of distribution among different villages so that there are no instances in which some villages eat bread without the austerity measures that must rule all our actions in the current fight against fascism and in other villages there is not enough to satisfy the most basic needs, and in order to motivate the production of ration cards in all those municipalities where conditions and special characteristics dictate the need to introduce them, I resolve:
> 1. There will be rationing of bread at a rate of 250 grams per person per day, throughout Catalonia.
> 2. City governments will not be supplied with flour if they have not implemented bread rationing according to the quantity established in the first article of this regulation within ten days of the publication of this order in the *Diario Oficial de la Generalidad de Cataluña*.

upon the proclamation of the Republic in 1931, he joined the BOC, participating in their action groups. After the Asturian revolution in 1934, he joined the Catalan Communist Party and at the beginning of the war was a prominent member of the newly formed PSUC.[12] Considered violent and unscrupulous, he was not an ideal candidate for police commissioner, although he held the position for almost six months.

The first significant disturbance of public order under Rodríguez Salas actually occurred far from Barcelona, in Fatarella, in the Terra Alta region of Tarragona. On 23 January, peasant opposition to the forced collectivisation of land provoked the intervention of the security patrols, and thirty peasants were killed.[13] The CNT, an ardent supporter of collectivisation, was soon blamed for the massacre, although there were several reports pointing to an authentic pro-Franco revolt in the Catalan rearguard.[14] In the end, the incidents in Fatarella caused a clear break between the CNT-FAI and the POUM, on the one hand, and the Esquerra and the PSUC on the other.[15] Shortly afterwards, on 19 and 21 February, another armed confrontation occurred, this time in Centelles, a village in the district of Barcelona. Several searches of local farms by security patrols led to the deaths of five peasants and the president of the Centelles Anarchist Youth Organisation (*Joventuts Llibertàries de Centelles*).

As a result of these incidents, at the beginning of February 1937, the Catalan UGT removed its members from the security patrols. On 1 March 1937, the *Generalitat* approved various decrees that dissolved the Catalan Security Office, the workers' and soldiers' councils, and all committees and bodies involved in public order, such as the security patrols. Then it created a single body for all matters of internal security.[16] Thus the security patrols and all the bodies formed during the revolution were formally abolished – although, in practice, the patrols did

---

12. See his biography in Martínez de Sas and Pagès (eds.) 2000.
13. There are several recent books, such as that by Josep Termes, which examine the events in Fatarella (Termes 2005). Termes's interpretation differs from mine, which can be found in Pagès 2004a, pp. 659–74.
14. This is the opinion, for example, of the delegate of the Catalan Office of Internal Security (*Junta de Seguridad Interior de Cataluña*), Tomás Fàbregas, a member of ACR, in his *Informació presentada pel delegat de Seguretat Interior de Catalunya, Tomàs Fàbregas, referent als fets ocorreguts al poble de la Fatarella*, 27 January, 1937, 8a.3, Archives of Montserrat Tarradellas Macià-Poblet.
15. For the analysis of the CNT and the POUM, see *Solidaridad Obrera*, 27 and 28 January 1937 and *La Batalla*, 27 and 29 January 1937, respectively. For the analysis of the PSUC, see *Treball*, 28 January 1937; for the UGT, see *Las Noticias*, 27 and 28 January 1937; and for the analysis of the *Esquerra*, see *La Humanitat*, 28 January 1937.
16. The decrees were published in *Diari Oficial de la Generalitat de Catalunya*, 4 March 1937. On 3 March, most of the newspapers made mention of the measures. *La Humanitat* (*Esquerra*), *La Publicitat*, and *Treball* (PSUC) wrote of them favourably, while *Solidaridad Obrera* (CNT) and *La Batalla* (POUM) were sharply critical.

not disappear. A few days later, an order announced that all arms and explosives in the rearguard were to be handed over to the *Generalitat*.

The PSUC offensive had the collaboration of the *Esquerra* and was reaching unprecedented dimensions in its struggle to re-establish republican and democratic normality and overturn revolutionary conquests. The POUM, now excluded from government, was openly critical of the advances being made by the counterrevolution.[17] Meanwhile, the military situation continued to pose problems. There was still little action on the Aragon Front, and the PSUC was blaming the defence minister, the anarchist Francesc Isgleas, for the inactivity. Then, on 13 February, Barcelona suffered its first bombing: an attack from the Italian ship *Eusebio de Savoia*. Nineteen people died and fifteen more were injured.[18] Over the next few days, Catalan villages like Port Bou and La Pobla de Segur suffered their first aerial bombardments from Italian planes, and the bombardment of Barcelona itself began on 6 March 1937.[19] Even though Franco's offensive failed against Guadalajara, saving Madrid once again, demoralisation was beginning to affect Catalonia. No doubt the disastrous fall of Málaga in Andalucía to Franco's army on 8 February contributed to this mood.

At the beginning of March, twelve tanks disappeared from a warehouse belonging to the *Generalitat*, and the incident had serious repercussions. The crime was attributed to the PSUC. Public accusations made against the PSUC by the POUM led to the temporary suspension of the POUM newspaper, *La Batalla*. Meanwhile, the PCE (the Spanish Communist party) and the PSUC intensified their campaign against the POUM, accusing them of being a counterrevolutionary party of Trotskyists. In the Stalinist language of the period, calling the POUM 'Trotskyist' was tantamount to calling them fascists.[20]

Adding to the tense atmosphere in Catalonia, the CNT ministers provoked a new government crisis when they abandoned their cabinet appointments on 26 March. Their resignations were a reaction to the growing success of the PSUC in dissolving what the anarchists considered to be the fundamental institutions of the revolution: worker-led militias on the front and security patrols in the rearguard. This time the crisis would be drawn out. After more than a week's

---

17. See Andreu Nin's article 'Ante el peligro contrarrevolucionario ha llegado la hora de reaccionar' ('In the face of the danger of counterrevolution, the time has come to respond'), *La Batalla*, 4 March 1937 (Nin 1937).
18. See *La Vanguardia*, 16 February 1937, and *Crònica diària*, 13 and 15 February 1937.
19. *Crònica diària*, 6 March 1937.
20. In the full session of the PCE Central Committee held in Valencia from 5–8 March 1937, José Díaz presented a document stating: 'Who are the enemies of the people? The enemies of the people are the fascists, the Trotskyists, and the *incontrolados*. It is a grave error to consider the Trotskyists part of the workers' movement. We are talking about a group without principles, a group of counterrevolutionaries classified as agents of international fascism' (Díaz 1939, pp. 428–31).

delay, new cabinet appointments were finally announced on 3 April that represented little more than an attempt to buy time. The appointments simplified the composition of the cabinet: Tarradellas became the Minister of the Treasury and Culture; Artemi Aiguader, Interior Security Minister; Francesc Isgleas Piernau, Defence Minister; Josep Juan Doménech, Minister of Economy, Public Services, Social Assistance and Health; Joan Comorera, Labour, Public Works and Justice; and Josep Calvet, Agriculture and Supplies.[21]

On the surface of things, the most noteworthy change is the replacement of the controversial Comorera, the PSUC leader, as Minister of Supplies by the *Rabassaire* Josep Calvet.[22] However, this cabinet reorganisation did little to ease tensions. On 14 April, confrontations broke out in almost all of Barcelona's markets due to a food shortage, and protests followed throughout the city. In the end, the government crisis was only resolved when on 16 April another cabinet was formed by reshuffling ministers and ministries.

First Minister and Finances	Josep Tarradellas i Joan (*Esquerra*)
Justice	Joan Comorera i Soler (UGT)(PSUC)[23]
Culture	Antoni Ma Sbert i Massanet (*Esquerra*)
Interior-Security	Artemi Aiguader i Miró (*Esquerra*)
Labour and Public Works	Rafael Vidiella i Franch (UGT) (PSUC)
Economy	Andreu Capdevila i Puig (CNT)
Agriculture	Josep Calvet i Móra (*Rabassaires*)
Health and Social Assistance	Aureli Fernández Sánchez (CNT)
Public Services	Josep Juan i Domènech (CNT)
Defence	Francesc Isgleas Piernau (CNT)[24]
Supplies	Josep Miret i Musté (UGT) (PSUC)

The political tensions that led to the government crisis at the end of March and beginning of April actually increased during the second half of April, compounding the already difficult military situation: Barcelona, Calella, and Mataró were bombed on 4 April, Colera and Llança were bombed on 16 April, and Barcelona was bombed again on 18 April. The attempt to create a viable government out of 'trade union unity' was failing, helping to weaken the CNT and strengthen the

---

21. *La Vanguardia*, 4 April 1937.
22. [TN] Replacing Comorera with Josep Calvet was truly a cosmetic change since, as Burnett Bolloten has shown, Calvet too was, secretly, a member of the PSUC (Bolloten 1991, p. 416).
23. [TN] In this chapter, as in the last, when the trade union representation has been used to designate the affiliation of a minister, I have added the individual's political affiliation, if it is the PSUC, in order to help clarify the process the author is describing regarding the Catalan communist ascendency in the *Generalitat*.
24. [TN] Not to be confused, as is often the case, with another anarchist, Germinal (Josep Maria) Esgleas Jaime.

PSUC. Instances of street violence broke out. Most notably, Roldán Cortada, secretary to the minister of labour and public works, was assassinated on 25 April when his car was stopped by several individuals in Molins de Llobregat. The culprits were never discovered.[25] On 27 April, armed confrontations in Bellver de Cerdaña and Puigcerdà between the police and anarchist militants ended with the death of the anarchist leader Antonio Martín. On 29 April, the *Generalitat* announced:

> The cabinet of the *Generalitat*, faced with such extraordinary circumstances in public order, cannot continue its work due to the pressure, danger, and disorder arising from the existence of groups that in some places in Catalonia attempt to impose their will through coercion, compromising the revolution and the war.
>
> Therefore, the government will suspend its session until all those who do not work for the cabinet of the *Generalitat* have left the streets, in order to dispel the uncertainty and alarm that Catalonia is experiencing at the present time.
>
> At the same time, the cabinet of the *Generalitat* has taken necessary measures to ensure the strict following of these orders.[26]

Because of the tension, the traditional workers' celebrations held on 1 May were cancelled. In a world where fascism confronted anti-fascism and reaction confronted revolution, Barcelona must have been the only city in anti-fascist Europe that did not see proletarian parades and hear impassioned revolutionary speeches. But in the tense climate of that 1 May, a celebration that brought the masses into the streets of Barcelona, where provocation could easily lead to violence, was considered too high a risk. At the end of April, the *Generalitat* renewed its demand that all arms in the rearguard be handed over to the government. But the revolutionary organisations knew that if they allowed themselves to be disarmed, they would lose any power they still held – and they knew that a revolution can only be won with arms. On 2 May, an editorial in the anarchist *Solidaridad Obrera* called for workers to keep their arms:

> It is great that those who handed arms over to the people to defeat fascism would try to take them away, when the people are the ones who captured the arms and own them! Comrades: arms are worth more than speeches. Do not let them disarm you under any circumstances!![27]

---

25. *La Vanguardia*, 27 April 1937. Several pages cover the assassination.
26. *La Vanguardia*, 30 April 1937.
27. *¡Estaría bueno que los que entregaron armas al pueblo para vencer al fascismo intentaran arrebatárselas cuando el pueblo las ha conquistado y son suyas! ¡¡Camaradas:*

At this stage, however, the forces of the counterrevolution, working to break CNT-FAI hegemony and force a return to 'republican normalcy', were not going to give up. The CNT no longer seemed as imposing as it had in the first few weeks of the war, while the PSUC had become a powerful party with a significant government presence: it had grown as those fearful of revolution had taken refuge in it. It had become the party of order and had decisively won its battle with the POUM. It mattered little that most of its leaders and members were recent converts to communism, while the POUM had, in large part, continued to preserve and maintain Catalonia's communist tradition. The help the PSUC received from its 'big brother', the all-powerful PCE, and from the 'proletarian fatherland', the Stalinised USSR, gave them the necessary credentials of purity and orthodoxy to present themselves as *the* party of the Catalan proletariat. The socialist-communist alliance that formed the PSUC had not been in vain. The PSUC considered itself to be the original, legitimate, and unique representative of the Catalan workers' movement. But it arrived later than the massive anarcho-syndicalist movement and even the POUM, a party that was not supported by any of the great workers' internationals even as it enjoyed significant support from numerous sectors of Catalan workers. As a result, Catalonia was an exception within the worldwide workers' movement. In no other country, in Europe or in the world, was there such a powerful anarcho-syndicalist movement, or a heterodox, non-Stalinist, communist party with real social influence, or an orthodox communist party (those of the PSUC would say 'popular frontist') that had done away with the organic presence of socialism.[28]

Like these parties, the Catalan revolution itself was an exception, and, like the parties, its singularity represented a 'problem' in a time of war and revolution, especially with so many international interests at play. Many – not just those in Catalan society who would be adversely affected by social transformation – perceived it as a threat: the Spanish Republic, the western democracies, and a Soviet Union directing an international communism that could not tolerate a revolutionary process that escaped its control and that, to a large measure, was the antithesis of what was happening in the USSR.

The seemingly irrational events of May 1937, describing what was essentially a mini-war within the broader Civil War, become more comprehensible when considered in their national and international context and their basis in class conflict. In the rearguard, different social classes had different strategies for fighting fascism, even though there were workers on both sides of the barricades. The

---

las armas valen más que los discursos. No permitáis que os las arrebaten bajo ningún pretexto!!'.

28. I have written about the uniqueness of the Catalan situation during the Civil War in Pagès 1990b, pp. 23–40.

class conflict being fought on the war front, in other words, had taken on a new dimension in the rearguard.

The chronology of the 'May events' is well documented. Around 3 p.m. on 3 May, Police Commissioner Rodríguez Salas, along with the police forces at his disposal, attempted to occupy the *Telefónica*, the telephone exchange building on the *Plaça de Catalunya* in Barcelona. The official version of events states that Rodríguez Salas's objective was 'to give the delegate appointed by the government possession of his charge' and that, in response, he and his forces were greeted by gunfire from the building.[29] The police managed to occupy the entry level of the building, anarcho-syndicalists fortified themselves in the upper floors, and news of the confrontation spread like wildfire. In just a few hours, barricades had formed in the streets around the Ramblas, and armed confrontations began to break out. Although no orders had been issued, CNT, FAI, and POUM activists hit the streets in order to answer the provocation and defend the revolution. At around 5:30 p.m., offices and stores closed, and at 7 p.m. public transportation shut down. Barcelona went on general strike. Events on that first afternoon and evening led to seven deaths. That evening, the CNT and FAI made the following announcement:

> Comrades: an incident occurred this afternoon at the *Telefónica*. Regional committees have responded immediately and taken measures to resolve the incident. All forces mobilised as a consequence of the conflict should now demobilise so that official forces can take charge and resolve the situation once and for all.
>
> These committees recommend that all groups aligned with them take note of this *communiqué* and adhere solely and exclusively to the committees' directions and agreements.[30]

The same evening, a delegation of the POUM's executive committee met with the regional committee of the Catalan CNT at the headquarters of the CNT's Defence Committee on the avenue *Via Laietana*. The POUM wanted to come up with a joint plan to save the revolution, but the anarchist leaders concluded that the new situation in the streets would be enough to force Companys to negotiate.

Nevertheless, the next day, confrontations spread throughout the city, from Palace Square to San Andrés and from Sants to Ciudadela Park. It looked as if no organisation was able to control its militants. The *Crònica diària* described a city experiencing a general strike, where only the war industries were running, and

---

29. *Crònica diària*, 3 May 1937. The same version also appears in *La Vanguardia*, 4 May 1937.
30. *Crònica diària*, 3 May 1937.

reported 'intense rifle fire between armed elements and the police and between fellow countrymen'.[31] That evening (4 May), political leaders representing different organisations spoke on the radio calling for calm: Calvet from the *Rabassaires*, Sbert from the *Esquerra*, Vidiella from the PSUC, Alonso for the local federation of the CNT, Zancajo from the UGT's executive, and Marià R. Vázquez ('Marianet') from the CNT's National Committee. A significant intervention came from García Oliver, who was the CNT minister in Largo Caballero's government at the time and was known for his oratory. Finally, the president of the *Generalitat*, Lluís Companys, spoke. Many CNT members listening to the radio pleas from the barricades were convinced that Alonso, Marianet, and García Oliver were speaking against their will while being held prisoner in the Palace of the *Generalitat*. That night the cabinet discussed the government crisis. The day had been especially bloody, with nearly eighty deaths.

In spite of the radio broadcasts, confrontations continued on 5 May and were especially violent around the offices of the organisations. At midday, the formation of a new cabinet was announced. It included Carles Martí Feced from the *Esquerra* in Interior, Finance, and Culture; Valeri Mas from the CNT in Social Services, Economy, Health, and Social Assistance; Joaquim Pou from the *Rabassaires* and Antoni Sesé from the UGT, both as ministers without portfolio. Sesé, who was both leader of the PSUC and secretary general of the Catalan UGT, was shot and killed in front of the offices of the CNT's Entertainment Union, on Caspe Street, while on his way to take up his new post. He was replaced by Rafael Vidiella, also from the PSUC. Shortly afterwards, on the avenue *Gran Vía*, Domingo Ascaso, brother of several anarchist leaders, was also killed. That same evening, radio broadcasts called for peace once again. Tarradellas spoke alongside Vidiella and other PSUC leaders as well as Marianet, Pere Herrera, and Federica Montseny from the CNT.

From the very beginning of the conflict, the CNT leaders had pledged their support for a return to normalcy. The response created confusion among the CNT membership, many of whom continued to believe that their leaders were prisoners and were being forced to make the radio broadcasts. A small tendency within the CNT, 'The Friends of Durruti', declared their opposition to the organisation's political collaborationism. On 5 May, the small group called for the creation of a revolutionary council, the execution by firing squad of those responsible for the attack on the telephone exchange, and the disarming of the Civil Guard. The group was immediately banned by the CNT leadership.[32]

---

31. *Crònica diària*, 4 May 1937.
32. For more on the 'Friends of Durruti', see Mintz and Peciña (eds.) 1978. And for a more recent account, see Amorós 2003.

At 3 p.m. on 5 May, the following was announced on the same official airwaves of the *Generalitat*: 'The Government of the Republic, on its own initiative, has taken charge of Public Order in Catalonia'.[33] Lieutenant Colonel Alberto Arredondo was appointed state delegate. At the same time, the Government of the Republic announced that it would be taking over the responsibilities of the Ministry of Defence in Catalonia by appointing General Sebastián Pozas head of the fourth military division. The two moves were highly significant, representing the loss of the most important responsibilities exercised by Catalans since the beginning of the war: public order and defence. The *Generalitat* had been in charge of public order since the passage of the Autonomy Statute in 1932, and the circumstances created by the military rebellion in July 1936 had, in effect, taken defence matters away from the Republican Government. On the same day these changes were announced, two warships dropped anchor in Barcelona's port, the *Lepanto* and the *Sánchez Barcaiztegui*. There were 56 fatalities reported that day. Newspapers on the next day indicated that by 8 p.m. on 5 May, a total of 136 people had died over the last three days: 128 could be found in the *Clínico* Hospital and 8 in the General Hospital of Catalonia. There were 191 injured.[34]

Fighting continued on 6 May, with the CNT calling the situation 'more serious than ever'. The body of an anarchist intellectual, the Italian Camillo Berneri, was discovered: along with Francesco Barbiere, he had been arrested by a UGT patrol. The UGT leaders expelled all leaders and members of the POUM, which, according to the PSUC newspaper, was 'the organisation motivating the counter-revolutionary movement these last few days'.[35] At 11 a.m., police seized the press of the POUM's daily, *La Batalla*, and more than thirty people were arrested. The POUM published a brief note from the party's executive committee, calling for workers to return to work immediately, to cease hostilities, and to abandon the barricades. They added that workers should nevertheless remain alert.[36] Rafael Vidiella and Federica Montseny called for calm once again on the radio. At 5 p.m., an official notice from the president's office of the *Generalitat* stated that no minister of defence had been appointed because the president had planned to exercise those functions himself, but that, given that General Pozas had been named head of the fourth military division, 'all powers and responsibilities of Defence will be exercised by him with the authority invested in him by military representatives of the Republic and, where necessary, the Government of

---

33. *Crònica diària* 5 May 1937. See also *La Vanguardia*, 6 May 1937.
34. *La Vanguardia*, 6 May 1937.
35. *Treball*, 7 May 1937.
36. *La Batalla*, 7 May 1937.

Catalonia'.[37] Despite the beginnings of a return to normalcy, fighting on 6 May resulted in forty-five more casualties.

Peace did return eventually to the streets of Barcelona, although there were still a few isolated casualties. On 7 May, the *Crònica diària* announced that all workers, without exception, had gone back to work. Public services and mass transit were up and running. Newspapers were being published. Stores, workshops, and factories were open. In the port, cargo was again being loaded and unloaded. The city had returned to its normal rhythm.[38] Police Commissioner Rodríguez Salas was relieved of his post, and Emilio Menéndez López took his place. That night, a few thousand Assault Guards arrived in Barcelona's port, having travelled up the coast from Valencia. Sent to take charge of public order, by the next morning they were walking the streets as if they were the true victors of a battle in which they had not even participated. The optimism of victory was shared by the communists of the PSUC. Meanwhile, the CNT-FAI and the POUM, more cautious, contended that, under the circumstances, there should not be winners and losers, victors and vanquished. But, a few days after the fighting was over, a dozen bodies were found in Cerdanyola: all of them had been members of the anarchist Libertarian Youth (*Joventuts Llibertáries*). Among the dead was probably Alfredo Martínez, who had been secretary of the anti-fascist Youth Alliance of Catalonia (*Aliança Juvenil Antifeixista de Catalunya*) and of the Revolutionary Youth Front (*Capdavant de la Joventut Revolucionària*).

The fighting was bloodiest in Barcelona, with more than two hundred killed, but other Catalan cities and towns had similar May events. There were confrontations in Tarrasa, Reus, Tarragona, Tortosa, Vic, and the region of Alt Empordá. In Tarragona, where, as in Barcelona, the telephone exchange was occupied, thirteen anarchist leaders were killed. In Tortosa, there were six deaths when the Assault Guards from Valencia passed through. Ten more were killed in Vic and Alt Empordá. CNT and POUM troops had nearly been remobilised from the front to take part in the fighting, but the good judgment of both organisations' leaders prevented it. There were nearly three hundred deaths during the painful days of early May, but there might have been more if the *milicianos* had not remained at the front.

---

37. *La Vanguardia*, 7 May 1937.
38. *Crònica diària*, 7 May 1937.

Chapter Eleven
The Consequences of the May Events

The May events in Catalonia had profound political repercussions both for Catalonia and for the Republic as a whole. Although the fighting was over, things did not return to how they were before the confrontations began, and there were clear winners and losers. The POUM lost the most: in an attack that represented the culmination of a defamation campaign initiated in January under the influence of the Soviet Union, it was depicted by the PCE and the PSUC as the sole organiser and *provocateur* of the clashes in Barcelona. The secretary general of the PCE gave the Stalinist line in a meeting that took place on 9 May in Valencia:

> In Spain, who but the Trotskyists has inspired the criminal putsch in Catalonia? *La Batalla* on 1 May is full of shameless incitements for the putsch-styled coup. Among other things, it says: 'The politics of the Popular Front led Spain down the road to the military coup of July 1936'. That is the same thing that Franco says, that his military coup was provoked by the formation of the Popular Front.[1]

On 13 May, *Treball*, the PSUC's daily newspaper, described the POUM as an 'organisation entirely complicit with secret fascist agents, a fifth column'.[2]

On 15 May, in a regular meeting of the Republican Government, Communist ministers Vicente Uribe and

---

1. Díaz 1939, p. 481.
2. *Treball*, 13 May 1937.

Jesús Hernández demanded that President Largo Caballero dissolve the POUM. They offered copies of the POUM newspaper, *La Batalla*, as proof for their demands. Largo Caballero's opposition to such an outlandish claim, described a few months later by the minister of industry, Joan Peiró of the CNT, was blunt:

> Caballero stated that any government that he presided over would not set the precedent of dissolving a political party for the motives that had been alleged. 'If there is anything criminal', he said, pointing to the copies of *La Batalla* on the table of the Council, 'then let it be sent to the Attorney General (*fiscal*) and let him dissolve the POUM and everything else proposed if there are sufficient reasons. But for me to ever let the Government do that...'[3]

Caballero's response cost him his position. Uribe and Hernández provoked a new government crisis that was resolved two days later with the formation of a new cabinet presided over by the socialist Juan Negrín. The new government formed by Negrín (President, Treasury Minister, and Minister of the Economy) was José Giral (State), Indalecio Prieto (National Defence), Manuel Irujo (Justice), Julián Zugazagoitia (Interior), Jesús Hernández (Public Education and Health), Vicente Uribe (Agriculture), B. Giner de los Ríos (Public Works and Communications), and Jaume Aiguader (Labour and Social Assistance). Significantly, the CNT held no portfolios in the new government, agreeing to participate only if Largo Caballero continued as President.

This was the government that would lead the repression against the POUM. On 28 May 1937, *La Batalla* was suspended. The police confiscated the daily and the POUM press on charges of 'incitement to rebel', after criminal proceedings had begun in the Supreme Court. The next day, POUM leader Julián Gorkín testified before court number 4 of Barcelona: he was charged with the same crime, a charge based on the publication of the article leading to the paper's suspension.[4] On 15 June, the government forbade all political action by the party, arrested its leaders, seized its offices, expelled its members from the city government and other committees, and suspended publication of the rest of its newspapers, of which there were several in Catalonia. On 16 June, the POUM's executive committee was arrested in Barcelona. Two days later, the offices of the chief of police announced the discovery of a spy network in Barcelona:

> Last night, in the offices of the chief of police, the following note was brought to our attention: For a few days, agents from Madrid have been working to uncover an important network of spies operating in Barcelona. After arriving

---

3. See Joan Peiró's 'La tragedia del POUM. El silenci seria una complicitat', published in the Mataró daily *Llibertat*, 8 July 1937 (Peiró 1937).

4. *La Vanguardia*, 28 and 29 May 1937. [TN] Gorkín, a pseudonym for Julián Gómez (1902–87), was a member of the POUM and a writer for *La Batalla*.

from the capital of the Republic, special agents, ably aided by agents from our own city, have succeeded in completely and rapidly exposing the extensive and complicated workings of this network.

In the course of providing this highly important service, numerous arrests have been made, including those of a significant and dangerous contingent of foreigners and of well-known members of a certain political party.

The evidence provided by the agents from Madrid against the individuals involved in this espionage was more than sufficient to demonstrate the need for the arrests carried out by the police. Statements by those arrested, as well as documentation found in the searches that have taken place here, have corroborated beyond any doubt the guilt of those arrested.

The names of those arrested and details of how the spy ring worked cannot be revealed publicly until all procedures and formalities related to the police investigation are fully completed.[5]

This announcement marks the beginning of one of the most disgraceful episodes of the Civil War – the persecution, even extermination, of a political party of committed and respected revolutionaries through accusations of pro-fascist espionage. The campaign waged by the PCE and the PSUC, aided and abetted by Soviet agents, had finally begun to bear results. It is obvious that practically no one believed a fable of such colossal dimensions, particularly those who knew the party's leaders: Nin, Andrade, Bonet, Gorkín, Jordi Arquer, Josep Rovira, David Rey, and others. These leaders represented an entire generation of revolutionaries, many of whom had come out of the rank and file of the CNT and had been activists since the beginning of the century. But few dared, publicly, to come out in their defence. The use of Soviet arms to effectively blackmail the Republic created numerous complicit relationships. And by the spring and summer of 1937, Stalin had achieved a considerable degree of influence over the Republican Government. As a result, hundreds of revolutionaries were thrown into prison, and some of them lost their lives.

The case of Andreu Nin, one of the POUM's most important figures, is the most well known. After his arrest along with the rest of the POUM's executive committee, he was immediately separated from them: while the rest of the committee was sent to Valencia, Nin was sent to the prison in Alcalá de Henares. There, the Soviet secret services, with Spanish help, faked an attempted prison-escape while Nin was being held at the estate of the aviation colonel Hidalgo de Cisneros and Constancia de la Mora Maura, two aristocrats and members of the PCE. The plan, 'Operation Nikolai', was concocted by Colonel Alexander Orlov,

---

5. *La Vanguardia*, 18 June 1937.

the chief of the Soviet NKVD in Spain.[6] The objective was to carry out a show trial (*magno proceso*) of the POUM in Barcelona, a trial that would conclude by identifying the POUM as a fascist party. The Stalinists had done essentially the same thing in Moscow against the 'Old Bolsheviks', friends of Lenin who were made to admit to being 'enemies of the people'. This time, however, the trial was derailed: rather than forcing Nin to openly make accusations against himself, the Stalinists came up with nothing. Instead, they buried Nin clandestinely on the highway to Perales de Tajuña, while they spread rumours that he had escaped to Salamanca (held by Franco) or Berlin.[7]

News of Nin's disappearance began to spread in July 1937. In a meeting held at Barcelona's *Olimpia* Theatre on 21 July, the anarchist leader Federica Montseny denounced his assassination:

> We have just been informed that the bodies of Nin and two other comrades have been found in Madrid. This news has not been confirmed, but until the Government says otherwise, telling us the whereabouts of Nin, we must believe that it is true. One cannot take a handful of men, going over the heads of a dignified people and ignoring their will, accuse them with impunity for something it has not been proven they did, and then stick them in a house prepared for the purposes of concealing them until they are taken out at night to be assassinated.[8]

In his writings during this period of the war, Manuel Azaña, President of the Republic, recalled the version that Prime Minister Negrín had given him on 22 July of Nin's 'escape' and subsequent capture by the German Gestapo.[9] The news was so alarming that the Justice Minister found it necessary to offer an official *communiqué* on 4 August:

> When this authority took charge of the official reports made by the police, acting under orders of the Office of General Security, regarding the subversive events this past May in Catalonia, and in relation to the information, documents, and accusations of espionage gathered in Madrid, which have previ-

---

6. NKVD, The People's Commissariat for Internal Affairs (also known as the GPU).

7. Although Jesús Hernández (PCE) reported this story in his memoirs (Hernández 1954), there was no documented proof confirming the story until the Soviet archives were opened. As the 1992 documentary film *Operació Nikolai* shows, the assassination of the POUM leader was based on a plot concocted in Moscow and directed from there. The film, directed by Dolors Genovés and produced by TV3 in 1992, was based on documents in the KGB archives.

8. The complete speech can be found in Liarte and Isgleas 1937. This passage is on p. 18.

9. See Azaña 1977, p. 165. When Negrín offered this version of the events, Azaña blurted back, 'Isn't that a bit novelistic?', revealing his disbelief.

ously been reported publicly, it was observed that among the detained placed at the disposal of the Justice Tribunals, Andrés Nin, former Minister of Justice of the *Generalitat* and leader of the P.O.U.M., did not appear.

With the collected information acted on, Mr. Nin, along with other leaders of the P.O.U.M., was arrested by the police of the Office of General Security, transferred to Madrid, and confined in a secure location prepared for such purposes by Madrid's Chief of Police. From this location he disappeared, and, to date, all efforts by the police to recapture him and his guards have been unsuccessful.

The situation has been brought to the attention of the Attorney General of the Republic, who has been ordered to urge the Tribunal of Espionage in charge to employ whatever means necessary to identify the location of Mr. Nin as well as the actions of all those who have participated in the crimes and who appear in the documents that incriminate Mr. Nin. The tribunal is currently familiarising itself with the contents and verifying the authenticity of those documents. None of this will hinder the efforts of the police, who are continuing their investigation in order to recapture the prisoner and subject him once more to the Republic's Justice Tribunals in the state prisons.[10]

Nin was not the only one assassinated. Other members of the POUM – including Joan Hervàs, Jaume Trepat, and José Meca, as well as distinguished foreigners like the Austrian Kurt Landau – were also victims of the Stalinists. Stalin's propaganda presented these crimes as acts of justice and presented the men of the POUM as criminals in the service of international fascism. Newspapers like *Treball, Mundo Obrero*, or *Frente Rojo* published forceful articles to this effect, and the communists even published special pamphlets to justify the murders. One pamphlet, *Spies in Spain*, listing a fictitious Max Rieger as author, had a prologue by the Catholic writer José Bergamín.[11] The French journalist Georges Soria published *Trotskyism in the Service of Franco: A Documented Record of Treachery by the P.O.U.M. in Spain*. Finally, the POUM was put on trial in October 1938. In spite of all the efforts of the Stalinists to discredit the POUM, the Tribunal of Espionage and High Treason found that 'all the POUMists were decidedly antifascist and have contributed with their efforts to the fight against the military coup'. It condemned them, however, for their actions during the May events, which represented an 'attempt to go beyond the democratic republic and to establish their own social system'. During the trial, there was no shortage of

---

10. *La Vanguardia*, 5 August 1937.
11. [TN] This pamphlet is mentioned by members of the POUM in a letter written from prison on 14 July 1938, included below in the appendix of documents.

testimonies – including those of Largo Caballero, Federica Montseny, Julián Zugazagoitia, Luis Araquistain, and Manuel Irujo – in favour of the accused.[12]

POUM members were not the only victims of the repression institutionalised after the May events. Those events gave the communists and the right wing of the PSOE, led by Indalecio Prieto, a useful pretext for getting rid of the leader of the Socialist Left, Largo Caballero, with whom they had numerous disagreements over military and defence issues. The Socialist leader was ostracised, his social and political influence ended. At the same time, the May events gave right-wing socialists an opportunity within the regulations of the party to mount an offensive in the party as well as in the socialist trade union – the UGT was dominated by supporters of Caballero – with the objective of eliminating once and for all what they considered to be the left-wing follies of so many of their militants.[13]

The May events also dealt a blow to the anarcho-syndicalists. The CNT, which had seemed an invincible giant when war broke out in July, turned out to have feet of clay. Undermining the party's influence was both the rise of the Catalan UGT – controlled by the PSUC – and internal disputes produced by the CNT's participation in government. After May 1937, not only was it possible to challenge the CNT politically, but it was also possible to arrest and imprison anarchists without the CNT-FAI leadership daring to protest. Catalan prisons had been filling up with members of the POUM, but now more and more anarchists were being 'welcomed' as well. Many anarchists were thrown into jail, accused of crimes committed in the first period of the war. That was the case, for example, with the lawyer Eduardo Barriobero, who had presided over the anarchist judicial body *Oficina Jurídica* in the first months of the war. Aurelio Fernández, previously a minister in the *Generalitat*, Manuel Fabregat, mayor of Granollers, and dozens of lesser known anarchist militants suffered the same kind of retribution. An assassination attempt on the president of the Barcelona High Court, Josep Andreu i Abelló, on 2 August 1937 intensified the repression against the CNT and FAI, whose members were accused of the crime.[14]

The CNT still had significant influence within the Catalan working class, as well as within the Spanish working class in general, but after the May events it completely lost the hegemony and moral authority it had enjoyed in the first months of the war. At the end of June 1937, a new crisis in the *Generalitat* was

---

12. The file, statements, hearing, and sentencing can be found in Alba and Ardevol (eds.) 1989.

13. [TN] Reflecting the radicalisation of the period, the PSOE had experienced significant growth during the first five years of the Republic (1931–6). Many of the new recruits were younger and more radical, tending to support Largo Caballero over the more conservative wings of the party.

14. See *La Vanguardia*, 3 August 1937.

instigated by Companys in order to end the provisional nature of the government that had been formed on 5 May, during the May events, and the crisis was resolved without the input of the anarchist union. On 28 June, Companys announced the formation of the new government. In his new cabinet, the CNT had equal representation with the *Esquerra* and the PSUC, the ACR was added to the list of parties with a ministerial portfolio, and Josep Tarradellas was no longer prime minister. The CNT opposed the proposal, and on 29 June, the new and final government of the war met without the CNT. Companys presided over the following appointments:

Interior and Social Assistance	Antoni Ma. Sbert, *Esquerra*
Finance	Josep Tarradellas, *Esquerra*
Culture	Carles Pi i Sunyer, *Esquerra*
Provisions	Miquel Serra i Pàmies, PSUC
Labour and Public Works	Rafael Vidiella, PSUC
Economy	Joan Comorera i Soler, PSUC
Agriculture	Josep Calvet, *Rabassaires*
Justice	Pere Bosch i Gimpera, ACR

With respect to the Republican Government, the CNT only returned in April 1938, when Negrín remodelled his government in order to project an image of unity among all the anti-fascist forces. Although the CNT's Segundo Blanco was a member of the new cabinet, the unity was far from being real.

As the CNT's influence decreased, that of the Spanish communists increased, both in Catalonia and in the Republican territory as a whole. In fact, the power of the PCE (in Catalonia the PSUC) grew so much that one historian, Josep Puigsech, has even concluded that the PSUC was 'the hegemonic party in Catalonia by the end of the Civil War'.[15] It is certainly true that both the anarchists and communists saw spectacular growth in membership. The PSUC expanded from some six thousand members at the beginning of the war to around sixty-nine thousand toward the end of 1938.[16] However, in no way did the communists ever grow large enough in membership to challenge the CNT's numbers at the time. More than anything else, what gave the communists hegemonic power under the Negrín government was Soviet aid. The arms Stalin sent to Spain came with an avalanche of military and civil experts, political agents, and spies who quickly wove a power structure that countered official Republican institutions. The Italian Palmiro Togliatti and the Argentino-Italian Vittorio Codovila were the real power brokers in the Spanish Communist Party (PCE), just as the French Communist Party member André Marty was the strongman in the International

---

15. See Puigsech 2001, especially pp. 145–7.
16. Puigsech 2001, p. 145.

Brigades and the Hungarian Ernö Gerö was the principal representative of the Third International in the PSUC and one of those responsible for the provocations that had led to the May events and the repression against the POUM.[17]

The Soviet network extended from the Soviet Embassy, under the direction of Ambassador Marcel Rosemberg, to the Russian Consulate headed by Antonov Ovssenko; from the Soviet secret police to their organs of repression, the *Cheka*, operating clandestinely within the country; and from the high military commands of the new Popular Army to the web of political operatives present in all army units. The network's objectives were to force a return to order, to centralise the war effort, and to put an end to all the 'revolutionary nonsense'. And finally, in keeping with PCE politics, now converted into the official line of Negrín's government, it worked to impose a unity of political and military command that implied the strengthening of hierarchy and discipline, both in the army and in civil life.

In spite of these efforts, parts of Catalan society remained immune to communist politics. One such area was the courts, even though they were militarising. Even Rafael Vidiella, PSUC leader and minister of labour and public works, noted the depth and persistence of the revolution in his comments on the courts' investigation of the clandestine graves and cemeteries that were used during the repression in the early part of the war. Vidiella stated on 7 September 1937 that 'the judges cannot consider accusations having to do with the revolutionary events provoked by the rebellious generals, since to do so would be to prosecute the revolution itself'. He added: 'The revolution does some things well and other things not so well, things that are not necessarily considered criminal, since all revolutionary uprisings break ties with the existing order, the formulas that existed before the revolution, just as they alter the norms of the existing justice system'.[18] Vidiella was reacting to judicial decisions that had also affected members of his party. The president of the Barcelona High Court, Andreu i Abelló, defended some judges by saying that they 'have never, for any reason, failed to fulfil their responsibility, and they have always acted within the guidelines of existing legislation while furthering their important work in the last year. I can give them nothing but my praise and congratulations'.[19] Just as they did in the trial against the POUM, the judges maintained an independence that no longer existed in other areas of Catalan society and politics.

---

17. See Radosh, Habeck, and Sevostianov 2002. See also Pagès 2003.
18. These statements have been saved in their entirety in the National Archive of Catalonia (Rafael Vidiella, 7 September, 1937, document 4.10.3, Archivo Nacional de Cataluña-Fondo Bosch Gimpera). Also conserved in the archives of the Minister of Justice of the *Generalitat* is documentation showing the impact of Vidiella's statements at the time.
19. Andreu i Abelló, 15 September, 1937, document 4.10.6, Archivo Nacional de Cataluña-Fondo Bosch Gimpera.

Another consequence of the May events was the progressive loss of power suffered by the Catalan *Generalitat*. In the early part of the war, Catalonia had reached levels of self-government unprecedented in its recent history. The *Generalitat* had already lost control of defence and public order during the May events, and afterwards its power declined even further. One of Negrín's stated objectives, the reinforcement of state power, had negative repercussions for Catalonia, which began to see its liberties threatened not only by the rebellious military generals but also by a central government determined to limit Catalan independence.

Shortly after Negrín's government was formed, Negrín himself explained to a foreign journalist his government's objectives. The *Crònica diària* summarised those aims as follows:

1. Unified command of land, sea and air.
2. Unitary command and state control of the war industries.
3. Political leadership by the cabinet.
4. Military leadership by the Chief of Staff.
5. No tolerance for disorder in the rearguard.
6. No tolerance for challenges to government authority.
7. Any citizen or committee with arms to be designated as traitorous (*faccioso*).
8. Protection for small industry, small farmers, and small property owners.
9. Use of all technological means for the agricultural cooperatives.
10. The government will not accept any mediation between itself and the insurgent traitors.[20]

For these reasons, many historians point to the May events as a turning point in the evolution of Catalonia and Republican Spain during the war. For some, it represents the triumph of the counterrevolution and the beginning of the end for the revolution's achievements. For others, the period after May 1937 represents the return to order and the end of anarchist disorder, exemplified by the definitive suppression of the security patrols. No one, however, disputes that the political situation in Catalonia after May 1937 was different, and not least because now it was revolutionaries who began to fill the jails.

---

20. *Crònica diària*, 21 May 1937.

Chapter Twelve
The Republican Military Offensives, Summer 1937

The significant changes in the Republican rearguard after the May Events profoundly affected the Aragon front. The front continued to suffer from the boycott decreed by the Republican Government, despite complaints from the anarchists and the Catalan government, both of whom appealed for arms in order to alleviate the troops' months of inactivity.[1]

It was only the overall military situation of the war, on all its fronts, that finally brought the stalemate on the Aragon front to an end. Until summer 1937, the

---

1. [TN] The arms boycott against the Aragon front and the politics behind it is addressed in the two famous accounts written by George Orwell and Felix Morrow. Morrow wrote:

> ... from September onward, there developed a systematic boycott, conducted by the government against the Aragon front. The artillery and planes which arrived from abroad, beginning in October, were sent only to the Stalinist-controlled centres. Even in the matter of rifles, machine guns and ammunition, the boycott was imposed. The Catalonian munition plants, dependent on the central government for financing, were compelled to surrender their product to such destinations as the government chose. The CNT, FAI, and POUM press charged that the brazen discrimination against the Aragon front was dictated by the Stalinists, backed by the Soviet representatives. (Caballero's friends now admit this.) The government plans for liquidating the militias into a bourgeois army could not be carried out so long as the CNT militias had the prestige of a string of victories to their credit. Ergo, the Aragon front must be held back. (Morrow 1974, p. 217).

And Orwell wrote:
> In order to check every revolutionary tendency and make the war as much like an ordinary war as possible, it became necessary to throw away the strategic opportunities that actually existed. I have described how we were armed, or not armed, on the Aragon front. There is very little doubt that arms were deliberately withheld lest too many of them should get into the hands of the Anarchists, who would afterwards use them for a revolutionary purpose; consequently the big Aragon offensive which would have made Franco draw back from Bilbao, and possibly from Madrid, never happened. (Orwell 1952, p. 68).

Republic had experienced little military success. While it had ended the siege on Madrid and won the battles of Jarama and Guadalajara in February and March 1937, these battles were defensive, doing little to earn the Republic any advantage over the enemy. Málaga had fallen to Franco in February, allowing him to consolidate his position on the southern front. The fall of Málaga was also significant because, as in Catalonia, most of Málaga's Republican forces were made up of militias, many of them anarcho-syndicalist. Since the government had shown little interest in organising Málaga's defence, the city's fall on 8 February, after a siege of three weeks, provoked criticism of all kinds against Largo Caballero's government. Then, beginning in March, Franco began an offensive against Bilbao that would turn into the prolonged 'Battle of the North'.

With the hope of alleviating pressure on Bilbao, the Republican Government, now under Negrín, decided at the beginning of June to attempt to reconquer Huesca. At the time, the troops on the Aragon front were experiencing a sort of hangover from the May events, and more than one writer has suggested that the Negrín government had another objective for the offensive: to distract the soldiers – mostly anarchists – from the strife just experienced in the rearguard.

Whatever their objectives, the government sent disciplined and well-equipped troops with abundant modern supplies from the central sector to aid the troops already at the front. The new troops were envied by the poorly dressed and poorly armed *milicianos* who had been wasting away on the Aragon front for months and who had come to be denigrated, especially by the communists, as 'the tribes' (*las tribus*). There was a stark contrast between the militias and the new battalions, of which the Twelfth International Brigade – commanded by the Hungarian writer Matei Zalka (General Lukacs), who died in the battle – was considered one of the best. One witness, the anarchist Pedro Torralba, explained, 'When they arrived and saw us, they looked at us above the shoulder, as we say in our land, and with a certain disdain and air of superiority, wanting to make sure we knew that they came from Madrid and that, compared to them, we were just simple peasants from the village and did not know how to fight or had not been fighting the war'.[2] The POUM's Josep Pané speaks of the admiration, envy, and sense of inferiority their militias felt before the new troops.[3] It was as if the newcomers wanted to show off the advantages of the new militarisation plan – the new 'Popular Army' – over the militia-army from the first weeks.

But the new army was not any more successful in the offensive against Huesca. The Francoists defending the city were inferior in numbers but well fortified, and they had detected the Republican army's preparations. The offensive began on 11 June with a generalised attack from all sectors of the front, and it was led by

---

2. Torralba Coronas 1980.
3. Coll and Pané 1978. See in particular pp. 176–9.

the new commander of the Eastern Army, General Sebastián Pozas. The first official *communiqué* was not issued until Sunday 13 June, when this reference to the offensive was published:

> An important operation on the Huesca section of the front has been initiated to test the troops, war materials, and fortifications of the enemy. Our forces performed efficiently and demonstrated once again their preparation and enthusiasm. Enemy lines were significantly penetrated and our troops inflicted many casualties and destroyed numerous fortifications. After carrying out this brilliant operation with the use of combat vehicles and an important air base, our forces returned to their base camps.[4]

A few days later, a second official *communiqué* seemed to predict an important success on the part of the Republican Army:

> The audacious strike carried out by our forces on the Hill of Martyrs has resulted in the capture of eighty enemy soldiers, twelve sergeants, three officers, and plenty of military hardware. After a forceful offensive with bayonets, our forces captured the enemy positions of the Santa Cruz and Punta Calvario hermitages, inflicting more than one hundred fatalities on the occupants, among them a captain, two lieutenants, and various lower officers, whose bodies have been collected by our Sanitary Services. Moreover, we captured thirty more soldiers, six machine guns, and all the armaments of the companies that held those positions.[5]

In spite of this account's enthusiasm, not one of the objectives leading up to the surrounding of Huesca was actually achieved. Only one manoeuvre was successful, and it was considered secondary to the overall strategy: the POUM partially succeeded in taking Green Hill (*Loma Verde*), but they had to abandon it in the end when the rest of the offensive failed.[6] After a long week of combat, the operation was considered a complete defeat, and around 19 June, calm returned to the front. The Republicans had lost one thousand men. In spite of the offensive's failure, a long article in the Republican press narrated its glories and included on the front page the text of a proclamation that had been signed by General Pozas and distributed behind enemy lines by Republican airplanes. The proclamation stated that the fall of Huesca was near:

> SPANIARDS IN THE REBELLIOUS ZONE.
> Do not doubt that Huesca will soon be ours. The more you resist, the more your houses and homes will be destroyed.

---

4. *La Vanguardia*, 15 June 1937.
5. *La Vanguardia*, 17 June 1937.
6. Coll and Pané 1978, pp. 184–8.

The tyranny you are suffering will soon end, but you must help us. Kill your assassins, and come over to our side.

This morning, a sergeant and thirty-four soldiers of the Twentieth Regiment were taken prisoner along with two lieutenant engineers. We received them with cries of 'LONG LIVE THE REPUBLIC!', to which they responded enthusiastically. With us, they are what they are, our brothers.

Do not doubt it. Huesca will be ours. Even more than you, your commanders know it. Do not let them sacrifice you for their cause.

'LONG LIVE THE REPUBLIC', 'LONG LIVE THE ANTI-FASCIST CAUSE', 'LONG LIVE THE INDEPENDENCE OF OUR DEAR SPAIN'.

General and Commander of the Eastern Army, POZAS.[7]

The intention behind publishing the General's proclamation and the accompanying articles seems clear: in the face of failure, it was necessary to boost morale and reinforce the Republican army's ability to fight.

Participating in the offensive was General Emilio Kléber (aka Manfred Stern), the International Brigadier considered the hero of the Madrid defence. In an extensive report written after he left Spain, he stated bluntly that 'the battle proceeded as badly for us as might have been expected'. He wrote of the Twelfth Brigade's loss of 'some 700 soldiers and many officials'; he stated, with no basis in fact and in a thoroughly Stalinist fashion, that members of the POUM militia had fired on soldiers of the International Brigade; and he complained of 'the damage done by the chief of staff of the Eastern Army, Lieutenant Colonel Guarner'.[8]

After the failed Huesca offensive, the ascension of the PCE/PSUC continued to affect the Aragon front. Most of the new troops for the offensive had come from the central sector and were aligned with the communists, and they wasted little time in taking advantage of their new dominance. On 16 June, while the offensive was still in full force, the commander of the POUM's Twenty-ninth Division, Josep Rovira, was arrested. Rovira had received two contradictory messages from the High Command that morning. The first congratulated him for 'the brilliant behaviour of the troops under his command that had occupied the objective indicated by Command'; the second simply stated: 'Present yourself immediately to headquarters. Signed, Pozas'.[9] A few weeks later, at the beginning of July, a direct order from the Ministry of Defence removed the Twenty-ninth Division from the front line and later dissolved the division entirely.

---

7. *La Vanguardia*, 19 June 1937.
8. See Radosh, Habeck and Sevostianov (eds.) 2002. For the references to the offensive on Huesca, see p. 403. ([TN] In the original English edition, the account is on p. 336 (Radosh, Habeck and Sevostianov [eds.] 2001).
9. Coll and Pané 1978, p. 203.

The communists next began a ferocious campaign to undermine the power of the anarchists on the front by attacking the reputation of the Aragon Regional Defence Council, the revolutionary government dominated by the anarchists that had ruled in Aragon since October 1936. In August, the communists called for the dismissal of its president, Joaquín Ascaso, accusing him of politically arbitrary and irregular rule. The attack satisfied the converging interests of the Communists, who were the most enthusiastic, the Republicans, and the right wing of the Socialist Party. Negrín's government prepared a decree to dissolve the council, but it delayed carrying out the decree for fear of an armed reaction from the anarchists. The decision had already been made, however, and so to prevent an anarchist response, Negrín's defence minister, Indalecio Prieto, sent eleven thousand men of a communist division to Aragon. The division, led by Enrique Líster, arrived outside Caspe, the new headquarters of the Aragon Regional Defence Council, on 6 August 1937. On 11 August, the decree was published, the Council dissolved, and the President arrested. The decree's text clearly shows that Negrín intended to further centralise the power of his government by eliminating yet another autonomous governing institution:

> The material and moral needs of the war demand, imperiously, that we proceed to concentrate state authority such that it can be exercised with unity of criteria and purpose. The division and subdivision of Power and of its resources has wasted, on more than one occasion, the efficacy of action, and even though this power is purely administrative, it has had deep repercussions for the waging of war.
>
> Aragon, capable of the highest human and economic contributions to the cause of the Republic due to the temperament of its people, suffers more intensely than any other the effects of this dispersion of authority, which damages both general and ideological interests. The harmful effects must end.
>
> The Aragon Council, whatever its efforts have been, has not succeeded in curing the problem. While the rest of loyal Spain is basing itself on a new discipline born of responsibility and effectiveness and in which there are many cases of sacrifice, Aragon remains outside of this centralising current, a current to which we will owe much for the promised victory.
>
> Upon preparing to resolve the crisis of authority that exists in Aragon, the government believes that it will only achieve its aims by concentrating Power in its own hands. And for this reason, with the cabinet's agreement, and by proposal of the President, I hereby decree:
>
> Article 1. The dissolution of the Council of Aragon and the suppression of the position of government delegate, the Council's president. Consequently, the government delegate in Aragon, Don Joaquín Ascaso Budria, and all other ministers of the Council, are also relieved of their positions.

Article 2. Aragonese territories pertaining to the authority of the Republic shall be under the jurisdiction of a governor general of Aragon, appointed by the government with the responsibilities of civil governors granted by existing legislation.[10]

Hundreds of anarchists were arrested in the days following the publication of this decree. Members of the CNT were excluded from town councils, offices of the regional CNT committees were occupied, and numerous collectivisations were destroyed.[11] Anarchist hegemony on the Aragon front was permanently disabled without the anarchists ever having mounted an armed response. On the same day that the Council was dissolved, José Ignacio Mantecón was named governor general of Aragon. A member of the Left Republicans (*Izquierda Republicana*), Mantecón's communist sympathies were well known.

In the meantime, the military situation worsened for the Republic. On 19 June 1937, Bilbao fell to Franco's army, and it looked like Franco's advance in the North would be unstoppable. The Republican offensive that had begun on 6 July at Brunete, on the Madrid front, did succeed in halting the enemy's advance, bringing about the retreat of Franco's troops and aviation toward the central sector. Specifically, the Condor Legion and two Navarrese divisions moved from their positions in the north. But the offensive only lasted one week, and on 18 July Franco initiated a counteroffensive that lasted until 26 July, when the fighting became less intense. The Republic lost around a hundred planes and twenty-five thousand men. Franco's army lost twenty-five planes and ten thousand men. On 14 August General Dávila took up the attack again, this time from the south and southeast of Santander.

In the hope of alleviating the pressure of Franco's offensive in the North, the Republican Government organised a new campaign on the Aragon front, this time against Zaragoza. The operation had two objectives: in addition to its military purpose, it was hoped that the offensive would distract soldiers from the recent political events in Aragon. If we are to believe Emilio Kléber, 'the Zaragoza operation had great internal political importance for the Communist Party because it presented an opportunity to end anarcho-Trotskyist-FAI dominance in Aragon'.[12]

---

10. Published in *La Gaceta de la República*, 11 August 1937. The decree was published the next day in *La Vanguardia*, 12 August 1937.
11. Casanova 1985, pp. 264–97.
12. See Radosh, Habeck and Sevostianov (eds.) 2002, p. 428 (p. 358 in the English edition, Radosh, Habeck and Sevostianov (eds.) 2001). [TN] Kléber (Manfred Stern) was a general in the International Brigades and was staunchly pro-communist. Assigning the triple name sequence 'anarcho-Trotskyist-FAI' to designate the formerly dominant power in Aragon is deliberately pejorative. In the end, Stern suffered the fate of many of Stalin's one-time allies, dying in one of the Soviet labour camps in 1954.

The Zaragoza offensive was organised by General Vicente Rojo, who was becoming the strategic leader of the Republican army, and it was carried out by Sebastián Pozas, in command of more troops than had ever been deployed on the Aragon front. The Fifth Army Corps had been transferred from the Central front, and new troops had arrived along with numerous foreign and Russian experts to make a grand total of eighty thousand men with one hundred tanks and nearly two hundred planes. Even though this time the Republicans were able to prepare their army in secret, the element of surprise did not stop Franco's army from keeping the pressure on Santander in the north. Santander finally fell on 26 August; sixty thousand Republican soldiers were taken prisoner.

As Rojo himself explained, the operation was supposed to consist of two simultaneous attacks, one from the north of Zaragoza and one from the south. From the north, the troops would have to break enemy lines in the direction of Zuera, from which vantage they could block reinforcements coming from Franco's army further north. At the same time, they would send a motorised brigade south towards Zaragoza. From the south, where the principal action was planned, the attack would be between Quinto and Belchite, with the objective of arriving in Zaragoza in the first three days of fighting.[13]

The offensive began on 24 August and was initially successful, owing in part to the element of surprise and the numerical superiority of the Republican troops. In the north, before midday, Zuera was taken. In the south, the front line was opened as planned; Codo fell on the left sector, but some units encountered resistance in nearby Belchite. On the right sector, Quinto was cut off from Zaragoza, and in the centre, motorised units headed toward Fuentes de Ebro, beating back a resistance that slowed them considerably. All in all, after forty-eight hours of fighting, the results of the offensive could not have been better for the Republicans. On the night of 25 August, the defence minister issued an optimistic *communiqué*:

> Today, with the same vigour, the Eastern Army's offensive in Aragon continued.
>
> The results of today's fighting were even more positive than those obtained on the previous day. Our troops have reached the Mediana, Rodón, and Fuentes de Ebro line.
>
> Codo and Quinto have fallen to us, as have all positions in the Pina sector.
>
> In Quinto, fighting was intense on both days. This town was defended by more than 1,500 well-prepared men with artillery and a great number of automatic rifles. The enemy offered strong resistance, and this has cost them enormous casualties.

---

13. Rojo 1975 [1942], pp. 103–8.

> Our troops took Quinto by assault. The last place of resistance was the church, where the Phalangists and the Civil Guard had taken refuge.
>
> Firing ceased late in the afternoon.
>
> Some of the defenders were killed, and the rest were taken prisoner. A number of these prisoners indicated that most of the rebel officers had secretly left Quinto the night before to find their way to Zaragoza.
>
> In Quinto, we have taken possession of six pieces of enemy artillery, many rifles, and some machine guns.
>
> The people of Quinto received the Republican troops with jubilation.
>
> In the Zuera sector there was intense fighting today, with communications still cut between Huesca and Zaragoza.
>
> In Pina the train station was occupied by a company of ninety men, fully armed.
>
> This morning, rebel forces tried to retake the station, but they were met effectively and forced to flee. They left forty rifles behind.
>
> In the Hermitage of Bonastre, also captured by our troops, we took possession of two cannons.
>
> More than one thousand heads of livestock have been captured. The casualties in our army, both yesterday and today, have been minimal.
>
> Republican aviation contributed effectively to the campaign. There were two air battles, and in one of them we lost one plane. Two rebel planes were shot down.[14]

After these early successes, however, problems emerged: the geography of the terrain was difficult, complicating transportation and bringing the advancing army to a halt just short of Zaragoza. Moreover, the Republican unit commanders lacked strategic training and did not know how to manoeuvre their troops in open terrain. Added to these difficulties was a critical strategic mistake: the Republicans prioritised the elimination of the small centres of resistance at the rear of the Republican vanguard over continuing the advance to Zaragoza. Hence, they focused their efforts at Fuentes de Ebro and, above all, in Quinto and Belchite. This is how the battle of Zaragoza ended up being the battle of Belchite, where Franco's local military garrison offered such stiff resistance that they were not defeated until 6 September. When the anarchist troops of the Twenty-fifth Division, led by García Vivancos, entered the village, they had to conquer it house by house. On 2 September, the defence minister's *communiqué* spoke of the troops of the Eastern Army fighting in the streets of Belchite, where Republican soldiers had occupied the seminary and the bullring.[15] Two

---

14. *La Vanguardia*, 26 August 1937.
15. *La Vanguardia*, 3 September 1937.

days later, Pozas sent a *communiqué* to President Companys stating: 'I have the great satisfaction of communicating to you that, after a hard fought battle, our forces have occupied the important fortified town of Belchite'.[16] But it was not until 6 September that an official *communiqué* announced the end of fighting:

> The small groups of rebels holding out in the houses of Belchite have been completely extinguished.
>
> Throughout the morning today, the enemy did not exhibit any activity except for the bombing over Mediana, which did not change the situation on our front line in any way.
>
> At the end of the evening, 672 prisoners from Belchite arrived at headquarters.
>
> The total number of military prisoners taken since the beginning of the operation on this front has surpassed three thousand.[17]

But that is when the Republican offensive stopped. After four days, the disorganisation and inefficiency had begun to wear on the attacking soldiers. The four days had also allowed reinforcements to reach Zaragoza's defenders, and two divisions from Madrid and substantial air support for the Francoists kept the Republican army, with no reserves, from advancing.

The operation could not have been more disappointing. It is true that the front line had advanced, and Codo, Quinto, and Belchite had been won. The victory in Belchite was, without doubt, the most significant. But Belchite, and this is no less important, was not occupied by the brand new shock divisions of the Fifth Army Corps, nor by the well-equipped International Brigades led by Soviet military experts. It was the 'tribes' of the first days who scored the most important victory of the campaign. Even General Rojo had to recognise that these fighters, 'with worse organisation and training, were able to achieve the best results'.

In the end, the advance ground to a halt, and Zaragoza had not been captured. While the combatants seemed satisfied with their partial success, Prieto telegraphed Pozas to state that 'so much effort to take four or five villages does not satisfy the defence minister or anyone else', and he blamed the failure of the campaign on 'political scheming' and the 'enormous number of Russian officials swarming Aragon, treating Spanish soldiers as if they were colonised subjects'.

In autumn 1937, adding insult to injury, two more partial attacks were carried out on the Aragon front. At the end of September, a Republican advance in the Jaca sector succeeded in occupying Bielsa Valley. In the middle of October, a new attempt was made on Zaragoza. This time, Soviet tanks led by Enrique Líster employed what was supposed to have been an important tactical innovation: infantry travelling while mounted on top of military vehicles. The armoured

---

16. *Crònica diària*, 4 September 1937.
17. *La Vanguardia*, 7 September 1937.

tanks, with soldiers travelling completely unprotected on top of them, ran smack into the defences at Fuentes de Ebro. Only half of the troops made it back. Even worse, the isolated operation did not form part of any general strategy or plan against Zaragoza.

In the end, the Zaragoza offensive failed to stop Franco's campaign in the north. Santander had fallen the day after the Republicans began their attack on Zaragoza, and only the region of Asturias was still in Republican hands at the beginning of September. After a new offensive by Franco, slower and more costly because of the difficult mountainous terrain, Asturias fell, too. The loss of the northern front deprived the Republic of an important industrial region, rich in raw materials. Furthermore, the Republic was left with seaports only on the Mediterranean coast. It would not take long for these circumstances to create all kinds of problems in the war-weary Catalan rearguard.

Chapter Thirteen
The Negrín Government in Barcelona and the Rupture of the Catalan Front

With Franco's victory over all of northern Spain, Catalonia would see its subsistence problems become even worse. Throughout the summer and autumn 1937, in step with the successive fall of territories to Franco's army, waves of refugees arrived in Catalonia seeking shelter. To the refugees that had come from Madrid, Castile, Extremadura, and Andalucía were added new refugees from the Basque Country (Euskadi), Santander, and Asturias. On 27 August 1937, the *Crònica diària* announced the arrival of fifteen hundred refugees from the Basque Country, one thousand of whom had already gone on to various villages throughout the Catalan region. Travelling through sections of France, three hundred more refugees arrived from the north of Spain.[1] A few days later, on 3 September, the minister of interior and social assistance, Antoni Maria Sbert i Massanet, announced that the number of refugees had risen to forty-five thousand, that the average number of refugees arriving each day surpassed two thousand, and that he would be adding to the Ministry a Refugee Commission. He added that the subsidy designated for municipal governments was insufficient for their maintenance and so the quantities would be increased by at least fifty percent, which would total a half million pesetas per day.[2] On 8 September, Sbert indicated that the number of refugees arriving in Catalonia daily had

---

1. *Crònica diària*, 27 August 1937.
2. *Crònica diària*, 3 September 1937.

risen to seven or eight thousand.³ The total number of refugees from the territories in question had reached more than six hundred thousand in November 1938, most of them women and children under fifteen. And there were still new waves of refugees to come.

The refugees' arrival caused a multitude of problems related to housing, food, schooling, health, and hygiene. Solving these problems – added to those already present in the Catalan rearguard – would be difficult, and the *Generalitat* could neither avoid stricter rationing nor prevent the appearance of speculators, who wasted little time in developing a black market in which consumers could buy at astronomical prices necessities that were scarce or nonexistent in stores. Soon, queues in front of food shops became a part of daily life in villages and cities, and unemployment began to rise. A shortage of coins led to the creation of a new monetary system based on IOUs, coupons, and cardboard coins issued by endless official and unofficial bodies – city governments, co-operatives, collectives, etc. – bringing on an inflation higher than Catalonia had ever seen.

Along with the refugees arriving from the Basque Country came the Basque government itself, to begin its long exile in Catalonia. This government's move to Catalonia, presided over by José Antonio Aguirre, began a period of extremely close relations and fraternal solidarity with the *Generalitat*. It even provided the *Generalitat* with a pretext for re-establishing a kind of religious normality in Barcelona: a Basque chapel was opened, and it seemed that Catholicism was returning to the city. The Church did not flourish, however: the vicar capitular of Barcelona, Father José María Torrent, opposed it, and he threatened to revoke the license of any priest who performed a public religious celebration.⁴ The period of religious persecution was long gone, but the church had chosen sides in the war, and its propaganda was fuelled by the image of an atheistic Republic made up of ferocious, priest-eating reds. Thus, the Vatican opposed the return of Cardinal Vidal i Barraquer to Catalonia, even though Vidal himself desired it. Vidal was one of the few prelates in Spain, along with the bishop of Vitoria, Mateo Múgica, who had not signed the collective episcopal letter supporting Franco's cause and baptising the war as a national liberation 'crusade'.

Along with the success of Franco's campaign in the north, the end of Republican offensives on the Aragon front, and an avalanche of problems in the rearguard, a new situation emerged that had significant political repercussions in Catalonia: in October 1937, the Negrín government moved from Valencia to Barcelona. The reasons for this second move (the first having been from Madrid to Valencia in November 1936) were twofold. First, for strategic reasons, Barcelona was considered safer militarily than Valencia. The second reason was even

---

3. *Crònica diària*, 8 September 1937.
4. Raguer Suñer 2001.

more important: the Republican Government was convinced that Catalan efforts in the war had been minimal and that, ultimately, the region had only created problems for the Republican cause. Negrín's larger motivation in the move was to use the presence of the Republican Government in Barcelona to reign in the Catalans and limit their governmental independence.

The measures taken by the Republican Government during the May events had already heralded its increased intervention in Catalan life and politics and had, in a way, even hinted at its eventual move to Barcelona. But the *Generalitat* did not find out about the move until the government began seizing buildings to house their offices. Suddenly, 250,000 government workers and their families landed in Barcelona, exacerbating the problems of a city already overburdened with refugees.

The move inevitably increased the friction between the two governments, because of both how and why the change was made. From the moment the move was decided, the Negrín government began the process of stripping the *Generalitat* of any real power. Even so, in public an attempt was made to portray the move as harmonious. When the new Republican Government was formed in May, Negrín sent a telegram to Companys expressing his desire to collaborate:

> President of the Cabinet [Negrín] to the honorary President of the *Generalitat* of Catalonia – Upon forming the new Government of the Republic, in yours and my name, I send to you, as official representative of Catalonia, a cordial greeting to the Catalan people, in whose loyal collaboration we trust to conquer fascism and ensure, by means of the revolutionary order demanded by Republican Spain, the social and political gains won at such great sacrifice. With regards, Juan Negrín.[5]

When, at the end of October, government employees began to occupy buildings and set up offices, Catalan president Companys's reaction was accommodating, at least in public. On 28 October, Companys described the government's arrival as 'a subject that we need not debate, nor even speak about, since the government may arrive whenever it wants, and it goes without saying that it will be welcomed'.[6] The minister of the interior announced on Radio Valencia:

> The government's trip to Barcelona fulfils a prior agreement and addresses an urgent need: that of protecting the Republic's progress regarding autonomous governments from stagnation caused by the difficulty of direct dialogue, which, of necessity, was altered when the Government moved from Madrid to Valencia.

---

5. *Crònica diària*, 18 May 1937.
6. *Crònica diària*, 28 October 1937.

> If Madrid can be sure that the government's move responded to strict national need, Barcelona, for its part, can see a strong indication of the government's true concern for Catalonia's particularities. The government need only remember that it consecrated these particularities by majority vote in the Constituent Assembly.
>
> Hidden agenda? None. Secret designs? None. Whether in Valencia or Barcelona, there is only one task, one goal that motivates the government: victory. Before this goal, all others are postponed, and all the nation's actions should serve it in the highest spirit of sacrifice.[7]

On 30 October, the president of the Republic signed the decree that established the Republican Government's new residence in Barcelona:

> In accordance with the Cabinet and as proposed by the President, I hereby decree:
>
> Article One. Upon publication of this decree in the *Gaceta*, Barcelona will be made temporarily the official residence of the Republican Government.
>
> Article Two. The President of the Cabinet is authorised to arrange the move of the different ministerial offices, in agreement with the respective ministers, however he deems is most appropriate for the fulfilment of those services.
>
> Issued in Valencia, 30 October 1937. Manuel Azaña; President of the Cabinet, Juan Negrín.[8]

The next day, Companys publicly confirmed Catalonia's strong support for the Republican Government, the president of the government, and the president of the Republic.[9] Negrín's response on 2 November, when he was already established in Barcelona, was:

> to greet the great city and autonomous Government with the loyal collaboration the cause demands and for which everyone makes every effort. The welcoming words from the honourable President of the *Generalitat* have been received as the indication of our affectionate cohabitation, which will alleviate the problems of the war.
>
> The Republican Government feels sure that this physical and spiritual partnership will be the beginning of a new period of struggle against the insurgents and invaders of the Nation and that the difficulties will be overcome quickly, thanks to the cordial renewal of the citizens' efforts and the co-ordinated use of our economic power. In this sense, the Republican Government has the honour of transmitting the satisfaction of his Excellency the Head of State,

---

7. *Crònica diària*, 28 October 1937.
8. *Crònica diària*, 30 October 1937.
9. *Crònica diària*, 31 October 1937.

who sees, in the perfect solidarity of the regions still loyal to the principles and rights of liberty, an indispensable condition for victory.[10]

So many promises of collaboration and demonstrations of affection could not hide the real tension between the two governments. In his memoirs, Julián Zugazagoitia, minister of interior in Negrín's government, describes the attitude of many of the Republican ministers toward Catalonia. He recalls Indalecio Prieto, for example, exclaiming in one cabinet meeting: 'If I were at liberty, I would not hesitate to go to Barcelona and shout in the Plaza de Cataluña that if the war is lost, it will be lost mostly because of the senseless and egotistical conduct of Catalonia'.[11] Zugazagoitia adds, tellingly: 'In the end, Negrín's violence was greater than Prieto's'.

The hostility of the president of the Republic, Manuel Azaña, residing in Barcelona since October 1936, was no less intense. Azaña's attitude can be seen in *La Balada de Benicarló (The Ballad of Benicarló)*, a short political play that he wrote in April 1937, although it was not published in its original version until the end of the war. A passage from Azaña's diary entry for 29 July 1937 reveals his perspective:

> Anyone who knows as much as I do knows that it is a historical law of Spain that Barcelona must be bombed once every fifty years. Philip V's system was harsh and unjust, but dependable and effective. It has worked for two centuries.[12]

According to Zugazagoitia's testimony, Negrín expected to resolve the problems that had arisen with the *Generalitat* when he moved to Barcelona, since his real objective was none other than 'to begin recuperating the power that the autonomous region had wrongfully assumed for itself'.[13] In other words, the move was about nothing less than stripping the *Generalitat* of its powers of self-government in order to further the centralisation of power desired by the Republican Government. Thus, Catalan nationalists sometimes contend that Catalonia was, in fact, occupied first not by Franco's army, but by Negrín's anti-Catalan government.

Soon, Negrín's interventionary policies gravely damaged the political power still wielded by the *Generalitat*. Already, in the courts, power had passed into the hands of the new tribunals put into effect by Negrín after May 1937; then, at the end of September, the Government took over the war industry in Catalonia. The *Generalitat* was losing power, its institutions progressively emptied

---

10. *Crònica diària*, 2 November 1937.
11. Zugazagoitia 1977, p. 343.
12. Azaña 1977, p. 184. [TN] Philip V, who reigned from 1700–46, had abolished the autonomous rights of the kingdom of Aragon, which included Catalonia.
13. Zugazagoitia 1977, pp. 343–4.

of content, and the shadow of the Republican Government, now in Barcelona, blocked their every move. It was not long before the Government took over the police and created a new counterespionage agency, the S.I.M. (*Servicio de Investigación Militar*), which quickly fell under the control of the communists.[14] In January 1938, the Republican Government dissolved the Supplies Department of the *Generalitat*, taking over its powers; two months later, it annulled the *Generalitat*'s control over transport. The Catalan government's resistance and anger toward the central administration grew with each development.

In response, the *Generalitat* attempted to show Catalonia's solidarity with the rest of Republican Spain. In December 1937, the *Crònica diària* published data, taken from the London paper *Daily Worker*, showing Catalonia's contributions in the war:

> On the Madrid front, 75,000 Catalans fought. Moreover, Catalonia has more than a million refugees who have fled the barbarity of the rebels. Catalonia has sent food worth 215 million pesetas to Madrid. That demonstrates the solidarity between Catalonia and the rest of the Spanish Republic.[15]

In this context, the measures adopted by the Republican Government provoked more and more irritation in the *Generalitat*. It was not just that two governments existing and functioning within one city would inevitably experience friction: the fact was that Negrín wanted only one government to hold sway over Republican territory, including Catalonia, and he had already ended concessions to the Catalan people's 'foolish' desires for autonomy.

On 23 April 1938, in the face of Negrín's obvious prejudice, Companys wrote a long letter of protest to the head of the Republican Government in which he denounced abuses of authority by the police – a continual problem throughout the war – and abuses within the central administration's justice system. He then profoundly lamented that 'as the days have passed and the concentration and absorption of powers has grown, the *Generalitat* has been converted into an institution lacking significance'.[16] For Companys, the *Generalitat* was being reduced to what the old provincial governments (*diputaciones provinciales*) had been. Catalonia was no longer consulted about anything related to the war: there was no Catalan under secretary of war, the *Generalitat* did not have representation on the High War Council, and the Catalan president no longer received confidential war dispatches.

---

14. The S.I.M. was created by decree by the defence minister, Indalecio Prieto, on 6 August 1937, with the objective of 'combating espionage, stopping acts of sabotage, and carrying out investigative and protective tasks related to all the armed forces in the Ministry's charge' (*Diario Oficial del Ministerio de Defensa Nacional*, 9 August 1937).
15. *Crònica diària*, 17 December 1937.
16. The letter can be found in Madariaga 1944, pp. 798–802.

Disregarding Companys's protests, Negrín continued stripping the autonomous government of power. According to Zugazagoitia, Negrín pronounced a veritable declaration of principles on the question of Catalan nationalism to his under secretary of the interior, Rafael Méndez, soon after the Battle of the Ebro began:

> I am not prosecuting a war against Franco... so that in Barcelona a stupid, hick-separatism might sprout. No way. I am fighting the war for Spain, and because of Spain. On behalf of her greatness, and so that she will be great. Those that think otherwise are mistaken. There is only one nation: Spain!... Before consenting to nationalist campaigns that will only bring dismemberment, which I will never permit, I would cede the way for Franco with no other condition than that he get rid of the Germans and Italians. As for the integrity of Spain, I am uncompromising and will defend it from those outside and from those within. My stance is absolute and will not be diminished.

Zugazagoitia comments: 'Azaña himself would not have expressed himself with more vehemence. On this subject, the two presidents were of the same mind'.[17]

A few short weeks after this speech, the Catalan minister Jaume Aiguader (of the *Esquerra*) and the Basque minister Manuel Irujo (of the PNV, the Basque Nationalist Party) provoked a government crisis. The cause was more or less the same as it always was. In two cabinet meetings on 9 and 11 August, extraordinarily controversial measures were adopted. At the first, Negrín proposed that fifty-eight death sentences given by the Court of Espionage and High Treason (*Tribunal de Espionaje y Alta Traición*) be confirmed. Although the record made of this adopted proposal merely stated that 'several death sentences have been approved for the crimes of desertion, high treason, and espionage', it appears that the decision was made with a great deal of controversy and argument.[18] The impact of the mass execution on 11 August – the last of its kind in Republican Spain – was enormous. Azaña's own indignation, reflected in his war diary, was considerable:

> Tarradellas tells me that yesterday they executed 58. Facts that Irujo sent me. Horrible. My indignation about all this. Eight days after talking about piety and forgiveness, they rub out 58 on me. Without telling me anything or listening to my opinion. I find out through the press after it was already done.[19]

At the second meeting two days later, on 11 August, the cabinet decided to seize all the war industries still controlled by the *Generalitat* and proposed to militarise

---

17. Zugazagoitia 1977, p. 454.
18. *La Vanguardia*, 10 August 1938.
19. Azaña 1977, p. 400.

the popular tribunals and the emergency tribunals by decree. According to Azaña, five ministers voted against the proposal because it was unconstitutional, and the president of the Republic himself refused to sign the decree.[20] Jaume Aiguader immediately resigned. His letter of resignation to the president of the Government, written the same day, states:

> Barcelona, 11 August 1938. – Your Excellency Señor Don Juan Negrín. – President of the Cabinet, – My dear President and friend: as I stated in the Cabinet, I have presented to my party for consideration the decrees agreed upon today. The Left Republicans of Catalonia Party [the *Esquerra*], which has always given its enthusiastic support to the Republic and has not shunned any sacrifice necessary for the war, regrets that the emphasis [of the cabinet] on a politics repeatedly shown to be prejudicial to the ideals we defend does not permit it to continue its participation in a government that approves and applies such decrees. Ruled by the demands of those I loyally represent, I give you my resignation as Minister of Labour and Social Assistance.
>
> It is with great disappointment that I share this with you. Not because of the responsibility that with more or less success, but always with the greatest seriousness, I have had during this time, but instead to no longer be with you and the other ministers, though you will always find me at your side in everything that might be beneficial for the Republic, and the ideals we have in common. – Your devoted friend, *Jaime Aiguader*.[21]

In solidarity with Aiguader, the Basque minister of justice, Manuel Irujo, offered his resignation as well:

> Barcelona, 11 August 1938. – Your Excellency Señor Juan Negrín. – President of the Cabinet. – My dear President and friend: the Catalan Minister Señor Aiguader has informed me that he has offered his resignation due to fundamental disagreements with the Republican Government's policies in Catalonia, policies that have culminated in the three decrees approved over his and my own protests in the cabinet meeting today. The intelligent course of action by Catalans and Basques, first seen with our resignation from the Parliament (*Cortes*) in response to the annulment of the Cultivation Contracts Law [*Llei de Contractes de Conreu*], demands that I follow the example of Mr Aiguader

---

20. Azaña 1977, pp. 399–400. According to the minister of agriculture, Vicente Uribe, there was a decree for the militarisation of the ports, which established that 'all industries involved in war production would be placed under the jurisdiction of the under secretary of arms', and other matters less important, but nothing related to justice or the tribunals. See *La Vanguardia*, 12 August 1938.
21. Aiguader's letter of resignation was not made public until days later, when a new government had already been formed. It was published by *La Vanguardia*, 21 August 1938.

and resign from my position as Minister. None of this will prevent me from reiterating to you, as a republican and as a friend, my loyal affection. – Sincerely, Manuel de Irujo.[22]

The two resignations, the culmination of a series of disagreements, led to a crisis in relations between the Republican Government and the *Generalitat*. Sometimes referred to by historians as a 'mini-crisis', it was resolved a few days later, on Wednesday, 17 August, with the appointment of two new ministers: Josep Moix, from the PSUC, and Tomás Bilbao, from the Basque Nationalist Action Party (*Acción Nacionalista Vasca*). Negrín wanted to maintain Catalan and Basque representation in his government, even if it was largely a fiction, and in a note on the crisis's resolution, he stated: 'The Government of the Republic hopes to clearly affirm once more its unshakeable respect for the character and rights of the autonomous regions, as it is satisfied to see continued Catalan and Basque representation in the heart of the Government assured, which maintains the Government's character as a national union and its will to sustain, along with regional liberties, the independence and existence of Spain'.[23]

When this statement was published in the *La Vanguardia* on 21 August (the paper was not published from 17 August through 20 August), the same page was filled with letters of loyalty to Negrín's government. It is especially significant that the expressions of loyalty came from the highest echelons of the PSUC, from Comorera, Vidiella, Valdés, and Serra Pàmies, as well as from the Catalan UGT. But the president's note was clearly formulaic: by losing the war industries, the *Generalitat* had just lost its last bit of control over the direction of the war. In the end, the government crisis of August 1938 represented the culmination of this period of intergovernmental tensions – made worse by the Republican Government's Spanish chauvinism – altering and damaging Catalan autonomy.

During this period, from the end of September 1937 to the middle of August 1938, the military situation on the front and the situation in the Catalan rearguard declined dangerously. In the military campaigns of 1937, from the Battle of Brunete (June–July 1937) on, the superiority of the insurrectionary army was undeniable, thanks to Italian aviation and the German Condor Legion. The planes supplied to the Republic by the Soviet Union did little to diminish that superiority. The Republic suffered significant losses: the disappearance of the northern front had made it possible for Franco to move his northern troops to other fronts. The Republic's efforts to create a modern, disciplined army under a centralised command had not produced the desired results.

---

22. *La Vanguardia*, 21 August 1938.
23. Ibid.

Then, at the end of 1937, Franco proposed a general offensive on Guadalajara, with the ultimate objective of moving on to conquer the capital, Madrid. In the face of this threat, which was circulating in the form of a rumour in the Republican territory, the Republic decided to carry out its own attack on Teruel, the only provincial capital in Aragon that had not already been the object of a general offensive. In order to prevent an assault on Madrid, the Republic would have to prepare in secret and attack before Franco began his offensive.

The offensive against Teruel was planned by General Vicente Rojo and led by Colonel Hernández Saravia. It began with forty thousand men on 15 December and caught the enemy by surprise. The enemy defence line was broken in three places, and, at the end of just a few days, Teruel was surrounded by a pincer movement of the Republican army. On 21 December, external resistance was defeated, and the next day the city was taken by Republican troops, although Colonel Rey d'Harcourt, commander of the town's garrison, did not surrender until 8 January 1938.

The campaign had been a huge success, and the euphoria in the Republican territory could not have been greater. Teruel was the first provincial capital taken by the Republic, and the victory added fuel to the belief that the Republican army had regained its ability to go on the offensive. Apart from having achieved a strategic objective, the attack had stopped Franco's offensive against Madrid.[24]

But the euphoria only lasted a few days. Franco moved reserve troops immediately from their destination in Madrid to the Teruel front on 27 December, initiating a counter-offensive led by General Dávila. Dávila led Valera and Aranda's Navarrese divisions and had the help of the Condor Legion. Thus began the Battle of Teruel, one of the hardest battles of the war, marked by an intense cold that dipped to minus 18 degrees Celsius. On both sides, many troops froze to death.

After a few days of inactivity due to the heavy snow that fell over the city on New Year's Eve, Franco's counter-offensive began again in the middle of January 1938. On 7 February, his divisions broke the Republican lines, and in two days the Republicans suffered fifteen thousand casualties. Seven thousand more were taken prisoner. Under constant bombardment by air and artillery, the Republicans could no longer respond to the counter-attack, and finally, on 21 February,

---

24. The euphoria could be seen in most of the Republican press. *La Vanguardia*, on 22 December 1937, headlined with 'Teruel for the Republic!', and on the next day led with 'Republican Flags in Teruel'. The *Crònica diària* of 21 December stated: 'In the whole city there were delirious demonstrations of enthusiasm, and on the faces of people in the streets could be seen satisfaction for the brilliant victory of the Republic's arms'.

they evacuated the city, abandoning much of their military hardware. Fourteen thousand five hundred Republican soldiers were taken prisoner.[25]

The Battle of Teruel left the Republican army exhausted and gave Franco's army greater room to manoeuvre. Having regained the initiative, Franco led a general offensive against the entire Aragon front, with the aim of pushing the line of defence as far back as the Mediterranean Sea. He concentrated a good number of his troops (the Moroccan and Galician corps, along with the Italian Corpo Truppe Volontarie – CTV) to the south of Zaragoza under the command of General Dávila. Dávila had at his disposal 100,000 soldiers, seven hundred Italian airplanes, two hundred and fifty German airplanes, nearly two hundred tanks, and one hundred and fifty pieces of artillery. The Republicans had thirty-four thousand soldiers and seventy-four pieces of artillery. The offensive began on 9 March and had an enormous impact: the next day Belchite fell, and on the 15 March, with a general collapse of the Republican army, the entire territory as far as Caspe and Calanda fell to Franco. An unprotected front of sixty kilometres opened toward the sea.

With this phase of the offensive a success, Franco began an attack to the north of Zaragoza with the Moroccan, Aragonese, and Pyrenees corps, while continuing his campaign through the south. At the end of March 1938, there was fighting on the entire front, from the Pyrenees in the north to the Maestrazgo range in the south and east of the region. In spite of the resistance mounted by the Republican army, the Nationalists' advance, though slow, was unstoppable. On 3 April, Franco's troops entered Lleida and Gandesa, advancing the front lines into Catalan territory. A few days later, with the conquest of Balaguer, Tremp, and Camarasa, Barcelona was left cut off from the important hydraulic power centres of the Pyrenees. In the south, Republican commander Enrique Líster was able to stop the advance of the Italians in Tortosa, but on 15 April, Franco's

---

25. On 22 February, the government announced the evacuation of Teruel in a long message stating that: 'the evacuation has taken place in perfect military order, without loss of troops or war materials and in accordance with the preparations made by commanders. The bravery of the Republican troops could not defeat the large quantity of German and Italian hardware used by the rebels to their advantage, an advantage guaranteed by the policy of "non intervention"'. The article making the announcement in *La Vanguardia* also mentions that:

> The evacuation of Teruel has, militarily speaking, secondary importance, and does not undermine the effect and advantage gained by its capture by the Republican army. Thanks to the capture of Teruel, the offensive the rebels were preparing against Madrid was frustrated, forcing them to give up on their plans and instead respond to ours. Without the superiority – which will not last long – of airplanes and artillery that the rebels have been able to boast, thanks to Germany and Italy, the soldiers of the Republic who were forced to surrender Teruel would not have evacuated the city' (*La Vanguardia*, 23 February 1938).

Galician Corps pushed as far as Vinaroz, on the Mediterranean Sea. On 19 April, sixty kilometres of coastline were occupied by Franco's troops. They continued down the Valencian coast with the hope, ultimately frustrated, of making it to the region's capital. Instead, they stopped at the rivers Segre and Ebro, but Catalonia had been cut off from the rest of Republican territory. One of Franco's first measures after invading Catalonia was to abolish the Catalan Autonomy Statute, thus sending a clear message about his intentions regarding the Catalan people. The decree abolishing the statue was dated 5 April 1938.

Franco's offensive on the Aragon front was accompanied by frequent air attacks in the rearguard by the Italian air force. Already in January 1938, there had been six hundred civilian victims of the air attacks in Barcelona alone. At the end of February, the press published these statistics on the bombing in Catalonia: 17 bombing campaigns from the sea, 212 air bombings; 5,024 bombs landed, 398 mortar shells, 1,542 killed, 1,978 injured, 361 buildings totally ruined, 1,495 buildings partially ruined. The affected cities were Tarragona, Lleida, Reus, Tortosa, Guíxols, Palamós, Cambrils, Figueres, Badalona, Portbou, Colera, Puigcerdà, Mataró, Vilanova i la Geltrú, Roses, el Vendrell, el Masnou, l'Hospitalet, Castelldefels, Flix, Aitona, Tremp, Vallcarca, Calella, Sarrià de Ter, Premià de Mar, Camarasa, and Mollet.[26] In the final phase of the offensive, the bombings became even more intense. The bombings of Barcelona between 16 and 18 March were particularly horrible: with a thousand victims, they provoked a series of international protests against what was considered a crime against humanity. Barcelona became the first large city not on a war front and with no special strategic significance to become the victim of indiscriminate bombing. As such, it presaged a practice that would be common a few years later during the Second World War.

The defence minister of the Republican Government published a note on the night of 17 March regarding the bombing suffered by Barcelona in the previous 24 hours:

> No justification can be found by looking for actions of a similar nature committed by our forces, because our loyal air force is completely occupied on the military fronts. In fact, it has even abstained from responding to the constant air attacks that almost all population centres up and down the coast have suffered. These attacks have had no military objectives – since there are none in the city centres, where there are no enclaves of war industry of any kind: their sole objective has been to harvest death in the civil population. The rebel air force, based on the island of Mallorca, formed by Italian and German airplanes, and piloted by aviators of the same nationalities, carried out a furious

---

26. *Crònica diària*, 28 February 1938.

bombing of Barcelona last night and today. The bombing had one thousand victims and destroyed a great number of buildings. In all of these bombings, the target was the most densely populated areas of the capital, on which enormously powerful bombs were dropped.

The rebel air force has caused more deaths today than any since the beginning of the war and the start of the criminal aggressions against defenceless cities.

One of the bombs that exploded in the middle of the street killed almost everybody waiting in line for the streetcar; another fell, setting a city bus on fire filled with passengers who all died torn to pieces or charred.

At midday 252 dead and 535 injured were admitted into various morgues or hospitals; but as a consequence of the most recent bombing, verified later in the afternoon, the numbers rose considerably, to roughly four hundred deaths and six hundred injured at the time of this notice (9 pm).

The attacks that began last night at 10 pm lasted for more than three hours, continuing almost uninterrupted. They began again this morning at 7:40 am, again at 10:25 am, and then once again at 2 pm. All of the bombings were done from an altitude of at least five thousand two hundred metres.

Our air defence offered energetic response against the airplanes, downing one last night and another this morning. Both fell into the sea.[27]

In spite of the international protests, the air bombing did not stop. On 31 May, the civil population of Granollers witnessed an inexplicable attack on the town's centre that left more than two hundred killed and innumerable injured. This attack spurred protests as well, but to no avail.[28]

---

27. *La Vanguardia*, 18 March 1938.
28. For more on the bombing, see Garriga i Andreu, Homs i Corominas, and Ledesma i Pardo 1989, pp. 224–35. On the bombing in Barcelona and Catalonia, see Villarroya i Font 1981 and Solé and Villarroya 1986. And for more recent work, see Solé and Villarroya 2003.

Chapter Fourteen
The Battle of the Ebro and the Deterioration of Conditions in the Rearguard

As Catalonia's hungry and fearful civil population became more demoralised, and conflict between the *Generalitat* and the Republican Government intensified, military defeats on the front led to further political difficulties in the rearguard. Someone had to be blamed for the disaster of Teruel and the crumbling of the Aragon front, and the PCE and the PSUC had no trouble finding a scapegoat: the socialist defence minister, Indalecio Prieto. Prieto had been an ally of the communists in their fight against Largo Caballero, but he had tried to block the communists' rise to power within the Republican army. He was notorious for his disagreements with the communists over matters of defence.

On 16 March 1938, a week after Franco's offensive against the Aragon front, a cabinet meeting held in Barcelona's Pedralbes neighbourhood was interrupted when a demonstration organised by the communists demanded the expulsion of the government's 'treasonous' ministers. The reference to Prieto was clear. According to the next day's newspapers, the demonstration had been called to 'express the desire of mothers that the fighting continue until total victory is achieved and fascism completely annihilated'. The demonstrators, 'carrying expressive placards, posters, and banners', began their march on the Fourteenth of April Avenue – now Barcelona's Diagonal Avenue – at the Pedralbes Palace. A commission including Dolores Ibárruri (PCE), Mariano R. Vázquez (CNT),

Felipe Pretel (UGT), Perrero (FAI), Vidarte (Syndicalist Party), Serra Pàmies (PSUC), and Santiago Carrillo (*Juventudes Socialistas Unificadas*) met with Negrín to express the position of the demonstrators, summarised by the press as follows:

1. Against all agreements and pacts.
2. For fighting until the definitive crushing of Franco.
3. Against vacillators and traitors.
4. For a firm and focussed government, capable of achieving victory.

The notice in the press finished with the following description:

> The President of the Government pointed out to the demonstration's commission that nothing had changed his desire, stated clearly and emphatically in his last statements, to continue the fight to victory in our war of independence, and that he agreed with the wishes of the demonstrators.
>
> Upon rejoining the march, the commission informed the rest of the demonstrators of Mr Negrín's comments, which prompted great applause and shouts of support for the President of the Government.
>
> Soon afterwards, the demonstrators began their return march, breaking apart without violence and continuing to show their enthusiasm.[1]

Prieto's inveterate pessimism regarding the military situation was well known. Three days after the demonstration, *La Vanguardia* published comments that Prieto had just made for the British newspaper, the *Daily Express*. His remarks on the war included the following:

> We have just suffered a setback. We will not try to hide it. The enemy has opened a breach on the Aragon front, and the Italian divisions, aided by the German air force and artillery, have succeeded in advancing to the Western shores of the Mediterranean, in hopes of having the entire sea for themselves, and they are also approaching the eastern Pyrenees.[2]

This attitude gave Negrín a pretext to remove Prieto from government and assume the role of defence minister himself. The new government, formed officially on 6 April, dramatically changed the ministerial appointments. At the same time, with the inclusion of Segundo Blanco González, it brought the CNT back onto the Cabinet:

---

1. *La Vanguardia*, 17 March 1938.
2. *La Vanguardia*, 19 March 1938.

President and National Defence Minister	Juan Negrín (PSOE)
State	Julio Álvarez del Vayo (PSOE)
Interior	Paulino Gómez Sáiz (PSOE)
Justice	Ramón González Peña (UGT)
Agriculture	Vicente Uribe (PCE)
Health and Education	Segundo Blanco González (CNT)
Treasury and Economy	Francisco Méndez Aspez (*Izquierda Republicana*)
Public Works	Antonio Velao Oñate (*Izquierda Republicana*)
Communication and Transport	Bernardo Giner de los Ríos (*Unión Republicana*)
Labour	Jaume Aiguader (*Esquerra*)
Minister without portfolio	José Giral (*Izquierda Republicana*)
Minister without portfolio	Manuel de Irujo (PNV)

Negrín wanted to create at least the image of unity among all the political and social forces of anti-fascism, but the unity was probably only formal – and only possible due to the increasing danger posed by the enemy.

As 1938 progressed, only Negrín and the communists seemed to believe in the ultimate victory of the Republic. On 30 April, Negrín offered his 'Thirteen Points' for victory, a programmatic declaration with solutions for ending the war – a sort of proposal for achieving peace with the enemy – alongside a social and political reform programme. The goals, in summary, were as follows:

1. The absolute independence and integrity of all Spain will be ensured...
2. Our territory will be liberated from the foreign armies that have invaded it....
3. The state will be a strong, popular republic based on the principles of pure democracy....
4. A judicial and social framework, the work of the people's will, freely expressed by means of a plebiscite, will take effect as soon as the fighting has stopped....
5. There will be respect for regional liberties without infringing on Spanish unity....
6. The state will guarantee citizens' full rights in civil and social life, liberty of conscience, and freedom of belief and religious practice.
7. The state will guarantee private property legitimately acquired, within the limits imposed by overarching national interests and the need to protect producers....

8. Profound agrarian reform will eliminate the old semi-feudal landowning aristocracy that, lacking in human, national, and patriotic sense, has always been the largest obstacle to the development of the country's enormous possibilities....
9. The state will guarantee the right to work by means of proactive legislation and in agreement with the specific needs of the Spanish national economy.
10. The cultural, physical, and moral improvement of the race will be a principal and basic concern.
11. The army will serve the nation and be independent from political parties and ideologies.
12. The Spanish state will reaffirm the constitutional doctrine renouncing war as an instrument of national politics....
13. There will be broad amnesty for all Spanish people who wish to co-operate in the immense task of reconstruction and aggrandisement of Spain....[3]

The impact of Negrín's programme on the achievement of these objectives was minimal. And in response to the slogan 'Resist, resist, resist' – the famous triple 'R' of Negrín and the communists – it was not long before other proposals began to call for peace negotiations with the Francoists. The president of the Republic himself, Manuel Azaña, gave a famous triple 'P' speech interpreted by more than one commentator as the antithesis to Negrín's proposals. Delivered in Barcelona's historic government chamber, Saló de Cent, during a commemoration of the second anniversary of the outbreak of war, 18 July 1938, the long speech ends with a profound statement in favour of peace:

> I believe that if out of this accumulation of evil something good can come, it will be with this spirit, and woe to those who do not understand it in this way. I do not have the optimism of a Pangloss, nor will I apply to this Spanish drama the simplistic doctrine of the saying 'there is no evil from which good does not emerge'.[4] It is not true, not true. But there is a moral obligation, above all for those who suffer from war, when it finishes as we hope it does, to take from the lesson and from the muse of learning the best thing that we can. And when the torch passes to other hands, other men, and other generations, may they, if they ever feel their enraged blood boil and once again the Spanish temper burns with intolerance and hatred and gains an appetite for destruction, think of the dead and listen to their lesson: the lesson of men who fell in the heat of battle, fighting magnificently for a grandiose ideal, and who now, covered in mother earth, are no longer hateful or angry. They send

---

3. *La Vanguardia*, 1 May 1938. This edition of the newspaper published the manifesto in its entirety with numerous commentaries.
4. [TN] *No hay mal que por bien no venga*, a well-known Spanish expression.

us, with their flickering light, calm and remote as a star, the message of the eternal fatherland that says to all its children: Peace, Piety, Pardon (*Paz, Piedad, Perdón*).[5]

In a climate of growing tensions, dissonance and suspicions in the Republican camp, the Negrín government carried out the most ambitious and spectacular military operation of the whole war: an attack on the entire line of the Ebro front. The attack had complementary objectives: militarily, it was designed to prevent the fall of Valencia, which the Francoists assumed would happen on 25 July 1938. Also, the attack was designed to gain time for a total reorganisation of the Republican army, with the hope of getting resources from abroad. There would be other advantages. If successful, the operation could result in Catalonia being rejoined with the rest of Republican Spain. The operation also might strengthen the will to fight, a will that had been deeply damaged by constant failure, and prevent what seemed like the Republic's slow, inevitable death. And the Republic's capacity to go on the offensive might get the attention of the Western democracies which, given the political crisis in Central Europe, could finally decide to intervene on behalf of the Republicans. Or at least, if the war dragged on in Spain, it could be brought into the broader European conflict. Finally, the operation could bring enormous prestige to the Communist Party, since most of the commanders of the Ebro Army were communists.[6]

The attack was prepared secretly and meticulously by General Vicente Rojo, beginning in June 1938. His aim was to break through the Ebro front in the sector between Xerta and Faió, approach the Fatarella mountain range from the North and the Pàndols and Cavalls ranges from the South, and surround the region between Ascó, Camposines, Benisanet and the Ebro river. From this position, the army would advance even further toward the lines of Fatarella-Vilalba-Batea and Corbera-Gandesa-Bot. Two secondary moves accompanied this main operation: an attack to the north between Faió and Mequinenza that would cut off Franco's communications, and an attack from the Amposta sector in the south that would divert attention toward the coast and facilitate victory in the mountains. The operation would be carried out by the recently formed Ebro Army, led by Juan Modesto with the troops of Enrique Líster (Fifth Corps), Manuel Tagüeña (Fifteenth Corps), and Etelvino Vega (Twelfth Corps).

After a few weeks of intense preparations, during which the army built bridges, footbridges, and boats of all kinds to cross the river, the operation began at 12:15 am on 15 July 1938. Six divisions of the Ebro Army crossed the river at twelve different points and caught the enemy by surprise. In less than one week they

---

5. *La Vanguardia*, 19 July 1938.
6. Cardona 2006, p. 252.

had occupied all the cities and villages on the right banks of the Ebro, the Cavalls and Pàndols ranges, and held back the offensive before Gandesa and Vilalba dels Arcs, where resistance from Franco's army was fiercest. Only the southern operation failed, when the strongly reinforced 105th Moroccan Corps confronted it with intense machine gun fire. The Fourteenth International Brigade, formed primarily by Belgian and French volunteers, was nearly decimated.

Franco's reaction to the Republican advance was swift: he began intense bombings of the bridges to prevent the arrival of more Republican troops, and by opening the reservoirs of the Pyrenees, he caused an artificial rise in the river that washed away the Republic's bridges. However, all the Republican troops had already crossed, and they were positioning themselves on newly conquered territory that offered ideal conditions for defence.

The Battle of the Ebro lasted until 15 November. It was the longest and bloodiest battle of the war, and both sides suffered profound losses. The Republic was gambling not only with its prestige, but also with its military capacity and, in no small measure, its survival. At the same time, the battle displayed Franco's obsession with never ceding an inch to the enemy: rather than accepting his army's new positions on the Ebro in order to proceed with his attack on Valencia, he chose to halt his other operations, concentrate his entire air force on the Ebro, and wage an offensive to reconquer the lost territory. General Rojo gave this unforgettable description of the battle from the perspective of the Republicans: 'The Battle of the Ebro was incredibly bloody; the fighting lasted three and a half months with only brief interruptions on land and none in the air; it was a battle of resources, one in which narrow fronts, powerful weapons, and all manner of ingenuity for war were put into play, except for gases; a fight in which troops engaged in hand-to-hand combat with enemies that were better organised and had a higher morale; a horribly unfair fight with the terrible clash of men against machines, of fortification against destructive elements, of air power against land forces, of abundance against poverty, of stubbornness against tenacity, of arrogance against daring and – it is fair to say as well – of bravery against bravery, and of heroism against heroism...'.[7]

Franco's first counterattack came on 6 August, and it was followed by others that, like the first, came face to face with a well-protected Republican defence. After three months, the Republicans had hardly ceded anything. The battle for Corbera exemplifies the brutality: the Republic lost and reconquered Corbera four times on the same day before Franco finally won the town. Fighting face to face, continuous air bombing and artillery attacks significantly weakened both armies. However, while the Francoists had at their disposal sufficient reserves,

---

[7]. Rojo 1975, pp. 161–2.

abundant resources and superior aviation, the Republic had to face the battle under clearly disadvantageous conditions. There were no reserves to replace the casualties on the front line and no supplies to replace things that were destroyed or damaged. The bridges and boats for crossing the Ebro had to be rebuilt daily since they were always under air attack. And day after day, the Republicans waited impatiently for trucks to arrive from Barcelona with needed munitions.

Meanwhile, European developments were affecting the course of the war. On 29 September, at the Munich conference, Chamberlain, Daladier, Hitler and Mussolini discussed the Central European crisis resulting from Germany's claim of the Czechoslovakian Sudetenland for the Third Reich. The conference's resolution, the Munich Pact, was adopted quickly, a victory for Hitler and a humiliation for Great Britain and France, who agreed to all of Germany's demands. Czechoslovakia itself had no say in the matter. The pact made at the conference was presented as a guarantee for continued peace in Europe. Upon his return from Munich, Chamberlain expressed his opinion clearly: 'The settlement of the Czechoslovakian problem, which has now been achieved, is, in my view, only the prelude to a larger settlement in which all Europe may find peace'. Chamberlain elaborated, in a statement he signed jointly with Hitler:

> We regard the agreement signed last night and the Anglo-German Naval Agreement as symbolic of the desire of our two peoples never to go to war with one another again. We are resolved that the method of consultation shall be the method adopted to deal with any other questions that may concern our two countries, and we are determined to continue our efforts to remove possible sources of difference, and thus to contribute to assure the peace of Europe.[8]

As has been pointed out on so many occasions, the pact proved to be a fatal trap for Europe, one which exposed the politics of 'appeasement' advocated by France and Great Britain toward Germany.

For the Spanish Republic, the pact ended any hope for aid from the Western democracies. It was clear that neither France nor Great Britain would move to save the Spanish Republic and that they were leaving the road clear for Hitler to gradually gain control over Europe. And it was also clear that the result of the Spanish Civil War was not being decided on the field of battle: it had already been decided at the negotiation tables of European diplomats.

On 21 September, one week before the Munich conference, Negrín announced before the Assembly of the League of Nations in Geneva that the Republican Government was going to withdraw its army's international combatants:

---

8. Both statements were published in *La Vanguardia*, 1 October 1938. Here they appear in the English original. The first quotation can be found in Macklin 2006, p. 73; for the second, see Chamberlain 1939.

'The Spanish Government, in its desire to contribute not only with words but also with action to appeasement and to the 'detente' that we all desire, and resolved to do away with all pretexts for continued doubts about the purely national character of the cause for which the Republican armies fight, has decided to withdraw immediately and completely all non-Spanish combatants participating in the fighting in Spain in the ranks of the government, recognizing fully that this withdrawal will apply to all foreigners, without distinction of nationality, including all those granted Spanish nationality after 5 July 1936'.[9]

Negrín requested that the Assembly create an international commission to verify the complete fulfilment of the decision.

The measure was more symbolic than effective: perhaps Negrín naïvely expected reciprocation from Franco. The international volunteers were profoundly indignant over the measure, since it meant abandoning Spain without having reached their goal – that of achieving victory for democracy over international fascism. Many of them were fighting in the Battle of the Ebro at the time. Since there were no more than thirteen thousand of them, their withdrawal would not have significant military repercussions, and so, in the end, the decision affected the foreign combatants themselves more than anyone else. On 28 October, they were the object of a massive, affectionate farewell in the streets of Barcelona. More than three hundred thousand people spilled into the streets to hail the volunteers that had come to fight in Spain, while airplanes flew over the city disseminating a sonnet by the poet Miguel Hernández, homage to the fallen international soldier in Spain:

> If there are men who contain a soul without frontiers,
> a brow scattered with universal hair,
> covered with horizons, ships, and mountain chains,
> with sand and with snow, then you are one of those.
> Fatherlands called to you with all their banners,
> so that your breath filled with beautiful movements.
> You wanted to quench the thirst of panthers
> and fluttered full against their abuses.
> With a taste of all suns and seas,
> Spain beckons you because in her you realise
> your majesty like a tree that embraces a continent.
> Around your bones, the olive groves will grow,
> unfolding their iron roots in the ground,
> embracing men universally, faithfully.[10]

---

9. *La Vanguardia*, 22 September 1938.
10. *Si hay hombres que contienen un alma sin fronteras,*
    una esparcida frente de mundiales cabellos,
    cubierta de horizontes, barcos y cordilleras,
    con arena y con nieve, tú eres uno de ellos.

If Negrín's government had hoped to gain some kind of diplomatic advantage with the withdrawal, all it earned in the end was the surprise and sadness of the international combatants themselves.

The decision to withdraw foreign troops was made by Negrín at a moment when the Republican Army still considered success on the Ebro possible. But the equilibrium on the front was about to be broken. On 1 November 1938, Franco's army mounted a new offensive toward the Cavalls mountain range, and this time, surprisingly, they succeeded in occupying the position, forcing the Republican Army on a gradual retreat that would never be reversed. From 7 to 15 November, the entire Republican army re-crossed the river in an orderly fashion, re-establishing the front where it had been on 24 July. The battle resulted in fifty to sixty thousand casualties, with probably close to fifteen thousand Republican fatalities. Others estimate that there were thirty thousand casualties on Franco's side and sixty thousand on the Republican side. Moreover, the Republic lost around two hundred and fifty airplanes and irreplaceable war materials. Franco lost sixty airplanes.[11]

During the Battle of the Ebro, the situation in the Catalan rearguard worsened. The refugee problem, already severe, continued to grow with the arrival of a new wave of people coming from the rupture on the front: nearly forty thousand came from Aragon and more than one hundred and thirty thousand Catalans came from areas in Catalonia now occupied by Franco's army. The total number of refugees in November 1938 was slightly more than one million, and the significance of this number becomes clear when one considers that the population

> Las patrias te llamaron con todas sus banderas,
> que tu aliento llenara de movimientos bellos.
> Quisiste apaciguar la sed de las panteras,
> y flameaste henchido contra sus atropellos.
>
> Con un sabor a todos los soles y los mares,
> España te recoge porque en ella realices
> tu majestad de árbol que abarca un Continente.
> A través de tus huesos irán los olivares
> desplegando en la tierra sus más férreas raíces,
> abrazando a los hombres universal, fielmente.

(From *La Vanguardia*, 29 October 1938.)
An especially touching article was published in *La Humanitat* on the same day. [TN] The translation here of Miguel Hernández's poem is by Ted Genoways (Hernández 2001).

11. In his recent book, *Historia militar de una guerra civil: Estrategia y tácticas de la guerra de España*, Gabriel Cardona writes:

The exact statistics of the battle are unknown. One could estimate that the Republicans lost around 60,000 men to fighting, of those almost 20,000 were killed and the rest injured, sick, prisoners and deserters. The number of Nationalist soldiers lost to battle was similar, however, its fatalities were around 10,000, and the rest injured or sick. The Republicans lost 25 airplanes and the Nationalists around 60. The booty for the victors was great: 14 artillery pieces, 18 Russian combat cars in good condition and 17 needing repairs, 45 mortars, 181 machine guns, 24,114 rifles and great quantities of munitions, grenades, and explosives. (Cardona 2006, p. 299)

of Catalonia was three million in April 1936 – and that, by this time, the region had lost five thousand five hundred square kilometres to the Nationalists. In the course of the war, Catalonia had gone from a population density of 88 inhabitants per square kilometre to 150.[12]

It is not terribly surprising that hunger became the chief concern for citizens, especially in the bigger cities. Omelettes without eggs, the famous Ampurdanian 'tannares'; bread without wheat flour, heavy, black, and difficult to digest; crumbly cod, almost pulverised; lentils, the famous 'Negrín pills': all these made up the basic diet for the Catalan population. The *Generalitat*'s minister of culture recalled that at his son's wedding, celebrated that same year, the main dish was the everyday plate of cod served in sauce.[13] But food supply was not the only problem. Once Franco's army had occupied the power stations in the Pyrenees, energy restrictions became a constant feature. It was not just household energy use that was restricted: Josep Maria Bricall points out that, in the second half of 1938, Catalan industrial production declined so much that there could be no hope of recovery.[14] The buying power of Republican currency – especially with what was now a predictable and imminent defeat – provoked speculators to go on a feverish buying spree.

Catalan society was overwhelmed by war. The front was now on Catalan soil, bombings rattled the civil population, and Catalonia had fully mobilised. Ever younger men were drafted and sent to the front as the 'baby-bottle conscripts' (*quinta del biberón*), paying dearly with their blood during the Battle of the Ebro. Meanwhile, reservists older than forty were mobilised to carry out all kinds of work preparing fortifications and defences. The absence of young men in the cities and towns of Catalonia contrasted, more and more each day, with the presence of widowed women, hungry children, and the elderly.

This bleak panorama began to create a sense of defeat in both the political class and Catalan society more generally. The initial success of the Ebro offensive had inspired some hope, but now it became more difficult to believe that the war could be won. The government's slogan was clear, however: resistance was essential, whatever the cost... whatever the price.

'Defeatism', along with disseminating news about the military situation or about the army's failures, became crimes against the Republic, crimes prosecuted as forcefully – if not more so – than those committed by Franco's fifth column. In the last phase of the war, the S.I.M., with its semi-secret *Cheka* prisons, created authentic terror in the Catalan rearguard: arbitrary arrests, mysterious disappearances and clandestine executions all contributed to an environment that

---

12. See Roca 1983, pp. 108–9.
13. Pi i Sunyer 1975, p. 505.
14. Bricall 1970, pp. 47–50.

undermined the government's efforts to infuse the Catalan people with the will to resist. Repression had undergone a qualitative change. As we have already seen, the first few months of the war saw a popular repression, uncontrolled and severe. Now, at the end of the war, popular repression had been replaced by state and police repression, much more subtle, cerebral and directed – and eventually operating as an autonomous organisation within the state itself.

Unresolved political problems contributed to the rearguard's difficulties. There was still friction between the Republican Government and the *Generalitat*. Many distrusted the communists, who portrayed themselves as the most loyal champions of Negrín's government but who controlled the S.I.M.'s repressive measures and dominated positions of command in the army. Political dissidents were still being persecuted, as in the October 1938 trial against the leaders of the POUM for their role in the previous year's May events. The anarchist organisations were in crisis. The copious inventory of problems reflected a profound and irreversible crisis for the Republic.

In spite of all that plagued Catalonia in 1938, the *Generalitat* made enormous efforts in the area of education and culture, even succeeding in contributing to a significant, though momentary, flowering of Catalan creativity. They had lost control of the war industries, but with a spirit that revealed the desire to take advantage of one last occasion for the expression of Catalan national independence, even if it would only be fleeting, they created the Culture Services for the Front and intensified efforts in the field of education by building new schools and fostering the pedagogical innovations that had begun with the revolution. This important area of creativity and success was one of the few to escape the interference of the Republican Government.

Chapter Fifteen
The Occupation of Catalonia and Losing the War

Failure in the Battle of the Ebro led to the definitive collapse of Catalonia. Once the battle had ended and the Republican Army had crossed the river for the last time, the army defending Catalonia began a process of reorganisation under horrific conditions: many units did not have supplies to fight against the imminent Francoist offensive. According to a *communiqué* sent by Vicente Rojo to the president of the government and minister of war, Juan Negrín, on 6 December 1938, only one hundred thousand of the two hundred and twenty thousand men in the various army units in Catalonia were in any condition to fight.[1] The French border, where abundant war supplies sent from the USSR were being warehoused, was closed, and the Republican Army had to look on while Franco received deliveries from Germany, a compensation for mineral concessions made to Hitler.

Under these conditions, rumours spread like wildfire that Franco was preparing a final offensive against Catalonia, although the move was not certain: with the Battle of the Ebro over, Franco was also contemplating other possibilities, like launching a new attack on Madrid or mounting an offensive against Valencia. It appears that the Italian generals and some Spanish ones, conscious that the defeat of Catalonia would hasten the end of the war, were urging Franco to go on the offensive against Catalonia. Mussolini, at the same time, would augment his power in Europe by putting

---

1. Rojo 1974, pp. 64–72.

Italian and German troops in the Pyrenees on the French border.[2] From the Pyrenees to the sea, Franco's army – still led by Fidel Dávila, who was also Franco's defence minister – boasted three hundred thousand soldiers: the Urgel Corps under Muñoz Grandes, the Aragon Corps under Moscardó, Gambara's Italian CTV, the Navarra Corps under Solchaga, the Maestrazgo Corps under García Valiño, and the Moroccan Corps under Yagüe. The army had 565 artillery pieces and around five hundred airplanes.

As he had done on other occasions, Vicente Rojo prepared several Republican offensives on distant fronts in order to gain more time for the reorganisation of the Catalan defences. Motril was to be attacked on 8 December in order to put pressure on Málaga and the area South of Granada and to force Franco to move troops from Extremadura and Andalucía. Franco's troop movements would be used as part of the Republic's 'Plan P' to attack Córdoba-Peñarroya in the centre. The plan was never carried out, however, due to opposition from General Miaja and Admiral Buiza, and the operation was rapidly suspended, even though ships carrying troops had already embarked for the south. 'The Battle of Catalonia', as Rojo complained much later, 'was lost when the Motril operation was suspended'.[3]

Catalonia was left on its own, defended by an army that was a mere shadow of its former self, while the Republican armies of the centre had been able to reorganise themselves during the brutal Battle of the Ebro. Franco's army planned to begin the attack on Catalonia on 10 December, but stormy weather postponed the advance for several days. The Republican army, expecting the attack, sent dispatches reporting little movement: on 18 December, for example, the dispatch is limited to pointing out that 'operational activity on the different fronts lacks any importance'. The next day's dispatch is even more laconic: 'All is quiet on the different fronts'.[4]

On 23 December, however, ignoring the proposal coming from the Vatican for a Christmas ceasefire, Franco began his offensive against Catalonia at two points on the front: at Tremp, moving toward Artesa de Segrea and Ponts; and in the south, at Serós, moving toward Sarroca and Mayals. A dispatch from the front on that day describes the following military movements:

> Following intense artillery fire and constant action from Italian airplanes, the enemy has initiated an attack on the Catalan fronts. The forces of the invasion attacked the area of Tremp, where they were stopped by Spanish soldiers who inflicted countless casualties.

---

2. Cardona 2006, pp. 317–18.
3. Rojo 1974, p. 84.
4. See *La Vanguardia* of Tuesday, 20 December 1938, where the dispatches from the two previous days are published.

> Between Lleida and Balaguer, two units that tried to cross the Segre were decimated, and they retreated in disorder to their base of operations.
>
> In the area of Serós, the Italian divisions, reinforced with a great deal of military hardware, succeeded in occupying the crown of Serra Grosa, which was recaptured after a brilliant counterattack by Spanish soldiers.
>
> Among the captured prisoners were a Lieutenant and a Corporal with Italian nationality. Our forces have collected the body of Captain Giuseppe de Cola, also of the same nationality.
>
> The fighting, which has not seen a moment's interruption, continues with great violence at the time this dispatch was written.[5]

Thus began the Battle of Catalonia. In the first sector, the Eleventh Corps of the Republican Army fought well and offered a tenacious resistance, but at Segre the collapse was absolute: the Twelfth Corps was not able to withstand the attack carried out by Italian and Navarran troops at Serós. The troops' dispersal there opened up a profound breach, and the sector's only two reserve units were unable to stop the Francoists from passing through. In fact, the front essentially disappeared in this sector, and fighting continued in the open field, with all attempts at a counterattack by the Republican army thwarted by an enemy superior in number, in artillery, and with air support. On 11 January 1939, General Rojo calculated that his army had ninety thousand combatants, sixty thousand rifles and much less artillery than the enemy, with Franco's army holding a six to one advantage.[6]

Under these conditions, it would be difficult, if not impossible, to save Catalonia. The Republican offensive in the central sector, the last one of the war, was finally begun on 5 January and had no effect on the military situation in Catalonia. It ended in failure. The government had decreed a complete mobilisation that would resist to the very end, in the way that Madrid was defended at the war's beginning, but the idea was nothing but a wild dream that did not take into account the actual situation in Catalonia: an army that was rapidly disintegrating and an exhausted rearguard that after two and a half years of war had lost its capacity for resistance. The Battle of the Ebro had left Catalonia in such tatters that it had no time to recuperate before Franco's rapid offensive. Hence, Rojo's plan to organise machine gun battalions, each with 250 men recruited from political and trade union organisations, fell on deaf ears.

Sometimes the occupation of Catalonia has been described as a military parade. It is not hard to understand why: resistance was isolated and lacked coordination. But in spite of everything, there was an attempt to stop the offensive

---

5. *La Vanguardia*, 24 December 1938.
6. Rojo 1974, p. 105.

and re-establish a front line on the basis of successive orders from Republican command to fall back and regroup. As of 6 January 1939, Franco's offensive was unstoppable. From the south, the front was pushed to the Gayà River; in the centre, Franco's troops occupied Cervera; and in the north, fighting was concentrated around Pons. On 15 January, Tarragona fell, and the entire southern section of Catalonia came under Franco's control. On 18 January a meeting of Negrín's cabinet and President Companys judged the situation to be grave but not desperate. The war dispatch that went out on 19 January stated:

> The invaders and the Spanish forces at their command, aided by foreign artillery and aviation, have continued their attacks in the sectors of Bellver, Segur, Argensola, Santa Coloma de Queralt, and Rodoñá, advancing their lines in some of these sectors in spite of the tenacious resistance of our soldiers, who have suffered enormously. Anti-aircraft fire shot down a twin-engined 'Heinkel 111'. Republican airplanes responded very effectively, shooting down three 'Messerschmidt' planes in combat with a greatly superior number of foreign airplanes. All of our airplanes returned to their bases unharmed.[7]

The same day, *La Gaceta de la Republica* (*The Republican Gazette*) published an order from the president of the cabinet that required all men between 18 and 55 years of age to participate in fortification work:

> All citizens that find themselves in the rearguard will report to worksites, on a daily basis and at the times appropriate to the work they are doing, where fortifications are being built. At these worksites, they will be given materials and organised so that they can accomplish the work assigned.
>
> Carrying out this order will be an urgent part of the work currently being done for the immediate defence of the city of Barcelona, in accordance with the norms established by the military command of the city and the manner in which the work is organised. The military command of Barcelona will give instructions, which will be made public, for the regular implementation of the work referred to in this order.[8]

On the radio on Saturday, 20 January, President Companys called for a resistance that would seem more difficult with each day. It was, without his knowing it, his last message:

> In this war, Catalans, we are risking everything, even our name. I feel shame and immense pain rising in waves of anger and frustration when I think about the great extension of Catalan territory, from the regions around Lleida to Tarragona, that is already in the power of the invaders. My heart trembles to think

---

7. *La Vanguardia*, 20 January 1939.
8. *Gaceta de la República*, 19 January 1939.

about it. But Catalans, they will not advance further. Not one of us will rest; at all hours, all our energy, all our restlessness, all of our human power and even our superhuman power will close the door to the invader.[9]

Barcelona continued to fill with refugees from areas that were being lost to Franco. At the same time, a multitude of refugees began a painful march toward the north of Catalonia, heading toward France. The French border finally opened to allow the entrance of Soviet arms, but at this point it would do absolutely no good.

General Rojo gives the following description of Republican resistance in the face of Franco's advance:

> We had no army. The flood of men that showed up to fight were not good for much. Entire units like a battalion of border police, with commanders and soldiers, were given arms and, when they reached the front line around Garraf, did not withstand ten artillery shots and scattered before making contact: we had no confidence in any point of the front or in any of the new units. The arrival of arms did not help; it was too late. The machine gun battalions that were able to get arms were simply absorbed by the larger units. True, they carried out their duty, but only unintentionally; there were not enough of them to ensure the defence of the line by themselves. And as if that were not enough, the second batch of machine guns got to the units in unusable condition because they had lost their belts.[10]

The last planned attempt to stop Franco's army from entering Barcelona was at the Llobregat River. But when Rojo came up with this plan on the night of 23 January, everything, or almost everything, already seemed lost. The few Republican Army units ready to fight found themselves in conditions of scarcity and deprivation, and there were massive desertions in the rest of the army. A fight to the last man seemed virtually impossible. On 21 January, Negrín told Companys that it would be best if the two governments, along with the Basque Government, left Barcelona, and they began their departure the next day. Still, the cabinet had one last meeting on Sunday, 22 January, when it made various decisions that seemed useless at this point, like declaring a 'state of war' throughout the Republican territory. The next day, *La Vanguardia* published a proclamation from the Military Authority, signed by General Juan Hernández Saravia, commander of the armies of the eastern region, announcing that during the state of war, all rights and guarantees of the Republican constitution indicated in Articles 29, 31, 34, 38, and 39 were suspended, the Law of Public Order was

---

9. *La Vanguardia*, 21 January 1939.
10. Rojo 1974, p. 123.

in effect, and the Military Justice Code would be applied.[11] The newspaper also announced that, starting on 23 January, the Public Entertainment Regulatory Commission (*Comisión Interventora de Espectáculos Públicos*) had decided to suspend all public performances 'until the circumstances of the war change'. Another story, even more bizarre when one considers the anti-clericalism at the inception of the war, stated that the chapel of the Catalan Democratic Union (UDC) had celebrated a solemn mass on Sunday, 22 January to bid farewell to the soldiers that the army had recently mobilised.[12] On 25 January, the last day for Barcelona's Republican press, *La Vanguardia* published the wishful headline: 'Llobregat can be Barcelona's Manzanares', a reference to the successful resistance to Franco's siege of Madrid at the beginning of the war.[13]

After the three governments residing in Barcelona had fled the city, the Figueres castle became, for several days, the seat of the Republican Government.[14] Meanwhile, on 24 January, after occupying cities like Manresa, Martorell, Castelldefels and Sant Boi de Llobregat, Franco's army reached Llobregat. On the morning of 26 January, while the last Republican soldiers were leaving the city, Franco's troops began occupying positions on the outskirts: the Fifth Navarran Division occupied the Tibidado and Vallvidrera, General Yagüe's men reached Montjuïc Castle, the Fourth Navarran Division advanced from Montcada, and the Italians sent a motorised column from Terrassa. In the late afternoon, the enemy entered Barcelona and found a city that was almost deserted: any resistance was merely symbolic, and the population was demoralised and hungry. The only people who dared to go out into the streets were the fascists of the Phalange and the Francoists who had been in hiding since the beginning of the war. The city itself was in a state of ruin due to frequent, intense bombings. Between 21 and 24 January, Barcelona had been bombed on twenty-eight occasions: more than one thousand five hundred buildings had been damaged or destroyed, and thirty-six ships had sunk in the port.

On the same day, 26 January, Franco handed over the command of Barcelona to General Álvarez Arenas, announcing that he would lead the city equally in civil and military matters:

> The occupation of the great city of Barcelona, the culmination of the vigorous offensive of the Nationalist Army in Catalonia, raises problems whose complexity demands the coordination of various services under the sole command

---

11. *La Vanguardia*, 24 January 1939.
12. Ibid.
13. *La Vanguardia*, 25 January 1939.
14. [TN] The three governments referred to are the *Generalitat*, the Spanish Republican Government, and the Basque Government.

of a leader of high military rank that will take charge of the direction of those services.

By virtue of my authority, I hereby stipulate:

Article One. Don Eladio Álvarez Arenas, Brigadier General of Public Order of the National Government, will take charge of all military and civil forces and services in Barcelona, and he will exercise this responsibility until the government determines a replacement for this transitional régime.

Article Two. For the completion of his mission, he will have at his direct command:

1. The commanders of the occupation's columns of police and public order.
2. The commanders of the national services of security, the press, propaganda and their delegates.
3. The commanders of the national information service and the military police operating in the province of Barcelona.
4. The provincial commanders of the Spanish Traditionalist Phalange and the Assemblies of National Syndicalist Offensive [*Falange Española Tradicionalista y de las Juntas de Ofensiva Nacional Sindicalista (FET y de las JONS)*].
5. The commanding delegates of document recuperation services, industrial groups, etc.
6. The delegates and leaders of technical services of all sorts.
7. Bank representatives.

Article Three. In the exercise of his office, the commanding chief of all occupation services will have sole authority to dictate police edicts, government services and the organisation of social life.

From my Catalan front headquarters, 26 January 1939, the third year of victory,

Francisco Franco Bahamonde[15]

Another proclamation from General Fidel Dávila, published on the same day, established the first conditions of the occupation.[16]

The Francoist occupation of Catalonia was completed between 26 January and 10 February. It was characterised by the Republican Army's continuous retreat, by resistance at specific points (like Granollers and Montalt), designed to offer cover for the enormous exodus to France, and by Franco's air force repeatedly bombing the retreating Catalan rearguard.

---

15. *La Vanguardia*, 27 January 1939.
16. Ibid.

One of the most terrible aspects of this stage of the war in Catalonia was the indiscriminate and senseless bombing suffered by the civilian population. After the catastrophic war and defeat, and on top of a devastating exodus, the cities and towns of Catalonia suffered merciless air attacks. Arguably, the objective of the bombing for the first few days was to prevent fierce resistance as Franco's army advanced. But Girona, occupied on 4 February, was bombed on 27, 28, and 29 January, and again on 1 February; Figueres, through which some fifty thousand people passed each day on their way to France, was bombed on 26 and 30 January, and again on 3, 4, 6, and 7 February. Moreover, immense columns of civilians – including women, children, and the elderly – heading for the border, some on foot and others using whatever means of transportation they could find, many terrified by rumours circulating about outrages being committed by Franco's Moorish troops, were also systematically bombed and machine-gunned by low-flying Italian and German planes. No military justifications exist for this kind of action: it can only be explained by a thirst for revenge and destruction.

At the border, closed by the French authorities on 26 and 27 January, people waited in the hope that they would soon be able to cross. On 28 January, the border was opened to civilians, and a few days later, on 5 February, soldiers were permitted to cross. More than four hundred thousand people moved over the border into France in those days. Lluís Companys, the Basque president Aguirre and other members of the Catalan and Republican Governments crossed the border on 5 February, while Negrín, General Rojo and his staff crossed on 9 February.

The loss of Catalonia represented the final blow for the Republic, although the Republican Government, which returned to Spain after crossing the French border, still controlled a broad central zone populated by ten million people and an army of five hundred thousand men. With the French border opened, hopes of receiving Soviet aid actually increased. But the will to fight had collapsed, particularly after the loss of the 'Bastion of the Republic', as Catalonia had often been called. Moreover, political disagreements in the anti-fascist camp reappeared, more intense than ever. President Azaña resigned on 28 February, just a few weeks after crossing the border. Practically the only ones still urging resistance were Negrín and the communists, who believed that, once the rest of Europe's political conflicts had degenerated into open war, Spain's war could be integrated into it.

But they were alone in this perspective. Most, including some high-ranking commanders of the Republican Army, believed that prolonging the war would prolong a bloodshed that had become senseless, and they argued that it was time to negotiate an honourable peace with Franco. The positions taken on this issue had become irreconcilable, and the month of March, marking the end of the war itself, also delivered a sad epilogue to the disagreements that had existed in the Republican camp throughout the war. A revolt of the Republican Navy in Cartagena against the Negrín government was put down in a few hours, but not before much of the fleet had succeeded in fleeing for France. Next, Colonel Casado, along with a group of soldiers, socialists led by Julián Besteiro, and anarchists like the well-known Cipriano Mera, formed a National Defence Council (*Consejo Nacional de Defensa*) in Madrid, presided over by General Miaja. The council abolished Negrín's government, which was isolated in Elda and was starting the journey back into exile on 6 March, confronted the communist troops that were supporting Negrín, and initiated negotiations with Franco.

The council's attempts to negotiate with Franco were useless, however, because he would only accept unconditional surrender. On 28 March – the same day that Casado's Defence Council left Spain – Franco's troops entered Madrid without firing a single shot, and the next day, Valencia was occupied. On 30 March, the Italian Littorio Division occupied Alicante, where thousands of Republicans had concentrated in the vain hope that they would be able to flee via the port. On 1 April 1939, Franco issued his final 'victory' war dispatch, announcing the end of the war. On 9 February he had already proclaimed the notorious 'Law of Political Responsibilities', which aimed to 'make those pay who, with their actions or grave omissions, helped to foster the "red" subversion'. The law was used against the defeated from that moment on, inaugurating the ruthless dictatorship that would last almost forty years.

Conclusion
The Historical Significance of the Republic's Defeat

When Franco declared an end to the Civil War, Catalonia had already lived under the yoke of occupation for almost two months, in a state of physical and material defeat and moral and spiritual devastation. In Catalonia, no event of the last two hundred years has had the catastrophic consequences of the Republican defeat. The loss of autonomy is only similar to what happened in 1714, when Catalonia lost its government after the War of Succession. None of the civil wars of the nineteenth century, none of the periods of absolutist reaction and repression could compare to Catalonia's situation at that time. Even the harsh repression of the early dictatorship of Primo de Rivera (1923–30) looks tame compared to Franco's new dictatorship. Beginning in 1939, Catalonia, and by extension all of Spain, saw its historical development suddenly interrupted. It would be extremely difficult to recover from this historical rupture.

Some authors have argued that the rupture really occurred in 1936, when the war began. It is true that the Civil War had a significant impact on the political, social, and economic life of Catalonia. It created the context for a multifaceted revolution that unleashed a process of profound transformations, including a move toward self-government that was so thorough that it broke through the limitations set by the 1932 Catalan Statute. But, at the same time, the transformations were a consequence of both the historical moment in Catalonia and the conditions inherited from the preceding period. One cannot say that Catalonia improvised its 1936 revolution: the revolutionary aims of organising a new society, as utopian and un-realistic as they might seem now, had enjoyed a long tradition in the Catalan workers' movement. And in 1936, even with all the problems, impediments, and contradictions, workers tried to put their ideas into practice. The Republican period before the war had been a time of creativity, with a militant and imaginative workers' movement that, when it got the chance, made a good go of its historical opportunity.

Projects based on traditions from before the war made advances in other aspects of Catalan society as well. If Catalan women achieved new levels of emancipation, however minimal, it was because the women's liberation movement had reached a significant level of organisation and self-consciousness. If the war created the context for an expansion of Catalan culture, it was because the Catalan culture movement – begun with the famous *Renaixença* (rebirth) a full century earlier! – was enjoying its greatest ever popularity. Even in the field of pedagogy, renovation was not beginning at ground zero, but was built instead on a movement that had begun in earnest at the beginning of the century. Finally, one cannot explain the level of self-government achieved by Catalonia between 1936 and 1937 without considering the national emancipation movement that had pushed for a transformation of the state, and liberties for Catalonia, ever since the Restoration (1874).

The war offered the historical occasion for the development of a series of transformations based on previously conceived projects. Only those suffering reprisals and persecution – a not insignificant sector of Catalan society – could consider the war years a historical exception, a parenthesis in time when their privileges, power, and liberty were interrupted. In 1939, however, their liberty, power, and privileges were returned with interest.

For most of Catalan society, the trauma of defeat, interrupting a decades-long historical trajectory, grew much larger than what might be called the trauma of the Civil War. With a *coup de main* – or perhaps, more accurately, a strike of the sword – the occupation army tried to erase Catalan history and build, with decrees and the force of arms, a new reality, a new state, and a new way of living, feeling, and thinking that were completely foreign to Catalonia.

The trauma of defeat began with the massive exodus of Spaniards and Catalans – four hundred thousand to five hundred thousand of them – who crossed the Catalan border into France. Approximately one hundred thousand of them were Catalan, and they included the entire political class, members of the *Generalitat* and political party and trade union leaders; almost all of the Catalan *intelligentsia*; what remained of the Republican Army and the workers, peasants, office employees, and shop owners who fought in it; and the civil population in all its diversity, who feared the announced reprisals (on 9 February, Franco had promulgated the Law of Political Responsibilities) or who simply feared the rumours circulating about Franco's Moorish troops. They headed off to an exile where many would be killed in concentration camps and others would continue their fight for liberty in a new war. The bloody statistics of exile must be added to the deaths of the war itself: it has been estimated that thirty-eight thousand five hundred Catalan members of the Republican Army and two thousand nine hundred Catalan members of Franco's army were killed on the front. Another five thousand five hundred people were killed by the bombing campaigns and eight thousand five hundred by Republican repression. To these statistics we should add the number of victims caused by Franco's repression.

It was not long before those who stayed in Catalonia began to suffer persecution. As prisons filled, new ones were improvised, sometimes in convents and factory buildings. Concentration camps were opened and summary executions began. New legislation repressed those who had saved lives during the war. Denunciations were a daily occurrence, and it was difficult to find witnesses willing to testify so that the accused could avoid jail or execution. It is estimated that, with the war over, the number of prisoners in Spain rose to seven hundred thousand; official statistics state there were still 270,729 prisoners a year later, in 1940. In Catalonia, Barcelona's Modelo Prison won the unenviable prize for the most lock-ups. According to Martín Torrent, the prison's chaplain, thirty-five thousand prisoners passed through between 1939 and 1942, making it 'the largest captive population in the world'.[1]

Then there are those who died at the hands of Franco's repression. According to current estimates, around four thousand were executed by firing squad after official judicial proceedings. Nothing is known about the number of others who were assassinated without a trial and buried in mass graves. The statistics are especially high if we bear in mind the fact that the entire Catalan political class fled into exile. Those who did not, naturally, were the ones who had nothing to fear. As late as 1953, Catalonia still had firing squads that executed prisoners for causes stemming from the Civil War. According to official statistics, there were 543 deaths in prison between 1939 and 1953, and many others died due to the country's poor economic and sanitary conditions throughout the 1940s. Catalonia's population lost, as a direct consequence of the war, around one hundred and sixty thousand people – possibly even more – but to this number we should add the deaths caused by starvation, illness, and poor sanitation, the post-war calamities of Catalan society. Finally, the severe decline in birth rates due to the war also damaged Catalan society.

---

1. See Pagès 2005, pp. 130–2.

Hunting down 'reds' with the blessing of the Catholic Church also began in the Catalonia and Spain of 1939. According to an anecdote that was passed down to me through family tradition, the priest of the prison in Figueres used to harangue Republican prisoners waiting for the execution of their sentences with some comforting spiritual words of wisdom: 'Did you Catalans not want your house and garden?' he would ask, referring to the idyllic social model that President Macià had defended during the years of the Republic. The priest's answer to his own question left no doubt about his feelings: 'You already have the house right here, and the garden is being dug for you now'. The ineffable Martín Torrent considered the man condemned to death fortunate because he was the only human being that knew for sure the exact moment of his death: he was the only man with the 'incomparable fortune' of being able to answer the question asked by millions of people each day: 'When will I die?'[2]

While the new corporate state was being imposed, following the models established by European fascism, Franco decreed that liberalism, freemasonry, communism, and separatism were the bitter enemies of the new Spain. Thus the liberties that had been so difficult to win were abolished. The only political party that would be tolerated was the Spanish Traditionalist Phalange and the Assemblies of the National Syndicalist Offensive (*FET y de las JONS*), a hybrid party formed by decree in April 1937. Catholicism would be the only tolerated religion, with the new state being explicitly Catholic once again. The class struggle was abolished by decree. The trade union organisations were prohibited and persecuted, and workers were converted, euphemistically, into producers. Any institutions that remained from the autonomous political systems disappeared, while all manifestations of 'Catalanness' were persecuted.

Schools, churches, and media and propaganda imposed – sometimes willingly, sometimes because they had no choice – a new morality that was fundamentalist, reactionary and regressive. New rituals of citizenship were violently imposed, replacing the previous ones and penetrating all areas of public life. The obligatory roman (fascist) salute in schools, cinemas, and streets; the new hymns of the traditionalists, Phalangists, and monarchists, before which one had to stand at attention; and the sudden reappearance of the imperial flag that aimed to recall a 'glorious' past became normal in daily Catalan life. One typical poster placed throughout the region by the new forces of occupation showed two smiling young fascists giving the fascist salute and wearing their emblematic blue shirts with yoke and arrows. Doves of peace soared above them, and a lion stood in the foreground. The slogan read, 'Spain has arrived'.

---

2. Torrent 1942, p. 68.

The problem of hunger, which had persisted since the war, was not solved by the victors, despite the social auxiliaries and charity organisations that proliferated with the help of the Catholic church. These organisations proved more beneficial to state propaganda than to the hungry. In 1939 Franco inaugurated a new political and economic plan that he called 'autarky', remembered by those who had to experience it for its ration cards, its restrictions on the use of energy and its famous corruption schemes known as 'straperlo', which made the Phalangist bureaucrats of the new state rich. The country – that is to say, most of the country – went on experiencing hunger until well into the 1950s.

In the factories, the owners regained their power and imposed harsh working conditions, taking advantage of the prohibition of class-based trade unions to institute a vertical and corporative syndicalism controlled by the Phalange.[3] All the social, economic, political, and cultural advances that had been achieved before or during the Republican period disappeared without a trace. Catalonia, like the rest of the nation, was forced to live anchored in a remote and antiquated past for two long decades. When, with the help of the expansion of the international economy, modernisation finally did come, it carried an extremely high socio-political price tag. Immigration to Catalonia from other parts of Spain was high in the 1940s and 1950s, but the numbers were unprecedented in the 1960s. Immigrants, primarily from rural areas of Andalucía, Murcia, and Extremadura, were forced to pack up and leave their homes; then, in Catalonia, they were subjected to harsh social conditions and economic 'super-exploitation'. The population throughout Catalonia, but especially in the urban and industrial areas, grew enormously. The Franco régime saw in this immigration a way to end the 'Catalan Problem' once and for all, since the immigrant community was so large that it could perhaps, in the end, absorb the original Catalan population.

With no bodies of self-government, free political parties, trade unions, or mechanisms to defend its own culture; with attempts to resist from within persecuted; and with the Catalan language relegated solely to domestic and family use, Catalonia was forced to contemplate the end of its own history. The Franco régime, fully aware of its historical role, did not limit itself to destroying the workers' movement and restructuring Catalan society: it set its sights on destroying, pure and simple, the national character of Catalonia. Fernando

---

3. [TN] Traditionally, trade unions organise workers to defend or extend their economic or workplace interests *vis à vis* the bosses, or owners of the means of production. These unions would be considered 'horizontal' because they organise one social layer (workers) against another social layer (owners). Franco's vertical unions were organised by industry instead of by class. Hence, everyone in one factory or industry, from the highest-ranking boss to the lowest-paid worker, belonged to the same trade union. Naturally, these unions would be controlled by the highest-ranking bosses and serve their interests.

Valls Taberner, a moderate Catalan nationalist who later became a staunch Franco supporter, wrote that while Catalonia had followed the 'false route' of Catalanism in the previous decades, now it needed definitive reincorporation into Spain, 'with no other commander than the Caudillo, the forger of a Nation reborn and saviour of our traditional civilisation'.[4]

In the end, Catalonia came out of the Civil War doubly defeated: the working class and peasantry had been crushed, as in the rest of Spain, and its political autonomy was lost. Even today, more than seventy-five years after the outbreak of war, Catalonia has not completely recovered the evolutionary trajectory which was broken when Franco took power.

---

4. Fernando Valls i Taberner published the 'La falsa ruta' in *La Vanguardia Española*, 15 February 1939, just after the occupation of Catalonia. It was published later in his book *Reafirmación espiritual de España* (Valls i Taberner 1939). [TN] Fernando Valls i Taberner had been a leader of the Regionalist League (*Lliga Regionalista*), a conservative, pro-Catalan party.

Appendix of Documents

To complement this book, we thought it would be beneficial to publish a collection of documents, following the thematic outline of the book itself, to help the reader gain even more insight into the Civil War in Catalonia. We have been extremely selective in choosing the texts, limiting ourselves to testimonies and other documents from the period to give a sample of the writing on a variety of issues, from the street fighting of the first day, 19 July, to Catalonia's occupation by Franco.

A. The Failure of the Military Insurrection in Barcelona
(Thematic Correspondence to Chapter Two)

When army units participating in the uprising against the Republic tried to take to the streets in Barcelona on 19 July 1936, they had to confront fierce resistance from the workers and from popular organisations, as well as from the security forces of the Catalan government, the *Generalitat*. There were different points in the city that saw fighting, but it was the *Eixample*, and especially the central squares known as the *'Plaça de Catalunya'* and the nearby *'Plaça de la Universitat'*, that became the most important sites of the struggle. The *Vanguardia*'s on-the-scene reporting from Sunday, 19 July, published on Wednesday, 22 July, captures the intensity of the fighting right up until the final surrender of General Goded, the designated leader of the uprising in Catalonia.

* * *

(From *La Vanguardia*, 22 July 1936)

All Saturday night one could see on the *Ramblas*, other central streets of the city and in the working-class districts a kind of animation, an effervescence among the people walking in the streets.

All night, rumours circulated that the soldiers in the barracks in the suburbs were going to come out that same night to join in the uprising against the Republican régime.

One of the details revealing that the movement was starting was the confiscation and collection of private automobiles by the workers' organisations and political organisations.

Along with other precautions, the Republican authority requisitioned arms in all of its branches in Barcelona.

The first hours of the early morning passed with nothing happening; in fact, some went so far as to say that the subversive movement would not happen in Barcelona.

The Subversive Movement Begins

At 4:45 in the morning, gun shots rang out on the *Plaça de la Universitat*. Meanwhile, shots were heard in the upper part of the city. The subversive movement had begun in our city, starting with an open shootout between our Assault and Security Guards and the subversive forces from the Pedralbes Barracks, where the Thirteenth Infantry Regiment was housed, and the soldiers from Tarragona Street, the Tenth Cavalry Regiment. Thus began the fighting.

The subversive troops succeeded in advancing through the streets of the Left *Eixample* toward the interior of the city, some of them headed to the *Plaça d'Espanya*, while another column of subversive troops arrived at *Plaça de la Universitat* after having exchanged fire with elements belonging to the Centre of Left Republicans (*Centre d'Esquerra Republicana*) from near the same square.[1] They also clashed with a section of the Assault Guards that had succeeded in passing down Cortes Street.

These subversive troop sections were seconded by a nucleus of civilians (*paisanos*) in uniform, giving the fascist salute.

Both the subversive troops and these *paisanos* occupied the *Plaça de la Universitat*, where they placed machine guns and mortars and took over the university building.

After these actions described here, a good section of the subversive forces advanced in a column on the avenue leading from the *Plaça de la Universitat* toward the *Plaça de Catalunya*, where they arrived and saluted the Republic, and the commanding officers signalled that they had come out to defend the Republican régime. In the first few moments this created a situation where the subversive soldiers were confused with the loyal Assault and Security Guards who were defending the square.

---

1. [TN] The *Eixample*, or 'extension', refers to the area of Barcelona that was built to accommodate the rapidly growing city during the nineteenth century. In contrast to the narrow and often serpentine streets of the old medieval town, the *Eixample* reflects the rationalist spirit of the age, with streets and avenues forming a grid. The *Eixample* is divided administratively into the Left *Eixample* and the Right *Eixample*.

The Fighting Begins

The following is how soldiers sent by their commanders got to the *Telefónica* [the telephone exchange building] on the *Plaça de Catalunya*. The door was guarded by a group of *Generalitat* police agents and security guards who were watching over the building under the command of Lieutenant Perales. When the two groups of soldiers, loyal and subversive, found themselves mixed together, one of the highest ranking officials of the subversives demanded that the others surrender. The command was not obeyed, and once the police had recovered from the surprise, an armed confrontation began, and there were victims on both sides, among them the Lieutenant Perales.

Due to the numerical superiority of the subversive forces and the element of surprise, the rebels succeeded in occupying the telephone exchange building after a brutal fight.

At the same time, other rebel soldiers from the same column had succeeded in advancing as far as the *Plaça de Catalunya*, and they established defensive-positions in the buildings of the Colón Hotel, Army and Armada Circle, and the rooms of the *'Maison Dorée'* restaurant, where soldiers gathered. They placed several machine gun nests in the gardens of the buildings.

Another column of rebel troops made its way down Fourteenth of April [Diagonal] Avenue with the apparent intention of moving down to the *Paseo de Gracia* or through Lauria Street toward the centre of the city. It was forced to fall back and abort its objective after a fight that lasted for one and a half hours. A section of the loyal Assault Guards inflicted numerous casualties on the rebels.

More rebel troops who had left their barracks on Girona Street and others from the San Andrés Artillery advanced down the streets of the right *Eixample* toward the *Plaça d'Urquinaona*, intending to penetrate the city centre and take over the most important government centres. Before reaching this square, they met with energetic resistance from the assault and security guards, who were able to check the rebels with rifle and machine gun fire.

However, the fight lasted for more than two hours, giving the rebels time to set up several artillery pieces and a machine gun section on Cortes Street, between Claris and Bruch streets. While opening fire, they tried to advance, but the reaction of the troops loyal to the government was even more energetic and succeeded in halting the advance of the rebel forces.

At the same time, rebels in the *Plaça de Catalunya* attacked this group of Assault Guards with machine guns, hand grenades, and small artillery. Opposition from the insurgent troops diminished as the fighting wore on. The total dispersion of these troops occurred when the air force joined the fight on the side of the Republicans and demoralised the rebel cavalry with its machine guns, while causing numerous casualties among the rebels. In that part of the city, armed groups of workers and party militias joined the fight, and with intense rifle fire and sidearms, they attacked the artillery units from the flanks until the rebels scattered, leaving behind their cannons and munitions for the loyal forces.

At the same time, on the *Sans* highway, close to the *Plaça d'Espanya*, various political and workers' groups were trying to attack the rebels that had taken over the square. With cannon fire, the rebel elements were successful in making the workers' first attempt a failure. In the late afternoon hours on Sunday and after long hours of fighting with the participation of both popular elements and forces loyal to the Republic, the rebels were defeated.

The failure of the rebels' repeated attempts to advance down the *Puerta del Angel* Avenue, where loyal forces had congregated, just as they had in the *Plaça d'Urquinaona*, explains why the *Generalitat* Palace, guarded by the Catalan Government police (*Mossos d'Esquadra*), was never attacked at all.

The *Generalitat* President at the Police Headquarters

From the beginning of the subversive movement in the early hours of Sunday morning, Lluís Companys, *Generalitat* President, accompanied by high-ranking officials of the Catalan Government, moved to the Department of Public Order, from which, along with Señor Escofet, police chief, Señor Pérez Farras, and others, he directed the defence of republican and democratic institutions against the rebels.

Other Clashes

Also in the early hours of Sunday morning, heavy artillery forces advanced from the barracks on Icaria Avenue where they were housed. From the first moment, these forces were fired on by armed popular elements that made their advance difficult. They were successful in setting up artillery and firing on the Ministry of Interior. The Ministry's building was defended by Civil Guard forces, who offered strong resistance to the insurgent attack.

The Ministry was also attacked by forces from the barracks of the Fourth Division's military headquarters, where General Goded and his officials had shown up in the early hours of the morning.

The battle outside the Ministry of Interior lasted all Sunday morning, until the Civil Guard and other loyal forces, with the aid of air forces under the command of Lieutenant Colonel Díaz Sandino, which bombed the insurgents and completely destroyed the barracks on *Icaria* Avenue and the troops that were near the barracks and the ministry, achieved the complete surrender and capitulation of the rebel forces.

While the air forces were in action, a group of armed civilians, with the co-operation of a group of fishermen, attacked the above-mentioned rebels from the sea, and succeeded in gaining possession of numerous artillery pieces. A little later they even assaulted the Icaria barracks, where they seized all the arms, munitions, and military hardware.

When the movement began in different parts of the city as described here, several rebels positioned in the cupola of the Christopher Columbus monument began firing machine guns on groups of workers gathering across from the building for the Transport and Metallurgy Union and the local of the 'CADCI' [the shop and office workers' union], inflicting the first casualties of the day. The group of workers began to retreat toward the *Plaça del Teatre*, where they were again fired on with machine guns by other rebels who were strategically placed on a rooftop of the square. However, the worker and political party forces distributed up and down the *Ramblas* used the arms at their disposal and, supported by pairs of Assault and Security Guards, responded in such a way that the forces who had joined the subversive movement were unable leave the barracks housing the services of the *Maestranza* and Artillery Park. The rebels did succeed in setting up an artillery piece, using it to direct several cannon shots toward the *Ramblas*. Popular militias and loyal armed forces blocked the rebel artillery advance toward the *Plaça de Catalunya* with a persistent attack.

All morning long the insurgent forces who had positioned themselves on *Plaça de la Universitat* were under fierce attack coming from the streets leading into the square. These attacks, ever more intense, led to the first signs of the rebels' defection and crumbling of morale around one o'clock in the afternoon. The fighting got worse, even turning into man-to-man combat.

At two thirty in the afternoon, the soldiers, officers, and fascists wearing army-jackets, brown shirts, helmets, and belts, and with Army-issue firearms, sought refuge inside the University building.

This building was taken by assault shortly afterwards, leading to the arrest of all the rebel commanders gathered in the building.

The Civil Guard arrived when the attack on the University building began, and they took charge of those who were arrested.

As in all the places where rebel soldiers had surrendered, they were disarmed, discharged from duty, and set free on the spot, as had been ordered by the Government.

After 3 o'clock in the afternoon, the Civil Guard, Assault Guard and volunteer forces began an energetic attack against rebel forces that had taken strategic position on the *Plaça de Catalunya*.

In less than three-quarters of an hour, the rebels who had entrenched themselves in the middle of the square were defeated. Loyal forces had to act even more forcefully to dislodge the rebel troops who had established positions in the *Maison Dorée* restaurant, the Hotel Colón, and the Military Club (*Casino Militar*).

Moreover, maximum effort was needed to gain the upper hand over rebels defending their positions, especially those occupying the *Telefónica*.

The Civil Guard used cannons the rebels had abandoned on the *Plaça de Catalunya*, just across the street from the *Telefónica*.

From the *Plaça de la Universitat*, Señor Pérez Farràs, with backup from an artillery unit that had gone over to the *Generalitat*'s side and using artillery pieces that had been abandoned by the rebels, bombed the buildings where the rebels had found refuge. In the end, these rebels surrendered there as well.

At 4:15 on Sunday afternoon, the *Plaça de Catalunya* and especially the *Telefónica* came under the control once again of the régime's defenders.

The fighting was intense and bloody, especially during the hours that passed between the beginning of the insurgency and the surrender of the rebels. The appearance of the *Plaça de Catalunya* after that painful day of fighting gave a good idea of the tragedy that had taken place on this central square: numerous bodies of soldiers, guards, and officials; lifeless bodies of horses and mules strewn about the sidewalks and gardens. The damage done by both sides could be seen in several of the square's buildings, and it showed the battle's cruelty.

From five in the afternoon on, loyal forces helped by large contingents of popular militias fought to subjugate various nuclei of rebels who, in their attempts to escape, had dispersed to different points in the city.

At that hour, an attack was initiated with artillery fire upon the headquarters of the Fourth Division, where General Goded and his fellow officials involved in the rebellion could be found.

The loyal forces and popular forces entered the building under the command of Don Enrique Pérez Farràs, and they took the general and his officials prisoner.

All those who had been arrested, except for General Goded, who was taken to the *Generalitat* Palace, were sent to the prison cells of the police station.

In front of the radio stations' microphones, General Goded pronounced a few words stating that the rebel forces had failed, and ordered them to avoid more bloodshed.

A General Strike is Called

As was agreed by the workers' organisations, as soon as it was verified there were insurgent troops in the streets of Barcelona, a general strike was called and supported by all the workers' organisations. As it was a Sunday, the strike only affected the urban transport system and those establishments that were open on holidays, like bars, restaurants, etc. The taxi drivers returned their vehicles to the garages, and the city buses and streetcars stopped running at a determined hour. However, some streetcars that were already *en route* were simply abandoned by their conductors.

By order of the workers' organisations, a complete general strike will continue.

B. The Formation of the Catalan Central Committee of Anti-fascist Militias

(Thematic Correspondence to Chapter Three)

On 21 July 1936, in the face of a general collapse of Republican institutions, all of the Catalan anti-fascist forces decided to form the Catalan Central Committee of Anti-fascist Militias, which acted as the authentic and sole government of Catalonia until September 1936. The dominance of the anarchist organisations (the CNT and the FAI) and of the numerous workers' bodies gave the Committee a revolutionary character. A few days later, the press informed the public of the Committee's powers.

* * *

(Article by Manuel Moragues, published in *La Publicitat*, 2 August 1936)

The reader is already aware of the existence of the Catalan Anti-fascist Militias. However, it is very possible that the reader does not know the reason why they were created or the mission they have been given.

...The supreme authority of this Central Committee is represented by the Commissioner (*comisario*) of Defence. Next there is the delegation from the *Generalitat*, which represents the interests of the government, and a representative of the Department of Public Order. Forming a part of the committee are representatives from all the parties that form the Catalan Left Front (*Front d'Esquerres de Catalunya*) and from Catalonia's workers' organisations.

With this authority, the Committee has created different commissions, according to the needs that have arisen. There are commissions for transport, war, investigation, patrols and security, militia organisation (for Barcelona and surrounding regions), supplies, health, press and radio. All of these commissions, presided over by delegates from the political and workers' bodies that form the Central Committee, have delegates from each party that does not have, shall we say, the presidency of these commissions. In sum, all the agreements made by these commissions are automatically approved by all those organisations represented on the Central Committee since, as is logical, the delegates of all the parties participating on the commissions have the confidence, and represent the interests of, the party in whose name they act.

Having explained the secret of the strength and the authority of the Catalan Central Committee of Antifascist Militias, we will explain why the militias were created. In the first place, they were created to fight fascism and to help those places where fascist forces have yet to be defeated.

The current mission of the militias, after sending numerous men to the places where fascism is in power, is essentially to maintain order. At this time in Catalonia, the militias exercise the function of military police.

In the few days since they were organised, they have carried out many tasks. Barracks still need to be established to house militia members. So far, nonetheless, they have succeeded in disarming all of the snipers.

Another function of the militias is the formation of militia tribunals to hear the cases of those charged with espionage and desertion, as well as to try the prisoners of war taken during the rebellion.

The Committee will have the authority to seize anything needed to facilitate the work of its various bodies.

... The *Generalitat* will rely on its usual bodies to ensure public order, and it will have the aid of the militias in cases of provocation from the reactionary forces, since the militia forces are under its control. All armaments destined for war ends will be under the custody and control of the Central Committee of Militias, which has been delegated this task by the *Generalitat*.

... Every day, the Department of Patrols and Security arrests individuals who appear to be militia members but who turn out to be undocumented. Since they do not belong to any of the political or workers' organisations that form the Committee, they are armed without good reason.

Another task of the militias has been to recover everything they can that has been looted. These items have been turned in to the *Generalitat* and a receipt has been issued for them.

For this work, the militias request help from citizens and ask that if anyone hears of a place where looting is occuring, they immediately inform the Central

Committee of Militias. With utmost speed, the security patrols will go the place indicated with identification papers and photos. The patrols have orders to severely punish on the spot those attempting to alter the revolutionary order.

The militias are responsible both for people's lives and for their property. The Central Committee strongly recommends that manufacturers and store owners do not hand over anything to anyone who does not come with authorisation. Those who intend to confiscate items without the Committee's permission should be denounced quickly.

...The Supplies Commission will take care of distributing food to the militias stationed both in the city and on the war front. It will be in charge of meeting all of the supply requests made. It has, therefore, a close relationship with the War Commission and the Barcelona Militias Commission.

...The committee formed in each of Catalonia's villages will be responsible for the militia's supplies in those villages.

The committees in the villages are formed in the same way as the Central Committee of Militias. These committees will dispense official identification cards with a photo and a stamp corresponding to the village committee and to the Regional Militias Commission of the Central Committee, which in this way will control all the militias in Catalonia.

...The village committees will be under the direct control of regional commissions, which will resolve all issues for which it is not necessary to obtain authorisation from Barcelona's Central Committee. There will be thirty-seven of these regional commissions, based on the map of the proposed territorial divisions of Catalonia.

...The Health Commission of the Central Committee delegates the responsibilities of the Central Health Committee (set up in the Barcelona theatre) and is in charge of all health concerns in Catalonia. This Commission is in charge of all Catalan hospitals and clinics and has the authority to close any that operates outside its control. It will organise hospital trains going to the war front, supervise hospital statistics and hospitalisation of the injured, and take control over all surgical material both for the front and for the hospitals in the rearguard.

The Commission has also sent surgical teams to the hospitals in Lleida, Reus, Flix, Cariñena, Bujaraloz, and to the soldiers on the front, accompanied by nurses.

C. Popular Militias on the Aragon Front
(Thematic Correspondence to Chapter Four)

To fight the military insurrection, the Catalan trade union and political organisations improvised a voluntary army that very quickly came to be called the 'popular militias'. In summer 1936 they formed the Aragon front. The nature of these militias differed radically from the organisation and structure associated with a conventional army. Born of popular initiative, the first important contingent left Barcelona on 24 July 1936.

* * *

(from the *Crònica diària*, 24 July 1936)

This morning, a column of soldiers left Barcelona, sent by Catalonia to our brothers in Aragon to free them from the fascist yoke. The complicated preparatory tasks necessary for the organisation of such a diverse force and their supplies delayed the departure of the anti-fascist troops for a few hours. At least the delay gave everyone the opportunity to see the enthusiasm of the young soldiers, eager to begin the great struggle with the highest enthusiasm.

Around midday, the forces were ready to begin their march. The bulk of the column lined up between *Provenza* Street and the *Pi i Margall* monument. Commander Pérez Farràs and the CNT leader Buenaventura Durruti directed the preparations from one of the trucks distributing supplies to the militias. A military band from the Thirteenth Regiment helped raise the enthusiasm of the expedition's members.

The sidewalks of the street were filled with a multitude of people continuously applauding the brave fighters. The same enthusiasm and desire for freedom was everywhere.

This column was formed by ninety-six vehicles, among which were thirty automobiles and sixty trucks filled with militia members, several trucks with food-supplies, four CAMPSA (petrol) tank-trucks, an army tank with potable water, and about fifteen trucks carrying twelve modern artillery pieces and munitions. There were also fifteen military and Red Cross ambulances and several nurses. Commander Pérez Farràs and Buenaventura Durruti's car led the procession. One could also see several armoured trucks that had been built in the shops of Hispano Suiza over the previous few days, as well as a truck with telegraph equipment for establishing communications.

The urban militias are formed by members of the CNT, FAI, UGT, POUM, Communist Party, Catalan State Party (*Estat Català*), Socialist Party, *Esquerra*, soldiers, and Assault Guards. A large contingent of women form part of the expedition and show no less enthusiasm than the men. Many of them are wearing overalls (*monos*) and are armed with rifles. Added to the column are many foreign athletes who came to Barcelona to take part in the Popular Olympics.

At one o'clock sharp, components of the column began to leave in groups of seven or eight vehicles. The columns marched while singing the '*Internationale*', and the multitudes on the sidewalks, on balconies and in windows applauded enthusiastically and spurred the column on to combat the fascist uprising with shouts for liberty.

The first column, composed of more than four thousand men, is led by Commander Pérez Farràs and the Lieutenant of the Civil Guard, Pere Garrido. It is composed primarily of CNT members. It has eight artillery pieces and 60 machine guns. The second column has three thousand members and is led by Commander Salanova and Captains Ortiz, García Miranda, and Navarro. They are accompanied by Lieutenant Macià and Sáenz Daza, Sub-lieutenants Moreno, Calzada and Tomás, Machine Gun Lieutenant Riutort, and Machine Lieutenant Gómez.

The second column is formed by the soldiers from the Alcántara Regiment Number Fourteen and members of the CNT, the *Esquerra*, and the Catalan State Party. It has fifty machine guns and several mortars.

The third column is composed of three thousand members under the command of Del Barrio, Arquer, and Josep Munienda. In its ranks are members of the POUM, the UGT, the Socialist Party, and the Communist Party. It also has sixty machine guns, a mortar section, and another section of 'Lafitte' bombs. In this third column, there is a large group of miners from Sallent and Súria as well as from Asturias – the Asturian miners were in Barcelona for the Popular Olympics –, well-equipped with dynamite and organised as shock troops.

D. Public Order in the Catalan Rearguard
(Thematic Correspondence to Chapter Five)

Public order proved a major problem in the Republican rearguard after war broke out. All the Catalan trade union and political organisations made appeals of all kinds to avoid the excesses being committed indiscriminately by groups of *incontrolados*. After the formation of the Unity Government in September 1936, the Committee for Catalan Internal Security (*Junta de Seguridad Interior de Cataluña*) was established. In October 1936, the committee's first appeal made it clear that it was assuming exclusive power over all things related to public order.

* * *

(from the *Crònica diària*, 24 October 1936)

Citizens: The Committee for Catalan Internal Security, created by the Cabinet of the *Generalitat* and in agreement with the Internal Security advisor, addresses everyone as follows:

With the speed demanded by present circumstances, bodies and committees are forming that are charged with giving form and stability to the massive task of social and economic transformation that, to the world's admiration, the Catalan people are bringing about.

Among these bodies, the Committee for Catalan Internal Security was one of the most needed. One of the most delicate aspects of all revolutionary movements is the defence of the present state of things, born of the revolution itself. This is a difficult problem and susceptible to errors, many of them irreversible.

Within even the most elementary understandings of revolution, the following is a logical and predictable occurrence: when the people break from the strictures of the past, all kinds of passions and hatreds accumulated over centuries of oppression are unleashed. It was logical and even necessary that things would happen as they have. The people could not go about the task of reconstructing a new life with hearts full of anger. It was necessary to become unburdened. Those who have suffered the consequences have no right to complain, since they are only harvesting that which they were eager to sow.

Another natural consequence of all revolutionary movements is the creation of *guerrilleros* who, from the very first moment and with no more control than their own revolutionary consciences, set about clearing the path for the triumphant revolution and who, thanks precisely to these quick and categorical actions, achieve victory. The success of any effort lies in the opportunity taken.

For these reasons, what at first is understandable and justified can endanger the revolution when it goes beyond the limits of opportunity. To prevent this danger comes the Committee for Catalan Internal Security, which will continue the work of defending and stabilizing the revolutionary order according to the needs of the moment. It always balances humanity and severity, with the result being none other than justice, justice, and justice.

This Committee, like all the revolutionary bodies being created, comprises representatives from all the political and trade union organisations of the Catalan anti-fascist front. It brings together, therefore, every assurance that it will inspire the people's utmost confidence in the exercise of the delicate task that it has been assigned. For the Committee for Catalan Internal Security to carry out its duties, all political and trade union organisations represented on the committee must offer their support and make sure that, from the moment it forms, no one under any pretext intervenes in those tasks that are the exclusive charge of this committee, tasks for which this committee was created. Isolated actions had their moment, and we are the first to recognise their significance and value. But now we must work together responsibly, and doing otherwise could cause serious harm. If we do not proceed in this manner, we will fail at our task. And it will not be on account of the Committee, but instead because the organisations that created it did not know how to give it life. The help that the organisations must offer the Committee for Catalan Internal Security cannot be simply formal. It is critical that the people feel that the Committee exercises maximum authority, so that its decisions will be followed by everyone.

We hope that everyone, citizens and anti-fascist organisations, recognising the significance of this time, will give us their strongest and most unselfish support so that the revolution can continue on its triumphant course.

E. The Municipalisation of Housing

(Thematic Correspondence to Chapter Six)

The social and economic revolution that Catalonia experienced in the first months of civil war was multifaceted, and it played itself out in many different sectors. After the Collectivisation and Workers' Control Decree, one of the most important decrees called for the 'municipalisation' of housing, which attempted to resolve a problem that had affected the Catalan popular classes for decades. After an intense debate lasting until 11 June 1937, the new decree was announced, going into effect immediately and collectivising urban space for the first time in history. Here we publish that historic decree as it appeared a few days later in Barcelona's *La Vanguardia* newspaper.

* * *

(*La Vanguardia*, 19 June 1937)

At the beginning of the fascist uprising, the government of the *Generalitat* did not hesitate to reduce rents for urban properties, understanding the people's desire to free themselves from one of their most burdensome sources of exploitation.

Yet, while echoing the will of the people, the government was not unaware of the move's inevitable consequences. The interests of capital, already fearful in these circumstances, did not dare commit to new investments or put more money into projects that were already begun. And if there was no chance of lucrative gain – the only incentive that might induce the capitalist class to take risks – then it was logical that the construction industry would become more paralysed each day.

With the aim of making sure that workers' needs were not denied, and to avoid the losses that abandoning all construction would have meant for the country, it was necessary to take steps to ensure that all building owners would continue investing resources to finish work on constructions already begun. But many of those who had begun works found themselves lacking in the liquid assets that they had counted on being able to gather, and so it was necessary for the *Generalitat* to play a role in organising loans and pledges to avoid the potentially disastrous consequences.

At the same time, many of the works started have been completed, and in spite of the number of workers employed in defence work and those who have gone to the front, the number of construction workers forced into unemployment goes up every day.

As a result of all of this, the *Generalitat* finds itself in a position of having to use important resources in order to complete projects not yet finished and provide jobs for unemployed workers. Meanwhile, the increasing pressures of the war suggest that all resources should be used exclusively in the fight against fascism.

It is indispensable and urgent that we find a rapid solution to these exceptional circumstances. If we consider that the benefits to be gained from urban properties do not depend exclusively on capital investment, and we instead see property as intimately connected to the municipality, a factor that is not the fruit of the proprietors' efforts, we will conclude that it is the municipality that will benefit most.

From these considerations we have drawn the conclusion that we must municipalise urban property. However, so as to not suffer the defects of bureaucratisation, we have decided it would be best to municipalise through a body that will have sufficient flexibility and agility to withstand the fluctuations that the urban housing stock faces on account of the rise, stagnation, and drop in the city's population. Hence, the body will have to be directed from a practical (*técnico*) point of view, without the city government losing its influence and control. With these aims in mind, the Housing Board (*Consejo Directivo de la Caja Inmobiliaria*), which will be the body in charge of this task, shall have representatives from the two trade union organisations, the National Confederation of Workers (CNT) and the General Union of Workers (UGT), as well as from the city government itself.

Therefore, in view of the report from the Catalan Economic Advisory Council (*Consell d'Economia de Catalunya*), a proposal from the Economic, Finance, and Justice Ministers, and in agreement with the cabinet of the *Generalitat*, we decree:

Chapter One: Municipalisation of Urban Property

Article 1. For the purposes of this decree, property will be classified as follows:

a) Utilitarian: those properties used directly by the proprietor.
b) Lucrative: those properties that brought in rent for the proprietor prior to 19 July 1936.
c) Philanthropic: those properties used, without the payment of rent, by someone other than the proprietor.

Article 2. Urban resources in the region of Catalonia are now property of the city governments (*Ajuntaments*), each of which will appropriate the properties within its municipal boundaries.

Excluded for municipalisation will be properties designated as utilitarian and also those utilitarian-lucrative properties that earned in June 1936 twenty-five pesetas or less per month in towns with fewer than fifteen thousand inhabitants, and fifty-nine pesetas or less per month in towns or cities with more than fifteen thousand inhabitants, except in Barcelona, where the rate will be set at one hundred pesetas or less per month.

Utilitarian-lucrative properties that earn their proprietors more than the quantities mentioned in the previous paragraph will be municipalised, but the proprietor may continue using, without payment, those portions reserved for personal use. If the proprietor dies, this right may only be bequeathed to the proprietor's children, parents, or spouse.

Chapter Two

Cajas Inmobiliarias *(Real Estate Banks)*

Article 3. To affect the transferral and management of urban property, city governments will form an autonomous administration called *Cajas Inmobiliarias* (Real Estate Banks), the functions of which are defined in the following articles:

Article 4. The *Cajas Inmobiliarias* shall be controlled by a Board of Directors comprising a president and the following representational distribution: one third, representatives of the city, made up of town councillors.

Two thirds, representatives of the trade union organisations, the CNT and UGT, distributed proportionally according to the number of affiliates of each federation in the locality.

Article 5. The number of board members shall be determined in accordance with both the preceding article and the following scale:

In municipalities with fewer than fifteen thousand inhabitants, there shall be six members. Nine members in municipalities with fifteen thousand inhabitants or more, with the exception of Barcelona.

Fifteen members for the city of Barcelona.

The president of the board shall be the mayor or a person delegated by the mayor and chosen from among the city councillors.

Article 6. The *Cajas Inmobiliarias* shall have an Administrative Department as well as a Works Department.

The Administrative Department shall be in charge of the following:

a. Appropriation of urban properties within municipal boundaries, in agreement with Article One.
b. Appraisal and compensation.
c. Distribution of properties in accordance with provisions for the occupation of real estate, classifying the properties as housing, industrial sites, sites for social organisations (trade unions, co-operatives, mutual organisations, cultural organisations, etc.), and sites to be used for social services.
d. Treasury.
e. Statistics.

The Works Department shall be in charge of the following:

a. Preservation, repair, and adaptation of buildings.
b. The construction of buildings.

Works and administrative personnel for the *Cajas* shall be appointed in accordance with the Rules of Procedure, which will also establish the qualifications by the personnel.

Article 7. The *Cajas Inmobiliarias* shall also be in charge of administering the utilitarian properties as well as the utilitarian-lucrative properties that have not been municipalised, and they shall be able to charge property owners up to five percent of the property's net earnings for administrative costs. For utilitarian properties, net earnings will be figured out by applying the norms set by the *Cajas Inmobiliarias* for calculating occupancy rights, defined in article 15, to the value of the property as deduced from the taxable assets.

Chapter Three: Compensation for Private Property

Article 8. Properties whose owners have been determined by the popular tribunals to have taken part in the uprising shall become the property of the government of the municipality in which they are found, without compensation to the former proprietors.

Article 9. The *Cajas Inmobiliarias* shall be in charge of compensation to proprietors not involved in the uprising. These proprietors shall be issued property-bonds that shall grant the owners a 4 percent annual repayment for twenty-five years, and which shall be registered, immune from seizure, and non-transferable unless the title owner dies, in which case the matter will be settled by law. These bonds shall expire after twenty-five years and shall then be placed, following the guidelines outlined in Article 10, in credit establishments determined by the *Cajas Inmobiliarias*.

Article 10. The *Cajas Inmobiliarias* will deposit, in the name of the former proprietors of the municipalised properties, property bonds for the value of the properties on 20 June 1936, calculated on the basis of the taxable assets listed in the land registry offices, and reduced by:

a. Five percent to make the buildings habitable, preparing them for industrial, social, and hygienic use.
b. A fractional part of the total value of the property used by the former proprietor, in cases referenced by the third paragraph of Article 2.
c. The quantity for contributions to the war specified for everyone in Catalonia and as established previously in a report from the Economic Ministry.
d. The value of the unpaid mortgage.

The *Cajas Inmobiliarias* shall not apply this article to empty lots until there has been construction on them, accepting as the value the amount paid for the lot as documented in public records before 19 July 1936.

Article 11. The collection of amortisation payments derived from the possession of property bonds held by proprietors not involved in the uprising will not exceed the following quantities for each owner:

Two hundred pesetas per month in towns with fewer than five thousand inhabitants; four hundred pesetas per month in towns of more than five thousand and fewer than fifteen thousand inhabitants; six hundred pesetas per month in towns and cities with more than fifteen thousand inhabitants, with the exception of the city of Barcelona; and eight hundred pesetas per month for the city of Barcelona.

Exempt from these limitations are foreign nationals, savings banks (*Cajas de Ahorro*), welfare banks (*Cajas de Previsión Social*), mutual organisations and popular co-operatives, insurance companies, credit organisations and, in particular, the Official Bank of Small Business Loans (*Caja Oficial de Descuentos y Pignoraciones*), and the *Generalitat*'s Regulatory Office for Salary Payment.

The Cajas *Inmobiliarias* shall be in charge of quantities that building contractors have yet to collect on properties that have been municipalised. The debts shall be settled with property bonds that may, under exceptional circumstances, be used to settle the debts of those contractors with the Regulatory Office for Salary Payment and the Bank of Small Business Loans.

Chapter Four: The Repayment of Debts, Liens and Burdens on Urban Properties

Article 12. Ground rents on municipalised property are abolished in favour of the respective *Caja Inmobiliaria*, without right to indemnification.

Article 13. For the purposes of compensation, the mortgages that encumber the collectivised buildings shall be considered real estate and, therefore, reducing them to property bonds shall also subject them to the deductions indicated in Article 10.

Article 14. All of the property bonds granted to the same owner, whether for the amortisation of a property or a mortgage, will be included in a single bill with the purpose of establishing the limits indicated in Article 11.

Chapter Five: Occupancy Fees – the Unification of Payments

Article 15. The occupation of urban properties can only be authorised by the *Cajas Inmobiliarias*, which will issue vouchers in duplicate for the corresponding occupancy contracts.

The *Cajas Inmobiliarias* shall automatically and immediately notify the public about available properties when they are vacated.

Occupancy fees charged by the *Cajas Inmobiliarias* will take the place of the old rent, and all of the taxes that encumber urban property will be calculated by the Works Department of the *Caja* and will be made up of:

a) Location fees.
b) Building fees.

Location fees will be instituted in the form of payments per square metre of land occupied, and these payments will vary according to the zones established by each city government for that objective, after receiving a report from the *Caja Inmobiliaria*.

Building fees will be calculated on the basis of a percentage of the building's value.

Occupancy fees may not exceed, in general, the rents that were paid in June 1936. When the Works Department reports that the rent established by a property's previous owner was clearly lower than that which results from applying the general norms established, setting a higher occupancy fee requires the agreement of the board of the *Caja Inmobiliaria*, and this agreement must be confirmed by the city government.

Article 16. For its internal organisation, the *Cajas Inmobiliarias* will break down the occupancy fees into the following parts:

a) Amortisation
b) Conservation and Adaptations
c) Risk (fires, explosions, etc.)
d) Administration
e) New constructions
f) Housing Tax
g) National and *Generalitat* taxes, to be overseen by the *Cajas Inmobiliarias*

Article 17. The sum of the amounts charged by the city governments as taxes or fees related to urban property, both those relating to the leaseholders (tenancy, etc.) and those relating to the former proprietors (construction and expansion permits, etc.), will be replaced by the national tax.

The city governments will set the national tax in their revenue budgets, based on a percentage of the occupancy fees, and they may not impose any other tax on the construction.

The total state tax cannot be lower than the revenue obtained for those items by the municipal administration in the fiscal year with the greatest return in the five-year period before this decree takes effect.

Article 18. The income from occupancy fees, in line with Article 16, items b and c, and the part proceeding from item a, cannot be designated by the *Caja Inmobiliaria* for anything other than finding work for the construction branch, for as long as anyone in that branch is unemployed.

It will be necessary to officially regulate the total number of construction workers in order to appropriately balance productive power with consumer power.

Article 19. The *Cajas Inmobiliarias* can neither sell nor rent construction sites, but they can give permission to occupy after receiving the corresponding fees. All provisional occupancy permits for a construction site will be issued with the condition that they may be annulled by the *Caja Inmobiliaria* if and when the site is needed for new buildings.

Article 20. Every individual or corporation wishing to build a utilitarian structure has the right to have at their disposal a site or land parcel that is not occupied or contracted, requesting it from the *Caja Inmobiliaria* and following the official ordinances in effect as well as construction norms. Neither the *Caja* nor the city government may charge any kind of fees for the building permit. If construction has not begun within the time frame previously set by the city government, or if, once begun, the construction does not progress at a normal pace, this permit will become void.

Utilitarian buildings that have been constructed on sites given by the *Caja Inmobiliaria* will only pay the occupancy fees that correspond to 'location fees'. When the city government, the *Generalitat* or the state applies for a building site, the *Caja Inmobiliaria* must grant it without receiving any kind of fee, as long as the buildings constructed have objectives that are of a public character.

Article 21. Every individual or corporation that wishes to occupy a building will request to do so from the corresponding *Caja Inmobiliaria*. The order in which the requests are made will determine who is given the right to occupy the requested buildings, and the only extenuating circumstance considered in the turn of occupancy will be:

a) The minor importance of the construction work, if the building has to undergo reforms, and
b) The extent of public interest when if it is for an industry.

Article 22. Everybody must pay occupancy fees for the building that they occupy, and neither the city government nor the *Caja Inmobiliaria* may cancel the occupation fees or the arrears.

In order to affect the payment of delinquent accounts, the *Cajas Inmobiliarias* may appropriate, using legal means, up to twenty percent of the debtors' total income. If this maximum does not cover the occupancy fees, the *Cajas Inmobiliarias* may obligate the citizen debtor to live in another building with occupancy fees no higher than twenty percent of his or her total income.

Article 23. No occupant has the right to sublet all or part of the building that is the object of their residency contract; they may, however, join together with two or more applicants to request possession, and in this case the contract will be extended to include the names of all of the people who have joined together, within the limitations set by the rules of procedure.

Article 24. The resident of a building shall be evicted only for the following reasons:

a) When the building has been designated for ends other than those specified in the residence contract.
b) When the resident makes reforms or does construction without the permission of the *Caja Inmobiliaria*, at which point the resident will be held liable, even to the point of having to return the building to the same state as before.
c) When the majority of those living in a building determine, for justifiable reasons, that one of the residents should be obliged to leave.
d) When the occupant has sublet all or part of the property.
e) When the city government needs the locale in order to help improve public benefit.
f) When the building is dilapidated.
g) In the case described in the second paragraph of Article 22.

In the first four cases, the occupant does not have the right to any kind of indemnification. In contrast, the *Caja Inmobiliaria* can hold the occupant liable for any compensation resulting from the breach of regulations.

In the other cases, the *Caja Inmobiliaria* must provide the resident with a new residence with similar conditions, granting compensation.

Provisional Articles

Article 25. The city governments will draw up, as quickly as possible, the rules of procedure for the respective *Cajas Inmobiliarias*, adapting the procedure to meet local needs and to satisfy the provisions of this decree.

Article 26. When a former proprietor is granted, as compensation, property bonds for more than one *Caja Inmobiliaria*, the proprietor must declare this circumstance to the central organism created by the Finance Department of the *Generalitat* of Catalonia.

If the sum of amortisation payments to be covered is greater than the maximum amount provided for in Article 11 or as corresponds to the greatest of the populations, the total payments cannot exceed this maximum limit, and the parts accredited by the different *Cajas* will be made *pro rata*, according to the values of the buildings that have been municipalised in each municipality.

Article 27. Before the *Cajas Inmobiliarias* referred to by this decree are created, their functions will be carried out in the interim by the commission created by decree on 1 February of this year (*Diario Oficial*, 3 March), which is formed by representatives of the *Generalitat*, the Construction Syndicate of the National Workers Federation [CNT], and the Construction Syndicate of the General Workers Union [UGT].

Barcelona. 11 June 1937. Lluís Companys; Rafael Vidiella, Justice Minister;

Carlos Martí y Feced Finance Minister; Valerio Mas, Minister of the Economy.

F. The Fatarella Incidents

(Thematic Correspondence to Chapter Ten)

Problems of public order in the Catalan rearguard persisted throughout the entire war. First there were the excesses committed in the summer of 1936, primarily by the *incontrolados*; later, omnipresent security patrols and friction between the different Catalan political and social organisations became commonplace until well into 1937. The confrontations that took place in the town of Fatarella (in the Terra Alta region of Tarragona) on 23 January 1937 were the culmination of a problem that would never be resolved. In the two texts here, the CNT and the UGT give their respective, clearly contradictory interpretations of the events.

* * *

(From the CNT's *Solidaridad Obrera*, 26 January 1937)

The fascists of Fatarella. The 'Fifth Column' rises up in arms in Fatarella (Tarragona) against the CNT and the FAI.

Our Information

This past Saturday, a 'fifth column' rose up against sections of the *Confederación Nacional del Trabajo* (CNT) and the *Federación Anarquista Ibérica* (FAI) in Fatarella, an important agricultural town in the province of Tarragona.

The first thing done by the fascists, followed by other political groups, was to arrest and disarm several comrades of the CNT and the FAI.

Most of our comrades managed to get out of town, armed, and they found refuge in the countryside, where they prepared defences. These comrades soon got help from CNT and FAI workers in nearby villages.

When news of the fascist uprising in Fatarella got to Barcelona, our comrades Aurelio Fernández, General Secretary of the Committee of Internal Security, and Dionisio Eroles, Head of Public Order, prepared to send a contingent of forces to put down the rebellion. Two trucks with comrades from the security patrols and several cars with agents from the investigation and guard unit (*investigación y vigilancia*) left for Fatarella.

When the security patrols got to Fatarella, the fascists refused to let them enter the town while armed.

The fascists, in defence positions on all the houses, fired in a cowardly manner on our heroic security patrol comrades and the agents from the investigation and guard unit. Shortly afterwards, two trucks arrived with a company of Assault Guards, which proceeded to return fire when they got to the town's entrance.

The fascists resisted fiercely, but our comrades of the security patrols and Assault Guards succeeded in taking back much of the town.

Using loudspeakers, our comrades invited women and children to evacuate the town. More than five hundred people did so.

If it is necessary, CNT and FAI comrades from the entire region will go to Fatarella to help the comrade agents from the investigation unit, the Assault Guards and the security patrols.

The UGT's Generous Offer

Our comrade Dionisio Eroles, Head of Public Order, has informed us that the comrades from the UGT in Tarragona and Ascó communicated by telephone early yesterday morning to say that they were prepared to collaborate with the CNT and FAI in order to put down the fascist uprising in Fatarella.

The CNT and the FAI expressed gratitude for the generous offer, especially since parties interested in fostering disunity among the workers' front had spread rumours that the rebels in Fatarella were from the UGT.

Anti-fascists have not been involved in these lamentable events. These things can only occur in towns that were decidedly right-wing in political orientation, as was the town where these events occurred.

When this paper went to press, we were told that the fascists have been totally defeated.

Official Note on the Incidents

On account of the incidents that occurred in the town of Fatarella (Tarragona) and led to open conflict, forces have been sent to re-establish order along with representatives of the ministers and the Committee of Internal Security, as well as representatives from those workers' and political organisations represented in the Catalan *Generalitat* government, those which have intervened to re-establish normality.

Once this has been achieved, information will be made available and necessary measures will be taken to insure that what happened in this town will be avoided elsewhere.

(And from the UGT's *Las noticias*, 28 January 1937)

On the Fatarella events

The UGT, PSUC, and JSU of Tarragona and Reus met to deliberate over the painful events that occurred in the town of Fatarella and agreed to make the following public statement:

1. According to sources, last Saturday, as a consequence of a long period of disagreement between the UGT and the CNT in Fatarella, our comrades, who represented the majority of the town and who did not wish to accept the impositions or demands of the minority, which hoped to go around all of the established principles of the Collectivisation Degree from the Catalan *Generalitat*, disarmed and provisionally detained some comrades from the CNT, without committing any acts of aggression.

2. The CNT comrades in the provinces, upon learning of what had happened, instead of communicating with the UGT provincial representatives or the functioning liaison committees, mobilised rapidly with the obvious intent, according to information gathered in official centres, of attacking the town of Fatarella themselves and assaulting our comrades, who, besides being the majority in Fatarella, represented almost entirely the legally constituted authority.

3. In light of the imminent danger of a serious confrontation, an agreement was made in the office of the Commissioner of Public Order in Tarragona, with the help of comrade Aracil as delegate of the Head of Public Order of Barcelona, to send a CNT delegation from Tarragona and Reus that would attempt to calm down the CNT comrades trying to involve Fatarella. Once this was achieved, UGT comrades from Tarragona and Reus would enter Fatarella to pacify and calm nerves and then take care, in a friendly way, of any excesses that might have been committed.

4. Upon arriving at a point about two kilometres from Fatarella, the UGT and CNT delegates were surprised and disappointed to hear that some agents of Barcelona's patrols, along with some CNT comrades from the provinces, had tried to enter the town, contrary to what had been agreed upon, causing a confrontation in which one individual from the patrols was killed and another injured.

5. In light of the violent situation created, UGT delegates considered any conciliatory action absolutely impossible, particularly given the excited state of those involved in the siege and the almost certainly heightened emotions of the combatants.

6. After hours of fighting, during which both sides suffered casualties, the comrades of Fatarella turned themselves in on the edge of town as the Assault Guards approached.

7. Afterwards, Fatarella suffered repressive measures that we do not wish to evaluate until the results are known.

8. Most of the victims, many of them well-known leftists, cannot be crudely labelled as fascists, as it appears some would like to do.

9. From the outset of the conflict the local committees, keeping in mind first and foremost the supremely important needs of the anti-fascist cause, and taking care to consider the need for close unity of the trade unions, avoided intervening by sending any of our comrades from surrounding villages. Unfortunately, this attitude was not answered in kind.

Tarragona and Reus, 27 January 1937.

G. The May 1937 Events

(Thematic Correspondence to Chapter Ten)

Political disagreements that had existed since the beginning of the war among the different Catalan political forces brought about an armed confrontation in Barcelona at the beginning of May 1937. On one side were the CNT-FAI and the POUM, and on the other were the PSUC, the *Esquerra*, and the *Generalitat*. In the chronicle offered here, published by the *Generalitat*'s Department of the Presidency, we can read the official version of the events of 3, 4 and 5 May 1937.

* * *

(From *Crònica diària*, 3, 4 and 5 May 1937)

3 May 1937

At midday, following government orders, the General Commissioner of Public Order (Police Chief) and his agents presented themselves in the building of the *Telefónica* on the *Plaça de Catalunya* to give the delegate appointed by the Government his charge.

The forces who accompanied the Commissioner were fired upon from several places inside the *Telefónica*.

In the late afternoon, after several discussions between the delegate of the Interior Minister and those resisting the orders to comply with the government's demands, those resisting abandoned the building, which was subsequently occupied by the forces of Public Order.

This incident led to a series of lamentable episodes that occurred in several parts of the city. Numerous groups of armed people moved through Barcelona's streets, especially in the neighbourhoods and adjacent towns. In some places, barricades were constructed. At around 5:30 in the afternoon, shops, offices, and stores closed, giving the impression of a general strike.

Following orders from the Ministry of Internal Security, the following message was sent out over the radio in the early evening:

'The Minister of Internal Security is pleased to announce that the incidents in the *Plaça de Catalunya* concerning the orderly intervention at the *Telefónica* have been resolved'.

The organisations CNT-FAI made the following public announcement:

"From the regional committees of the CNT and the FAI to all members in Catalonia:

Comrades: This afternoon an incident occurred in Barcelona in front of the *Telefónica*. The regional committees intervened immediately and took steps to resolve the incident, retiring all of the forces mobilised due to the incident so that the committees in charge can resolve the issue definitively.

These committees responsible for resolving the crisis recommend that all members and membership bodies pay close attention to this message and listen exclusively to the instructions and agreements coming from these committees.

The secretary, on behalf of the regional committee of the CNT.

The secretary, on behalf of the regional committee of the FAI."

As a consequence of the incidents and the anxiety they caused in the street, the Palace of the *Generalitat* took adequate security measures.

4 May 1937

Several lamentable episodes that occurred towards evening yesterday, Monday, when it seemed that, with the resolution of the incident at the *Telefónica*, calm was returning, caused a complete shutdown of the city.

All public transportation stopped. The closure of stores, warehouses, shops and offices was absolute. Newspapers are not being published. The only work that was being done was in the factories of the war industry. Distribution of food was handled as usual and water, gas and electricity services continued as well.

Apart from ambulances and cars for doctors, the only automobiles that moved about were occupied by the police, committee members, and members of trade union organisations.

Throughout the entire day in different parts of Barcelona, gunfire was exchanged between armed groups and the police as well as between countrymen. In many parts of the city, barricades were constructed.

The number of people killed and injured due to these events is significant.

At one o'clock in the afternoon, from the Palace of the *Generalitat*, where at the very beginning the President of Catalonia gave appropriate orders for the quick suppression of the conflict, a radio message was sent warning everyone about orders that might be broadcast by certain groups and organisations.

5 May 1937

The government of the *Generalitat* was formed provisionally at three o'clock in the morning with Antoni Sesé representing the UGT, of which he was Secretary General.

While travelling by car at midday to occupy his position as minister, Mr Antoni Sesé was assassinated by unknown assailants with pistols. As a consequence of the attack, two police agents who accompanied the minister were also killed.

When news of the assassinations was announced, the entire city was saddened.

Message broadcast at 3:05 in the afternoon:

> In light of the current circumstances, the Republican Government, on its own initiative, has taken charge of public order in Catalonia. The Republican Government, with more resources than the *Generalitat*, will be able to take on the challenges of the moment.
>
> This is not the time for debate. The only thing that can and should be done in the face of the supremely important circumstances of the war against fascism is loyal and resolute collaboration with the Republican Government. Long live the Republic!
>
> The *Generalitat*'s resources and troops, alongside the Republic, will not take long to stabilise the situation. We recommend that everyone remain calm. We recommend that everyone give up their arms. We must put a stop to the fratricidal fighting. There have been enough disturbances in the street.
>
> Long live the Republic! Long live Catalonia!

H. Repression Against the POUM

(Thematic Correspondence to Chapter Eleven)

One of the consequences of the May events was the repression of the Workers' Party of Marxist Unification (POUM) by the new Republican Government led by Juan Negrín. Its local offices were closed, its press was shut down, and many of its members were incarcerated. The repression culminated with the assassination of its most important leader, Andreu Nin, and the trial against the party in October 1938. The letter printed here, written from Barcelona's state prison by important POUM leaders, denounces the subjection of the organisation's members, the slander coming from the Communist Party, and the interference of the Soviets, who hoped to stage a show trial against the party.

* * *

(From a typed letter found in the General Archives of the Civil War, Salamanca: 'Presos del POUM', document B 1568.)

State prison, Barcelona

14 July 1938
The Honourable President of the Republic
The Honourable President of the Government
The Honourable President of the Cabinet
The Honourable President of the *Generalitat* and of the Basque Country
To the Committees of the Anti-fascist Organisations and Parties,

We the undersigned, long-time militants in the workers' movement and founders and leaders of the POUM, have already suffered imprisonment for thirteen months. We were arrested on 16 June 1937. Two days earlier we had received a verbal promise from Mr. Julián Zugazagoitia, then Minister of Interior, that the matter of the suspension of our newspaper, *La Batalla*, would be addressed, and, if possible, resolved at the cabinet meeting on 18 June. The minister added: 'If it were my choice, I would authorise the publication of the newspaper tomorrow'. There was no time to address the matter, and there was an attempt to prevent the Editor in Chief of *La Batalla* from appearing freely, with the executive committee's consent, before Barcelona's popular tribunal #1 in order to respond to the wicked accusations that have been hurled upon us. The absolution, which seemed inevitable, would have completely shattered the plot the Communist Party has been preparing for months in order to destroy our party. The police agents obedient to the Communist Party came expressly from Madrid and Valencia to unleash relentless repression against the POUM. Any POUM militants and sympathisers that could be found were arrested as 'fascist spies'. For example, at the very moment that a fascist bullet on the Eastern front was putting an end to the life of Commander Cahué, a member of our central committee, he was being hunted down as a 'fascist spy'. All of our offices and social centres have been raided, as have some of our private residences, from which objects of value have disappeared: typewriters, fountain pens, clothes, even soap and cologne.... Our publishing house, 'Editorial Marxista', has been confiscated and sold off for virtually nothing, the principal works of Marx, Engels, Rosa Luxemburg, Lenin, Kautsky and Bebel branded as 'Trotskyist'. These acts were the prelude of what was going to happen next. The repression was going to be bloody – and it was, calculated and bloody.

Andrés [Andreu] Nin was kidnapped and assassinated by soldiers when he was in prison in Alcalá de Henares. We have the right to say that he was assassinated until those responsible for jailing him can prove otherwise. Months later, the Austrian Marxist writer, Kurt Landau, was kidnapped in Barcelona. He has not reappeared: surely, he too has been assassinated. Meanwhile, the brother of our government representative Joaquín Maurín lies dying in a hospital bed, watched over by two policemen, and Maurín himself is a prisoner in Zaragoza or Salamanca. Shortly afterwards, a long-time worker militant and one of the combatants in the heroic days of the militia, our Commissar Marciano Mena, was executed in Lérida. Months later, on the Eastern front, two of our long-time members, Hervás and Trepat, the former a nephew of ex-Commissar General and government representative Crescenciano Bilbao, were shot in the back. On 8 May of this year, our comrade Francisco Pina Orce, along with eleven other prisoners, was executed in the labour camp Omells de Nagaya, in the province of

Lérida. Commander Astorga, who capriciously had them shot, had the audacity to boast to our comrade that he had held the order to set him free in his possession for the last three days.... Who can doubt today, in anti-fascist Spain and abroad, that our party is the 'martyr of the Civil War'?

And what of us? For the last 13 months we have been moved from one prison to another. We have been acquainted with some sixteen different jail cells. We were set free from Valencia's Modelo Prison, the seventh of our long list, and at the moment of our exit, in the doors of the prison, we were kidnapped, transferred to Madrid and thrown into a basement without light or ventilation. No doubt we were destined to suffer the same fate as Nin. Though disgraceful, this is not even the worst of it. The monstrous thing is that, while a judge and special prosecutor appointed by the government prepared our case, the Communist Party's press, with representatives in this same government, were able to wage, day after day and with no restrictions, an unprecedented campaign, beyond words or description, while preventing us from defending ourselves and everything we stand for. Some decent newspapers – from Madrid, Valencia, and Barcelona – have mountains of galley proofs for articles in our defence or simply in defence of justice that the censors will not allow published. This fact dishonours forever that institution.

The campaign and the repression did subside a little for a while. Lately, it has become more intense again. For the last couple of months, POUM members have been hunted again. In Barcelona's Modelo Prison and in this, the state prison, there are already quite a few of them, most of whom were volunteers for the militias or who have occupied public positions of responsibility ever since the beginning of the movement. For more than a year, several foreign comrades have been imprisoned in the women's prison, and for the last couple of months, Andrade's and Bonet's partners have as well, along with a girl less than eighteen years old who was sentenced to six years for the simple act of reading a newspaper. And the campaign against us goes hand in hand with the repression. Once again we are going to be the target in the Communist Party's papers and their elections. Added to the same slanders as always, they have now added a new one, and it is a shocking one: we in the POUM are responsible for the fall of the Eastern front. And from newspaper articles and flyers, we have grown into a book, translated into several languages. Lately, they have begun selling *Spies in Spain* (*Espionaje en España*). The title is false and misleading, the author's name is a lie, and the publisher does not exist. So many lies can only serve to mask more lies. Why does the Communist Party not show its face in this vile libel of the POUM? Are they perhaps afraid of the scandal that will ensue if they publish the documents that form the basis of their accusations? This is a serious matter, extremely serious. The Communist Party has succeeded in taking over and using the police and the censors as it wishes. Now it has done the same with the justice system. This book is proof of that fact. Who issued these documents? What magistrate has gone outside of justice? Another example: the prosecutor in charge of our case has written his conclusions. Reading them is embarrassing. It is nothing more than a retelling of the libellous accusations. What is the government doing about such a scandal? What are the high authorities of the Republic doing? And what are the anti-fascist parties and organisations doing? We understand perfectly that ever since the beginning of this matter there have been protests and anxiety among workers and liberals around the world. Their good sense is based on legitimate emotions in the face of an undeniable truth: the rationalisations of a party, or even better, those of a foreign dictator, have become the rationalisation of the State in anti-fascist Spain. How can the international workers' movement be made to believe that the problem of independence is being fought over in Spain? And if all this had led the dictator in question to send the necessary material to destroy fascism in our country, perhaps our sacrifice would have had at least some compensation. But has this been the case? No.

About a month ago we were officially informed of the next hearing of our case. Now there are rumours that there will not be a hearing at all this summer. Why? How long will this situation be prolonged? Is it not about time that we put an end to this scandalous comedy? We are about to mark the second anniversary of the glorious July days [of our revolution]. All of us were directly involved in those events. We all put our lives at risk to fight fascism. Among all the hundreds of comrades who died and of whom we are proud, the first one killed in Barcelona on 19 July was one of ours – the secretary of our youth organisation – as was the only one who died in Valencia. The first anniversary found us in one of Madrid's '*checas*', threatened with execution. Will we have to spend the second anniversary in prison? We take full responsibility for what we are saying when we ask this question. If so, it will be a mark of shame on anti-fascist Spain, on those who govern, and on its political parties and organisations, whom we hold responsible for what is happening, like the Communist Party itself and those who command here and from the outside. From the POUM detainees

Former members of the executive committee: Andrade, Gorkin, Bonet
W. Solano, former Secretary of the Iberian Communist Youth
David Rey, former member of the Barcelona Committee
Juan Farré, former secretary of the Lerida provincial committee
Juan Quer, former secretary of the Girona provincial committee
José Escuder, former editor-in-chief of *La Batalla*

I. The Abolition of the Catalan Autonomy Statute
(Thematic Correspondence to Chapter Thirteen)

One of the justifications used by the army officers for their rebellion against the Republic was that Spain was in danger of disintegration owing to separatism. The Spanish right wing's Castilian chauvinism (*Españolismo*) and anti-autonomism had a long history. Hence, one of Franco's first commands when he arrived in Catalonia on 3 April 1938 was to abolish the Catalan Autonomy Statute, which had been approved by the Republican Government in 1932.

* * *

(from the *Boletín Oficial del Estado*, 8 April 1938)

Ministry of the Interior. Law to abolish the Catalan Statute.

The national uprising signified a rupture in the political order with all the institutions that implied the negation of the values that the uprising was trying to restore. And it is clear that whatever conception of local life might inspire future norms, the Catalan Statute, regretfully conceded by the Republic, lost its validity in the Spanish legal system after 17 July 1936. Therefore, it should not be necessary to make any declarations on the matter.

But the arrival of our glorious military on Catalan territory poses a problem that is strictly administrative, that of determining the practical consequences of the statute's repeal. Consequently, it is important to re-establish a régime of public law that, in accordance with the principle of national unity, returns to the provinces the honour of being governed on equal footing with their sisters in the rest of Spain.

Therefore, at the proposal of the Ministry of the Interior and with previous consideration by the Cabinet, I hereby proclaim:

Article 1. State, provincial, and municipal administration of the provinces of Lérida,[2] Tarragona, Barcelona and Girona will adhere to the same norms applied to all other provinces.

Article 2. Subject to the dismantling of the régime established by the Catalan Statute, the responsibilities and exercise of all legislation and the services that were ceded to the Catalan region by the law passed on 15 September 1932 will revert back to the state, which holds these rights in all the common-law territories.

I hereby proclaim this law, in Burgos, 5 April 1938, the second year of triumph.
Francisco Franco

Minister of the Interior
Ramón Serrano Suñer

---

2. [TN] Franco uses the Castilian 'Lérida' rather than the Catalan 'Lleida' here, in keeping with his opposition to the use of Catalan.

J. The Battle of the Ebro

(Thematic Correspondence to Chapter Fourteen)

In July 1938, the Republican army launched its largest offensive of the war. The crossing of the Ebro river caught the enemy army by surprise. Franco, who never accepted the loss of even an inch of land, responded to the Republican offensive by concentrating his troops on the river. The battle of the Ebro would be the longest battle of the Spanish Civil War. This newspaper article chronicles the crossing of the Ebro by the Republicans during the first days of the offensive.

* * *

(From *La Humanitat*, 30 July 1938)

Republican Soldiers Cross the River

The Ebro River, with its hanging bridges and its banks guarded by rifles and protected by machine gun nests hidden in the underbrush, had interrupted the enormous struggle in March in the sector from Mequinenza to Amposta.

Faced with this deep and wide band of water and mud, the invaders stopped their hurried plunder.

Our soldiers, their spirit of resistance firm, waited with impatience for the precise hour when they would put their boats to water, set up gangways and footbridges, and leave the river in their wake.

Finally the hour arrived. A few minutes earlier, news of the order spread. The command was met with every fighter's enormous enthusiasm and infinite happiness:

'We are crossing the Ebro! ...'

Preparations for the attack were accompanied by words of joy, bursting forth from every soldier's throat. Immense and unanimous joy, which was tested later in the difficult, harsh battle that forced the invader to flee in disarray in various sectors of the fight.

How It Began

Dark night; of an anxious silence, where it seemed that even just breathing would reveal you to the enemy.

The banks of the river were covered with rifles and outstretched arms that dragged boats and latched the cables for the hanging bridges. With each man in his place, the attack and reconquest began.

In this task, one had to fight with alert senses, because the difficulties were enormous. One of them – the first – was there, in the river itself, not at all easy to cross in the rush of the attack and with rapidly improvised methods for crossing. And this was even more difficult if the enemy had the easy target of thousands of heavily encumbered men who could not cross from one side to the other in just a few moments.

But an avalanche of will and enthusiasm was leaping to the conquest. Our arms against the enemy could not have been more effective. The evening before, the surprise and the difficulties provided by the Ebro's natural defences had been overwhelming. But these defences were overcome by the titanic efforts of thousands of patriots.

Soldiers, Sailors

The enemy was vigilant.

They believed – so we are told by the men of the Battle of the Ebro – that it was a changing of the guard.

When they began to organise their defence, with anguished hurry, with the desperation of failure, it was already too late.

On the river there was an avalanche of boats. Rowing at top speed, the Republican soldiers carried with them the fervour of victory all the way to the very banks where the invaders shielded themselves with their weapons.

And with the soldiers of these divisions went sailors as well, who, in a battalion that today shares the glory of the attack on this front, came to fight, tenacious and victorious, on the banks of the Ebro.

Once on the other side, a good number of soldiers began, under desperate enemy fire, the necessary task of connecting the hanging bridges, extending over the river the entire communication system that would aid the attack and the advance.

Battalions and brigades continued to cross the river.

When the first foreign airplane appeared, when the hanging bridges came under their gun sights and they were burned by machine gun fire, licking the jackets of the people's soldiers, one soldier, speaking for all, bellowed with enthusiasm the desire of each and every man that crossed the river or was waiting to cross. He answered the enemy machine gun fire with these words:

'Comrades: who cares if we do not have their foreign guns; it does not matter how many they have! Onward!'

His cry received a thundering reply, enthusiastic voices that drowned out the thundering explosions and noise of the guns hoping, in vain, to block the crossing of the soldiers who were overtaking enemy defences.

Men Swimming Across the River

This battle fervour, this uncontainable desire to reconquer land that the invader has stolen and to aid, with supreme effort, the soldiers fighting in the Levante, assumed enormous proportions in the Battle of the Ebro which are still difficult to describe, because we are still receiving news without full details.

But acts of heroic fervour have occurred in formidable proportions.

Acts like that of the battalion that could not wait for the moment when its men could cross the river, one by one, on the bridge that had just been hung, and could not wait either to be taken across on boats, so the men jumped into the water and swam across the wide and strong current of the river.

Feats of epic proportions by all the soldiers of the army of the Ebro, who spent hours accomplishing their first, elemental objective: crossing the river. They have demonstrated the extent of the powerful morale of Spanish fighters and the extent also of their strength and their will to fight and reconquer.

K. Disagreements Between the *Generalitat* and the Republican Government

(Thematic Correspondence to Chapter Fourteen)

Relations between the *Generalitat* and the Spanish Republican Government grew more tense as the war dragged on. Gains made for Catalan self-government in the first months of the revolution were never recognised or accepted by the Republican Government. As soon as it could, the Republican Government began to intervene in Catalan politics: in May 1937, the *Generalitat* lost control of its police and of defence matters. In October 1937 the Republican Government moved to Barcelona and intervened even more directly in Catalan public life. In a speech before Parliament, which had met in the *Pins del Vallès* (*Sant Cugat del Vallès*) monastery on 30 September 1938, Juan Negrín, President of the Republican Government, offered the following version of the government crisis of August 1938 and of the government's relations with the *Generalitat*.

* * *

La Vanguardia, 1 October 1938

The Three Decrees that Led to the Ministerial Changes in August

On 20 August, ministerial assignments were changed. I offer here a succinct explanation for the change: Three decrees were approved by the cabinet: one pertaining to the militarisation of industry, another pertaining to what we might call the militarisation of the Special Justice Tribunals, and the third pertaining to the Minister of Justice's creation of a special court for contraband and capital evasion cases in Barcelona. The *Esquerra* believes that one or more of these decrees represents, or could represent, a reduction in the *Generalitat*'s powers or at least a lack of consideration for the responsibilities carried out by the *Generalitat*. After a brief absence of two days, I found upon returning to Barcelona that Mr. Aiguader had resigned and, in solidarity with him, Mr. Irujo, another of those who have closely collaborated with this government since its beginning. In a letter, Mr. Irujo said that he lamented having to resign and that the government could certainly count on his collaboration from the outside, but that in the end he was only following the political line of the minority Basque nationalists at the time of the Cultivation Contracts Law. I have spared no effort in keeping these two friends and collaborators, first, because I appreciate and hold in high regard the work we have done together, and second, because their resignations might have political consequences. I convinced Mr. Aiguader. Of course, since the resignation of Mr. Irujo was due to the resignation of Mr. Aiguader, I concentrated my efforts exclusively on trying to hold onto Mr. Aiguader. I believe that I even convinced him that none of the three decrees, the one for militarisation of industry, the one about capital evasion and contraband, and the one, perhaps misnamed, for the militarisation of certain special justice tribunals, could be seen as minimising the powers established in the Catalan Statute, that the policy of the government and that my policy from the beginning was the utmost respect for the constitution and the statute. That I would not permit any infringement or weakening of the statute except for a single reason, and that reason only upon full consideration and agreement coming from those who ought to make such decisions, parliament, first and foremost, in those things that represent an absolute war necessity. I openly declared that it would only be a temporary measure, but that I believe there are issues, such as capital evasion, that are and have been, according to the law approved in the Constituent Assembly of Parliament immediately after it approved the statute, responsibilities that fall preferably to the central government. It continues to be the case that the reality of the central government's move to Catalonia does not imply that the Catalan tribunals or the courts of Barcelona should be the ones that have the final say in these matters. I would say the same if the Catalan appellate court or Barcelona's regional court ever had the misfortune to have to move to Albacete, Madrid, or Alicante. The issues that had not yet been settled in those high courts, issues that concerned them in particular, should not be decided by Madrid's Supreme Court, or Albacete's courts, or the courts of wherever they might be moved.

War Industries and the Militarisation of the Justice Tribunals

As for the war industries, there were no precepts in the constitution and no precepts in the Catalan Statute on which any of us might base our claim for the central government or the government of the *Generalitat* controlling or not controlling the war industries; but the war services (I myself was convinced and have been for a long time now, and even before me my predecessor, Mr Prieto) I believed that it was necessary and highly advantageous to place them under one command and to expedite even more rapidly the industrial centres that, actually, could not maintain themselves without economic support from the government and without the supply of raw materials and financial backing for the manufacture of products offered by the central government.

As for the third decree, the militarisation of the Justice Tribunals, about which there were no reservations – because as soon as experts on the matter raised concerns about whether the decree might contradict any of the articles of the constitution, the matter was turned over for further study – and no such contradictions were found, I mean, there are no issues that might make it necessary to have to manoeuvre around constitutional stipulations, to alter or otherwise make modifications to the decree (which I did not bring here today because it did not seem appropriate to do so without the Minister of Justice); as for this decree, I maintain that, finding ourselves at war, a war that has not legally been declared because of the special circumstances of this particular conflict, and since the tribunals deal with crimes that are exclusively of a military character, specifically military or having to do with the war, such as espionage, high treason, etc., the responsibility of government in the functioning of these tribunals, the role that the government legally has in these tribunals, by means of the state prosecutor, and finally, the responsibility in sentencing that falls on the government, all this leads to the conclusion that the government – in the sense that the decree grants it, which is through the proper institutional bodies – should be in charge and that if there are any contradictions with the Statute or the constitution, or any doubts to be considered, then the government would be obligated, in order to maintain control of the tribunals, to call for the declaration of a state of war, which, as long as it is in our hands, we would like to avoid, or at least postpone.

Political Understandings of the *Generalitat* and the Republican Government

My arguments with different friends about this matter were not without use, because they ended up telling me that, in the end, there was a more fundamental issue – that is, there were some deeper origins to the crisis, origins that I am going to mention now because I believe that in these questions, the best and simplest policy is to state things with absolute clarity: what we are talking about is different understandings held by some of the Catalan political parties and by the Republican Government about how to make possible the collaboration between the government of the *Generalitat* and the central government of the Republic. I have always believed and held that full authority and control over the politics of the state corresponded uniquely and exclusively to the government [of the Republic]. There may be other positions on this matter. Obviously, one could think that it is beneficial for the autonomous governments, especially in times of war, to function in agreement, to come to prior agreement on things, to consider and resolve, and later to put to further consideration who should have the responsibility of power, that it is the government of the Republic. It is possible, but of course I have said from the very beginning, before the government coming here to Barcelona, that this political position is possible, but it is not my position. Therefore, to follow this political position would be to do so without me. I believe that the place for each of the autonomous governments and the government of the Republic is well established, well defined by the constitution and the Statute. Within each entity's sphere of action, there are difficulties that arise due to the war. I understand perfectly the limitations that arise in civil life as a necessity of the war, above all when the war has the character of the internecine battle that we see in our country; but these are transitory matters, matters that we must tolerate if we wish to maintain unharmed the principle of respect for the Statute, as it has been maintained from the very first, and the principle of the Statute and the constitution.

I want to have and I believe that we do have the best cordial relations between the governments that coexist here in Barcelona: the government of the Republic and the government of the *Generalitat*, and I believe this for two reasons: one, because it is needed for the war; another, older if you like, because it corresponds to my beliefs and my own feelings. Perhaps I, a politician little adept at politics, and, if you would not give me a vote of no confidence, I would say a man who detests and loathes politics, perhaps I have lacked tact, the necessary ability to polish the edges of a cordiality that in me is probably a little rough. But this is a question of temperament; essentially, this cordiality is perfect, and respect for the principles of the Statute exists.

And if it did not exist based on a political position and on firm conviction, it would have to have been produced by the effects of the work carried out not only by the Catalan political parties who have all, almost all, acted as one man alongside the government in this cauldron of war, but also by the exemplary conduct of the Catalan people, whose feelings, tendencies, and particularities always, and now more than ever after this war, all Spanish people must respect. I believe it, because of my convictions and reasoning, but I also believe it because of profound and deep-seated feelings that did not need this war to be awakened. So I find myself deprived of the collaboration of my two dear friends and collaborators, Mr. Aiguader and Mr. Irujo, who, like Largo Caballero before, but in the government I preside over, from the first moment have shared difficult moments and taken on enormous historical responsibilities with me, perhaps on many occasions disagreeing with my judgment, and they are honoured and will always be honoured for knowing how to subsume their own judgment and their own personalities under the direction of the government.

L. Bidding Farewell to the International Brigades

(Thematic Correspondence to Chapter Fourteen)

On 28 October 1938, Barcelona bade farewell to the international volunteers who from the beginning of the war had come to fight for the Republic. The event was extremely emotional. All of Barcelona came out to say goodbye to the approximately thirteen thousand members of the brigades still in the Republican Army at that time. The account published in *La Humanitat* the next day captures that emotion.

* * *

(From *La Humanitat*, 29 October 1938)

The people of Catalonia will never forget the gesture of the free men who came from all over the world, from the very beginning of the war, to help us fight for the ideals of liberty and justice. Our people know how much the heroism of the International Brigades has contributed to blocking the greedy avalanche of fascism.

That is why the historical moment of the farewell to the truly voluntary forces that have fought in our ranks inspired one of the most emotional and impressive outbursts of support ever seen in our country. Everyone who participated will not easily forget yesterday's experience, not least the distinguished fighters from fifty-three different nationalities that received homage and gratitude from our people. A fitting farewell for the gigantic task they took on by coming to fight in our ranks.

Yesterday, anyone who doubted the anti-fascist fervour of the Catalan people would have received the biggest imaginable disappointment.

Nobody knew until mid-morning when the parade would start. It was finally announced only minutes before it actually began. People responded brilliantly, resoundingly, and unanimously, ... the answer to those who thought the Catalan people were recalcitrant and tired, when they saw the imposing spectacle of two columns of people on both sides of the street from 14 April Avenue to the *Pi i Margall* monument.

And the enthusiasm!...Words cannot describe the enthusiasm. It was so spontaneous, natural, effortless and free of posturing that we must emphatically renounce any attempt to describe it.

It is essential that we comment on the applause that our women offered to the international fighters. The refined sensitivity of our women was once again visible.

The most emotional moment was the appearance in the parade of the international fighters. Spectators burst into indescribable and uninterrupted applause for them. The faces of the heroes from fifty-three different nations reflected the intense emotion of the moment. Flowers, flags, and the shower of praise welcomed every one of their rigid and disciplined steps. Occasionally, a kiss or a hug from our women was a spontaneous, emotional prize for these months of suffering and fighting for the dignity of man and the liberty of all people.

One placard read: 'We thank you, brothers of Spain, for what you have taught us during these two years of battle'.

The modesty of the internationals. We underline it. We underline in every way the message of another placard: 'The best homage for our fallen will be a Republican victory'. And we must call attention to the moment in which, when the French contingent passed, the vibrant notes of the *'Marseillaise'* were welcomed with an extraordinary ovation. It is clear that, for us, the solidarity between people is no myth.

Our esteemed President of the Republic presided over the parade. The presence of Mr. [Don] Manuel Azaña was welcomed with ardent applause. His Excellency, pallid and emotional, returned the people's acclaim with deference. People cheered the great politician who – precisely because he is a great politician – has always been a sincere friend of our country [Catalonia].

We must also remark on the evidence of unanimous affection for President Companys. As always, the affection that our people feel for our President was unquestionably manifest.

Finally, we will describe – if we tried to describe every detail we would have to go on forever – the constant and uninterrupted enthusiasm of our people. One scene full of tender emotion: the moment when one fighter picked up and kissed a child. This reminded us that (even if there may have been unspeakable desertions, from within and from without) men with ideals, who put their convictions above all else, came two years ago so that Spain's children would never be an instrument of reaction or ignorance, so they could become citizens of a dignified nation, happy and free.

M. The Last Armed Resistance
(Thematic Correspondence to Chapter Fifteen)

Beginning on 23 December 1938, the Francoist offensive along the entire Catalan front and the enemy's advance throughout Catalan territory was unstoppable. To mobilise Catalan citizens, continuous calls were made for resistance at any cost. It was one last attempt to prevent what seemed to be the inevitable fall of Catalonia.

* * *

(Editorial published in the PSUC daily newspaper, *Treball*, 21 January 1939.)

We must fortify!

Each day, each hour, each minute that goes by, Catalonia's patriotic fervour against the invading hordes grows ever larger. Volunteers that enlist in the machine gun battalions; mobilisations taking position at designated gathering points; fortification workers with picks and shovels who hurry to make our land impregnable; women who devote themselves to the combatants and drive the machinery of production; selfless and heroic acts in the front and in the rearguard that proclaim the sublime nature of our struggle: all together, a popular uprising against the foreigners that have come to destroy our nation and to assassinate our women and children.

This patriotic fervour, this popular uprising must remain in the ascendency, accelerating its pace until the victory is assured, until Spain's independence and the liberty of Catalonia and the Catalan people are assured. We have outdone ourselves. But we must do even more. We cannot lose days, hours, minutes, or even seconds. Now is the moment for our greatest effort, and we must make use of our time and give everything we have and all our energy. We can and we must turn this brutal offensive of the invaders into their definitive defeat. All the people of Catalonia and Spain, no matter what their age or circumstances, must co-operate in the supreme efforts that we ask and require of our nation. So says President Negrín. So says, with the authority and emotion of the President of all the Catalan people, President Companys. It is necessary to resist the attack, whatever the cost, because after this triumphant resistance lies victory.

While the army selflessly and heroically fulfils its mission to stop the invading avalanche, all non-combatants have the immediate and inescapable obligation to aid, consolidate, and fortify this resistance. And this can be achieved by making fortifications. Using all our terrain, valleys and mountains, roads and highways, cities, towns, and farms, in order to block the path of the invader; joining granite walls of containment to the brave hearts of our soldiers; making of each town a castle and of our capital a fortress. Thousands of arms must work tirelessly to build fortifications. Let us raise mountains of steel, stone, and cement to stop the invaders. We must gain time: the freedom of our nation depends on our unspent capacity to resist, so that we can prevent crimes like those of Santa Coloma de Queralt and so that we can offer our children a future with peace, happiness, and progress.

Heroic combatants who sacrifice your lives to fight the assassins: resist!

Catalans, Spaniards, non-combatants: make our land impregnable! May our shovels and pickaxes, and even our fingernails – if necessary – move mountains against the invasion.

Let us defend Catalonia! Let us defend Barcelona! Let us lift our hearts high, higher than the walls we build! We must fortify!

N. Franco Occupies Catalonia

(Thematic Correspondence to Chapter Fifteen)

With the occupation of Barcelona by Franco's army on 26 January 1939, the first phase of the occupation of Catalonia came to an end. That same day, General Fidel Dávila issued a proclamation establishing the first regulations of the occupation. After Brigadier General Eliseo Álvarez Arenas was appointed head of the new Barcelona Occupation Services (*Servicios de Ocupación de Barcelona*), a new proclamation on 27 January set the occupying régime's regulations, which would be in effect in Barcelona until 1 August 1939. The preamble showed clearly the new régime's attitude towards Catalonia.

* * *

(From *La Vanguardia*, 27 January 1939)

The General Don Fidel Dávila Arroyo, General of the Northern Army, has issued the following proclamation:

I, Fidel Dávila-Arroyo, General of the Northern Army, hereby declare:

Now that the criminal effort by the powers that subjugated Catalonia in order to put it at the service of sinister and undignified plots has been annihilated, and the city of Barcelona has been rescued by the Nationalist Army, I order:

Article 1. The city of Barcelona and the other liberated Catalan provincial territories shall be reintegrated into the Spanish sovereign state, whose head is the

Generalísimo of the land, sea, and air forces, Captain General of the Army and the Navy, and National Chief of the Spanish Traditionalist Phalange and the Assemblies of National Syndicalist Offensive (*F.E. Tradicionalista y de las Jons*), his Excellency Don Francisco Franco Bahamonde.

Article 2. I declare invalid all orders and appointments made by the rebels holding power after 18 July 1936.

Article 3. All laws of the new state announced in the 'Official Bulletins' (*Boletines Oficiales*) will go into effect as of today. In agreement with the principle of national unity, the honour of being governed on equal footing with the rest of its sisters in the rest of Spain will be returned to the Catalan provinces (Law of 5 April 1938).

Article 4. Military jurisdiction will be exercised by the corresponding authorities and courts, as determined by the 28 July 1936 edict from the Committee for National Defence and other relevant regulations; in this region, permanent military tribunals will have jurisdiction over all crimes committed and will use emergency summary procedures.

Article 5. For the exercise of powers determined by the legislation in effect, all appointments deemed necessary will be made, and any disobedience of my orders or the orders of authorities or designated agents of authority will be considered acts of rebellion or treason, according to the circumstances, and will be brought before the permanent military tribunals, as will disobedience of any other order deemed necessary.

Article 6. All arms, explosives or incendiary devices, as well as valuable objects, documents and personal effects that are not legitimately possessed will be immediately turned over to the authorities and police. The sole act of disobeying this order, of failing to report immediately the known possession or concealment of such objects, or of aiding in the escape or concealment of the guilty, will itself be considered to be a sufficient motive for incurring the legal repercussions indicated in the previous Article, even without further criminal culpability.

Article 7. All authorities and governing bodies will answer directly to military advisors (*Auditoria de guerra*) regarding any matters relating to judicial procedures; for this reason, the illustrious territorial advisor will exercise not only his own powers but also those powers given by this order, subject to delegation with the requirement that they be used in accordance with the instructions he deems necessary.

Article 8. All prisoners and individuals brought before the court will be dealt with through the justice system and subject to military advisors, who will assign them to concentration camps or to other places to be determined.

I expect the most effective collaboration from everyone and assistance in the normal development of public services. Infractions against this patriotic duty will be considered an overt act of hostility against the state.

From my office, 26 January 1939, the third triumphant year

Fidel Dávila Arroyo
(Signed and sealed)

(From *La Vanguardia*, 28 January 1939)

Proclamation. Don Eliseo Álvarez Arenas, Brigadier General of the Spanish Army, Undersecretary of Public Order for the Nationalist Government, Head of Barcelona Occupation Services.

I hereby declare:

All Barcelonans and Spaniards who live in Barcelona:

The triumph of the *Caudillo* Franco has just given us the immense benefit of liberation and the highest honour: that the men and land of this hardworking and bountiful region become a full part, definitively and irrevocably, of the greatness and unity of the nation.

Let no one believe that – just because our arrival was preceded by the roar of cannons and the heat of battle – the law of conquerors will rule here. Let no one assume that the weight of the victors will fall heavily on the weak bodies of the defeated. Leaving aside for the moment the work that our justice system must take on concerning those guilty of the Spanish tragedy and the criminals responsible for non-political crimes, neither Catalonia nor the Catalans have anything to fear from this régime, inaugurated today in Barcelona with the great jubilation of a mother who finds her lost children.

Persuaded as we are of Catalonia's feelings for Spain and Spanish unity, in spite of the evil of some and errors of many, the *Caudillo* Franco offers the solemn promise of respecting in her everything that is intimately tied to her being and moral fibre but that does not fan separatist aspirations or imply an attack against sacrosanct unity. Be assured, Catalans, that the private and familial use of your language will not be persecuted; that the costumes and traditions through which you express the rich subtleties of a strong and firmly sensitive race will find in the new régime the warmest affirmation; and that your economy, the cornerstone of the Spanish economy, with which it forms an indivisible whole, will be rebuilt with urgency and Barcelona will once again be the centre of wealth and work that made it the most important place in the Mediterranean for centuries.

All Spain hopes that Catalonia, in the great task of national reconstruction, will offer along with her strength and wealth, as much as her strong economic sense, a patriotism revived and made fertile with the blood spilled in this crusade. And that quickly assimilating, with her intelligent capacity for understanding, the guiding principles of the Movement,[3] she shall be a decisive factor in the happy ending of the Great Nationalist Revolution.

But the circumstances experienced by a country immediately after a war like this one require us to go through a period of transition and recuperation, during which strong authoritarian principles, effective regulation, and an iron discipline in ensuring their strict observance shall facilitate a rapid return to normality.

For all the aforementioned reasons I command that:

Article 1. A state of war is declared in the entire nation, and this includes the liberated Catalan territory and the city of Barcelona.

Article 2. Public order and the re-establishment of civil life are subject to my authority. All other authorities, persons in official positions, public employees, corporations, businesses of all kinds and individuals must therefore obey and fulfil my direct orders and those conveyed by my representatives or delegates and must actively co-operate in the maintenance of public order and the security of people and things, and in the re-establishment of economic and domestic life.

Article 3. Anyone in possession of firearms and flammable or explosive substances must hand them over within twelve hours, with no exceptions, to those police stations with signs indicating that they are drop-off points. Only commanders, officials, soldiers, and militia members of the liberation army, and the police forces at my command, are exempt from this order.

Article 4. Requisitioned and placed at my command are all vehicles, communications devices of all kinds, radio stations, entertainment venues and

---

3. [TN] After Franco's victory, the fascist and corporatist 'Spanish Traditionalist Phalange and the Assemblies of National Syndicalist Offensive' (*Falange Española Tradicionalista y de las Juntas de Ofensiva National Sindicalista*) became known as simply 'The Movement' (*El Movimiento*), the basis of Franco's single-party state.

their facilities, and printing presses and engraving workshops, along with every kind of paper and wood pulp they use.

Article 5. Confiscated and placed under my authority are all commercial items, whether or not they are considered emergency items. Consequently, those possessing stockpiles greater than what is used for ordinary consumption must follow my orders and those of my representatives concerning these items, especially with regards to stocks, sales, prices, distribution, transfer, transport, and conservation.

Article 6. All information possessed by government offices, bodies, and departments, as well as by social, political, and syndicalist organisations, is also hereby confiscated. Removing, concealing, or otherwise preventing this confiscation is prohibited.

Article 7. Also confiscated, upon my orders and with the same prohibitions, are printed and graphic materials of all kinds, political and social propaganda, negatives and copies of cinemagraphic films, and gramophone discs.

Article 8. All seizures, requisitions, or dispossessions not ordered on my authority are prohibited. Similarly, all searches and arrests not carried out by my representatives, except in cases of crimes discovered *flagrante delicto*, are prohibited.

Article 9. Abandoned goods belonging to people who are absent must be scrupulously respected, with no one other than my representatives altering their current location.

Article 10. Those with goods that do not belong to them shall present a written statement about these goods to my representatives and shall be the custodians of those articles until further orders are received. This measure will be especially important for objects with historical, artistic, or other intrinsic value.

Article 11. All factories, workshops, and production sites shall begin running immediately or continue functioning if they have not suspended production. If difficulties or impediments to production arise, relevant parties are instructed to go to the Industrial Recovery Commission.

Those previously employed by the now defunct *Generalitat* according to the terms of the 15 January Order issued by the honourable chief minister of the government shall present themselves in their respective offices.

Article 12. All political or trade union activities outside the *Falange Española Tradicionalista y de las Juntas de Ofensiva Nacional Sindicalista* are prohibited. Complete faithfulness to the spirit of unification and brotherhood shall govern every statement and act of this organisation, and any sign of opposition that might sow discord or conflict among Spaniards is prohibited and will be considered treason and harshly sanctioned.

Article 13. Any insults or acts of aggression against soldiers, public employees or individuals belonging to the militias that took up arms to defend the nation will be considered to be insults against the armed forces and will be issued with summary judgments, even when no soldiers, public employees, or militia members were present during the act of aggression or insult.

Article 14. Public employees, authorities, or corporations that do not offer the immediate aid requested by my authority or that of my subordinates for the re-establishment of order or the execution of this proclamation's commands will be immediately suspended from their responsibilities, without freeing them from any corresponding criminal charges required by the military courts.

Article 15. All crimes covered in Articles V, VI, VII and VIII from the second treaty of the Code of Military Justice will be issued with summary judgments by the military courts.

Article 16. The following will also be handed over to the military courts and given summary judgments:

a) All crimes of rebellion, sedition, assassination, resistance, and disobedience against the ruling authority and its agents and other representatives as delineated in Title 3 of the Ordinary Penal Code under the category 'Crimes against public order'.
b) Attacks on the transportation or communication systems, services, and public offices or buildings.
c) Attacks on people or property for political or social motives.
d) Attacks carried out by way of the press or any other type of publicity.

Article 17. The following will be considered rebels under the Code of Military Justice and tried accordingly:

a) Those who propagate false or tendentious news with the aim of undermining the prestige of the military forces and of those who cooperate with the army.

b) Anyone possessing firearms and flammable or explosive materials without proper licence or authorisation.
c) Anyone who holds or attends a meeting, conference, or public demonstration without previous permission from the authority, applied for as required.
d) Anyone who commits a crime as understood in Article 16, items b), c), and d).
e) Anyone who in any way impedes or hinders the distribution of necessities, unjustifiably raises the prices of necessities, or contributes to their scarcity.
f) Anyone who restricts or impedes the freedom of hiring or working, whether he or she is an employee, an employer, or a worker.

Article 18. All documents or printed matter destined for public view must first be submitted in duplicate for censorship.

Article 19. Those setting up private radio stations will be considered rebels against the Code of Military Justice.

Article 20. The military courts will be authorised to hand over to the jurisdiction of ordinary courts cases initiated on the basis of the articles of this proclamation, provided that the military authorities determine that the infractions do not concern public order.

Article 21. Civil and judicial authorities will carry out their functions in everything that does not contradict the previous articles.

Article 22. This proclamation will take effect from the date of its publication.

Barcelona, 27 January 1939.

Brigadier General of the Spanish Army, Undersecretary of Public Order, Elíseo Álvarez Arenas.

Bibliography

Adín, Josep L., et al. 1989, *Col·lectivitzacions al Baix Llobregat (1936–1939)*, Barcelona: Publicacions de l'Abadia de Montserrat.

Alba, Victor and Maris Ardevol (eds.) 1989, *El proceso del P.O.U.M. (junio de 1937–octubre de 1938): Transcripción del sumario, juicio oral y sentencia del Tribunal Especial*, Barcelona: Lerna.

Alba, Victor et al. 1998, *Andreu Nin i el socialisme*, Barcelona: Publicacions Universitat de Barcelona.

Amorós, Miquel 2003, *La revolución traicionada: La verdadera historia de Balius y los Amigos de Durruti*, Barcelona: Virus.

Aracil, Rafael 1999, *Empresaris de la postguerra: La Comisión de Incorporación Industrial y Mercantil*, Barcelona: Cambra de Comerç, Indústria i Navegació de Barcelona.

Aróstegui, Julio 1996, 'La Guerra Civil, 1936–1939', *Historia de España*, 27, Madrid: Historia 16.

Aymaní i Baudina, L. 1935, *El 6 d'octubre tal com jo l'he vist*, Barcelona: Atena.

Azaña, Manuel 1977, *Memorias políticas y de guerra, II*, Barcelona: Crítica.

Bada, Joan 2011, *Societat i Església a Catalunya: cent anys entre Constitucions i dictadures*, Barcelona: Facultat de Teologia de Catalunya.

Balcells, Albert 1976, *Cataluña contemporánea, II (1900–1939)*, Madrid: Siglo XXI.

—— 1991, *El Nacionalismo Catalán*, Madrid: Historia 16.

Barrull i Pelegrí, Jaume 1986, *Les comarques de Lleida durant la segona república (1930–1936)*, Barcelona: L'Avenç.

—— 1995, *Violència popular i justícia revolucionària: El Tribunal Popular de Lleida (1936–1937)*, Lleida: Pagès.

Bolloten, Burnett 1991, *The Spanish Civil War: Revolution and Counterrevolution*, Chapel Hill: University of North Carolina Press.

Bonamusa, Francesc 1977, *Andreu Nin y el movimiento comunista en España (1930–1937)*, Barcelona: Anagrama.

Bonsón Aventín, Anabel 1994, *Joaquín Maurín (1896–1973): El impulso moral de hacer política*, Huesca: Diputación de Huesca.

Bricall, Josep Maria 1970, *Política económica de la Generalitat (1936–1939): I, Evolució i formes de la producció industrial*, Barcelona: Edicions 62.

Camps, Judit and Emili Olcina i Aya 2006, *Les milícies catalanes al Front d'Aragó (1936–1937)*, Barcelona: Laertes.

Cárdaba, Marciano 2002, *Col·lectivitats agràries a les comarques de Girona, 1936–1939: Pagesos i revolució a Catalunya*, Girona: CCG.

Cardona, Gabriel 2006, *Historia militar de una guerra civil: Estrategia y tácticas de la guerra de España*, Barcelona: Flor del Viento.

Casanova, Julián 1985, *Anarquismo y revolución en la sociedad rural aragonesa: 1936–1938*, Madrid: Siglo XXI.

Cardona, Gabriel, Francisco Espinosa Maestre, Conxita Mir, and Francisco Moreno Gómez 2002, *Morir, matar, sobrevivir: La violencia en la dictadura de Franco*, Barcelona: Crítica.

Castells i Duran, Antoni 1993, *Les col·lectivitzacions a Barcelona, 1936–1939*, Barcelona: Hacer.

—— 1996, *Desarrollo y significado del proceso estatizador de la experiencia colectivista catalana, 1936–1939*, Madrid: Nossa y Jara.

Cendra i Bertran, Ignasi 2006, *El Consell d'Economia de Catalunya (1936–1939): Revolució i contrarevolució en una economia col·lectivitzada*, Barcelona: Publicacions de l'Abadia de Montserrat.

Cercle d'Estudis Històrics i Socials 1986, *La Guerra Civil a les comarques gironines (1936–1939)*, Girona: Cercle d'Estudis Històrics i Socials.

Chamberlain, Neville 1939, 'Neville Chamberlain's "Peace for our Time" Speech', available at: <http://eudocs.lib.byu.edu/index.php/Neville_Chamberlain's_%22Peace_For_Our_Time%22_speech>.

Clara, Josep 1986, 'La Justicia Popular en Girona: La actuación del tribunal popular (octubre–diciembre de 1936)', paper presented at the conference 'Historia y Memoria de la Guerra Civil: Encuentro en Castilla y León', Salamanca, September.

Clara i Resplandis, J. 1990, 'Justicia popular republicana: Procesos contra militares en Girona (1936–1939)', *Justicia en guerra: Jornadas sobre la administración de justicia durante la Guerra Civil Española; Instituciones y fuentes documentales*, Madrid: Ministerio de Cultura.

Coll, Josep and Josep Pané 1978, *Josep Rovira: Una vida al servei de Catalunya i del socialisme*, Barcelona: Ariel.

Comité Ejecutivo del POUM 1936, 'Resolución del Comité Ejecutivo del POUM sobre el proceso y el fusilamiento, en Moscú, de 16 bolcheviques de la Revolución de octubre', *La Batalla*, 28 August.

Consell de l'Escola Nova Unificada 1936, *Projecte d'ensenyament de l'Escola Nova Unificada*, Barcelona: n.p.

Cornellà, Pere 1986, 'La constitució dels ajuntaments a la comarca del Gironès durant la guerra civil', in Cercle d'Estudis Històrics i Socials 1986.

Costa i Déu, Joan and Modest Sabaté 1935, *La nit del 6 d'octubre a Barcelona: Reportatge*, Barcelona: Tipografia Emporium.

—— 1936, *La veritat del 6 d'octubre*, Barcelona: Imprenta Clarasó.

Díaz, José 1939, *Tres años de lucha: Por el Frente Popular, por la libertad, por la independencia de España*, Barcelona: Ediciones del Partido Comunista de España.

Durgan, Andrew 1996, *BOC 1930–1936: El Bloque Obrero y Campesino*, Barcelona: Laertes.

Espinosa, Francisco 2003, *La columna de la muerte: El avance del ejército franquista de Sevilla a Badajoz*, Barcelona: Crítica.

Estivill, Ángel 1935, *6 d'octubre: L'ensulsiada dels jacobins*, Barcelona: L'Hora.

Fontana i Lázaro, Josep 1973, *Cambio económico y actitudes políticas en la España del siglo XIX*, Barcelona: Ariel.

Fradera, Josep Maria, Jesús Millán, and Ramon Garrabou (eds.) 1990, *Carlisme i moviments absolutistes*, Vic: Eumo.

Fraser, Ronald 1979, *Blood of Spain: The Experience of Civil War, 1936–1939*, London: Penguin.

Genovés, Dolors (director) 1992, *Operació Nikolai*, film, produced by TV3.

Guarner, Vicenç 1980, *L'aixecament militar a Catalunya i la Guerra Civil (1936–1939)*, Barcelona: Publicacions de l'Abadia de Montserrat.

García Oliver, Juan 1978, *El eco de los pasos*, Barcelona: Ruedo Ibérico.

Garriga i Andreu, Joan, Josep Homs i Corominas, and Joaquim Ledesma i Pardo 1989, *Granollers 1936–1939: conflicte revolucionari i bèl·lic. 1. El marc demogràfic i econòmic. Revolució i guerra*, Barcelona: El Racó del Llibre de Text.

Hernández, Jesús 1954, *Yo ministro de Stalin en España*, Madrid: NOS.

Hernández, Miguel 2001, 'To the International Soldier Fallen in Spain', in Genoways, Ted (trans.) 2001.

Genoways, Ted (trans.) 2001, *The Selected Poems of Miguel Hernández, Bilingual Edition*, Chicago: University of Chicago Books.

Lacomba, Juan Antonio 1970, *La crisis española de 1917*, Madrid: Ciencia Nueva.

LeBlanc, Paul 2009, 'The United Front Tactic', *Revolutionary Strategy: An Online Textbook*, available at: <http://revolutionarystrategy.wordpress.com/united-front/>.

Liarte, Ramón and Francisco Isgleas 1937, *El mitin del Olympia en Barcelona 21 de Julio de 1937*, Barcelona: T.G. Gosch.

Lorenzo, César M. 1969, *Les anarchists espagnols et le pouvoir, 1868–1969*, Paris: Éditions du Seuil.

Macklin, Graham 2006, *Chamberlain*, London: Haus.

Madariaga, Salvador de 1944, *España: Ensayo de historia contemporánea*, Buenos Aires: Sudamericana.

Malefakis (ed.) 1986, *La Guerra de España: 1936–1939*, Madrid: Taurus.

Maragall, Joan 1978, 'La iglesia cremada', *Elogi de la paraula i altres assaigs*, Barcelona: Edicions 62.

Martin i Ramos, Josep Lluís 1977, *Els orígens del Partit Socialista Unificat de Catalunya (1936–1939)*, Barcelona: Curial.

Martínez de Sas, María Teresa and Pelai Pagès (eds.) 2000, *Diccionari biogràfic del moviment obrer als països catalans*, Barcelona: Edicions Universitat de Barcelona; Publicacions de l'Abadia de Montserrat.

Massot i Muntaner, Josep 1987a, *El desembarcament de Bayo a Mallorca: Juliol–Setembre de 1936*. Barcelona: Publicacions de l'Abadia de Montserrat.

—— 1987b, *La persecució religiosa de 1936 a Catalunya: Testimoniatges*, Barcelona: Publicacions de l'Abadia de Montserrat.

—— 1988, *Vida i miracles del 'Conde Rossi': Mallorca, agost–desembre 1936/Màlaga, gener–febrer 1937*, Barcelona: Publicacions de l'Abadia de Montserrat.

Maurín Joaquín 1935, *Hacia la segunda revolución: El fracaso de la república y la insurrección de octubre*, Barcelona: Gráficos Alfa.

Mayayo, Andreu 1986, 'PSUC. 50 Anys. Els militants: Els senyals lluminosos de l'organització', *L'Avenç*, 95, July–August.

Mayayo, Andreu et al. 1986, *La nostra utopía: PSUC, cinquanta anys d'història de Catalunya*, Barcelona: Planeta.

Maymí, Josep 2001, *Entre la violència política i el conflicte social: els comitès antifeixistes de Salt i d'Orriols en el context de la Guerra Civil, 1936–1939*, Barcelona: Publicacions de l'Abadia de Montserrat.

Mintz, Frank and Miguel Peciña 1978, *Los Amigos de Durruti: Los trotsquistas y los sucesos de mayo*, Madrid: Campo Abierto.

Montero Moreno, Antonio 1961, *Historia de la persecución religiosa en España, 1936–1939*, Madrid: Biblioteca de Autores Cristianos.

Morrow, Felix 1974 [1938], *Revolution and Counter-Revolution in Spain*, New York: Pathfinder.

Nash, Mary 1999, *Rojas: Las mujeres republicanas en la Guerra Civil*, Madrid: Taurus.

Nel·lo, Oriol 1986, 'El govern local a les comarques gironines durant els primers mesos de la guerra i la revolució (juliol-desembre de 1936)', in Cercle d'Estudis Històrics i Socials 1986.

Nin, Andreu 1937, 'Ante el peligro contrarrevolucionario ha llegado la hora de reaccionar', *La Batalla*, 4 March.

Nin, Andreu 1936, '¿Por qué los sindicatos de la FOUS ingresan en la UGT?', *La Batalla*, 23 September.

Orwell, George 1952, *Homage to Catalonia*, Boston: Beacon.

Pagès, Pelai 1975, *Andreu Nin: Su evolución política (1911–1937)*, Bilbao: Zero.

—— 1986, 'El POUM en la guerra civil', *La guerra civil*, 11, Madrid: Historia 16.

—— 1990a, 'La adminstración de justicia en Catalunya durante la Guerra Civil Española, 1936–1939', *Justicia en guerra: Jornadas sobre la administración de justicia durante la Guerra Civil Española; Instituciones y fuentes documentales*, Madrid: Ministerio de Cultura.

—— 1990b, 'Les transformacions revolucionàries i la vida política: Catalunya, 1936–1939', *Acàcia: Papers del Centre per a la Investigació dels Moviments Socials*, 1: 23-40.

—— 1993a, 'Andreu Nin, Conseller de Justícia de la Generalitat de Catalunya', paper presented at the conference 'Jornades d'estudi sobre Andreu Nin' (1892–1937), Barcelona, March, 1993.

—— 1993b, 'Sacerdots i religiosos a la presó Model de Barcelona (1936–1939)', *I Congrés d'Història de l'Església Catalana: Des dels orígens fins ara; Actes*, 2 vols., Solsona: n.p.

—— 1996, *La presó Model de Barcelona: Història d'un centre penitenciari en temps de guerra (1936–1939)*, Barcelona: Publicacions de l'Abadia de Montserrat.

—— 1998, 'Andreu Nin, conseller de Justícia de la Generalitat de Catalunya', in Alba 1998.

Pagès, Pelai and Alberto Pérez 2003, *Aquella guerra tan llunyana i tan propera (1936–1939): Testimonis i records de la Guerra Civil a Catalunya*, Lleida: Pagès.

Pagès, Pelai et al. 2001, *Historia del moviment obrer als països catalans*, Valencia: Edicions del País Valencià.

―― 2003, 'Marty, Vidal, Kléber y el Komintern: Informes y confidencias de la dirección política de las Brigadas Internacionales', *Ebre 38: Revista internacional de la Guerra Civil*, 1: 11–25.

―― 2004a, 'La Fatarella: una insurrecció pagesa a la rereguarda catalana durant la guerra civil', *Estudis d'Història Agraria*, 17: 659–74.

―― 2004b, 'La justícia revolucionària i popular a Catalunya (1936–1939)', *Ebre 38: Revista internacional de la Guerra Civil*, 2: 35–48.

―― 2005, 'La presó Model de Barcelona a la postguerra', in Josep María Solé i Sabaté and Joan Villarroya i Font (eds.) 2005.

―― 2011, *Andreu Nin: Una vida al servicio de la clase obrera*, Barcelona: Laertes.

Peirats, José 1971, *La CNT en la revolución española*, three volumes, Paris: Ruedo Ibérico.

―― 2001–, *The CNT in the Spanish Revolution*, three volumes, edited by Chris Ealham, translated by Chris Ealham and Paul Sharkey, Hastings: Meltzer.

Peiró, Joan 1937, 'La tragedia del POUM. El silenci seria una complicitat', *Llibertat*, 8 July.

―― 1987 [1936], *Perill a la rereguarda*, Mataró: Patronat Municipal de Cultura de Mataró.

Pérez Baró, Albert 1970, *Trenta mesos de col·lectivisme a Catalunya (1936–1939)*, Barcelona: Ariel.

Pi i Sunyer, Carles 1975, *La república y la guerra: Memorias de un político catalán*, México: Oasis.

Piqué i Padró, Jordi 1998, *La crisi a la rereguarda: Revolució i guerra civil a Tarragona (1936–1939)*, Barcelona: Publicacions de l'Abadia de Montserrat.

POUM 1936, *El POUM ante la revolución español*, Barcelona: Marxista.

Pozo González, Josep Antoni 2002, 'El poder revolucionari a Catalunya durant els mesos de juliol a octubre de 1936: Crisi i recomposició de l'estat', doctoral thesis, Universitat Autònoma de Barcelona.

Preston, Paul 2012, *The Spanish Holocaust: Inquisition and Extermination in Twentieth Century Spain*, London: Harper Press.

Primo de Rivera, José Antonio 1966, 'Discurso de la fundación de Falange Española', *Textos de doctrina política*, Madrid: Sección Feminina.

Puigsech Farràs, Josep 2001, *Nosaltres, Els comunistes catalans: el PSUC i la Internacional Comunista durant la Guerra Civil*, Vic: Eumo.

Pujol, Rafael 1986, *Cataluña en la Guerra Civil española*, Barcelona: Biblioteca de la Vanguardia.

Queipo de Llano, Gonzalo and Ian Gibson 1986, *Queipo de Llano: Sevilla, verano de 1936; Con las charlas radiofónicas completas*, Barcelona: Grijalbo.

Radosh, Ronald, Mary R. Habeck, and Grigory Sevostianov (eds.) 2001, *Spain Betrayed: The Soviet Union in the Spanish Civil War*, New Haven: Yale University Press.

―― (eds.) 2002, *España traicionada: Stalin y la Guerra Civil*, translated by Juan Mari Madariaga, Barcelona: Planeta.

Raguer Suñer, Hilario M. 2001, *La pólvora y el incienso: La Iglesia y la Guerra Civil española (1936–1939)*, Barcelona: Península.

Reig Tapia, Alberto 1986, 'Represión y esfuerzos humanitarios', in Malefakis (ed.) 1986.

Riottot, Yveline 2004, *Joaquín Maurín o la utopia desarmada*, Zaragoza: Gobierno de Aragón.

Roca, Francesc 1983, *Política, economía y espacio: La política territorial en Cataluña (1936–1939)*, Barcelona: Ediciones del Serbal.

Rodrigo, Antonina 2002, *Una mujer libre: Amparo Poch y Gascón, Médica anarquista*, Barcelona: Flor del Viento.

Rojo, Vicente 1974 [1939], *¡Alerta los pueblos!: Estudio político-militar del período final de la guerra española*, Barcelona: Ariel.

―― 1975 [1942], *España heroica: Diez bocetos de la guerra civil española*, Barcelona: Ariel.

Rourera Farré, Luís 1992, *Joaquín Maurín y su tiempo: Vida y obras de un luchador*, Barcelona: Claret.

Rubió i Tudurí, Marià 1937, *La justicia a Catalunya: 19 de juliol del 1936–19 de febrer del 1937*, Barcelona: n.p.

Sagués San José, Joan 2003, *Una ciutat en Guerra: Lleida en la Guerra Civil Espanyola (1936–1939)*, Barcelona: Publicacions de l'Abadia de Montserrat.
Solano, Wilebaldo 2006, *Biografía breve de Andrés Nin*, Madrid: Sepha.
Solé i Sabaté, Josep María and Joan Villarroya i Font 1986, *Catalunya sota les bombes (1936–1939)*, Barcelona: Publicacions de l'Abadia de Montserrat.
—— 1989, *La repressió a la reraguarda de Catalunya (1936–1939)*, two volumes, Barcelona: Publicacions de l'Abadia de Montserrat.
—— 2003, *España en llamas: La Guerra Civil desde el aire*, Madrid: Temas de Hoy.
—— (eds.) 2005, *El franquisme a Catalunya (1939–1977)*, Volume I: *La dictadura totalitaria (1939–1945)*, Barcelona: Edicions 62.
Tarradellas, Josep, Josep Alegre, and Javier de Madariaga 2007, *La indústria de guerra de Catalunya, 1936–1939: L'obra de la Comissió, creada per la Generalitat, i el seu report d'actuació*, Lleida: Pagès.
Termes, Josep 2005, *Misèria contra pobresa: Els fets de la Fatarella el gener de 1937; Un exemple de resistència pagesa contra la col·lectivització agrària durant la Guerra Civil*, Catarroja: Afers.
Torralba Coronas, Pedro 1980, *De Ayerbe a la 'Roja y negra': 127 Brigada Mixta*, Burdeos: Torralba Coronas.
Torras Elías, Jaime 1976, *Liberalismo y rebeldía campesina, 1820–1823*, Barcelona: Ariel.
Torrent, Martín 1942, *¿Qué me dice usted de los presos?*, Alcalá de Henares: Imprenta Talleres Penitenciarios.
Ucelay Da Cal, Enric 1982, *La Catalunya populista: Imatge, cultura i política en l'etapa republicana (1931–1939)*, Barcelona: La Magrana.
Valls i Taberner, Ferran 1939, 'La falsa ruta', *Reafirmación espiritual de España*, Madrid-Barcelona: Editorial Juventud.
Vilar, Pierre 1986, *La guerra civil española*, Barcelona: Crítica.
Villarroya i Font, Joan 1981, *Els bombardeigs de Barcelona durant la guerra civil*, Barcelona: Publicacions de l'Abadia de Montserrat.
Zugazagoitia, Julián 1977, *Guerra y vicisitudes de los españoles*, Barcelona: Crítica.

Index

Abad de Santillán, Diego   35, 36, 49, 53, 76, 104
ACR (*Acció Catalana Republicana, Acción Catalana*)   14, 16, 36, 40, 41, 76, 94, 96, 108n14, 123
Aguirre, José Antonio   42, 137
Aiguader, Artemi   36, 37, 94, 101n14, 104, 107, 110
Aiguader, Jaume   118, 142, 143, 151, 217, 220
Alcalá Zamora, Niceto   14
Alcón, Marcos   37
Aldabaldetrecu, Cristóbal   47, 48
Álvarez Arenas, Eladio   165–6, 226
  Barcelona proclamation   228–32
Álvarez del Vayo, Julio   42, 94, 151
Ancien régime   6, 6n2
Andrade, Juan   119
  letter from prison   207–10
Andreu i Abelló, Josep   69, 122, 124
anticlerical violence   59–62
Anti-fascist Militia Committee
  See Central Committee of Anti-fascist Militias of Catalonia
Aragon front   37, 44–53, 98–100, 109, 126–35, 137, 146–7, 149, 150, 186–7
  arms boycott   126
Aragon Regional Defence Council   80, 130–1
Aranguren Roldán, José   22, 28
Araquistain, Luis   122
Arinzón i Mejías, Lluís   87
Arquer, Jordi   47, 48, 60, 119, 187
Arredondo, Alberto   115
Arxiu Nacional de Catalunya   3
Ascaso, Domingo   47, 114
Ascaso, Francesc   25, 28, 56
Ascaso, Joaquín   80, 130
Asens, Josep   35, 36, 37
Assault Guards   46, 116, 187
  Fatarella and   201, 203

military rebellion and   22–3, 26, 28, 177–8, 180
Asturias (October 1934 Revolution)   9, 10, 11
Autonomy Statute   11, 11n16, 15, 51, 115, 147, 211–2
Azaña, Manuel   8, 14, 16, 16 n. 22, 18, 18n25, 100, 120, 120n9, 139, 140, 142, 143, 152, 167, 222

Balada, Sergi   47
Baldomero Espartero, Joaquín   6n5
Barbiere, Francesco   115
Barcelona
  bombings of   147–8, 164, 167
  food shortage   105–7
  military rebellion   24–30, 176–82
  occupation by Franco   163–6, 224–5
Barrera, Martí   62, 76
del Barrio, José   6, 47, 48, 53, 187
Barriobero, Eduardo   97, 122
Basque government in Catalonia   137
Basque Nationalist Action Party   144
Battle of the North   126
Baudina, Aymamí   9
Bayo, Alberto   50–3
Belchite   132–4
Bergamín, José   121
Bernades, Vincenç   76
Berneni, Camillo   115
Bertran de Quintana, Josep Maria   71n20
Besteiro, Julián   168
Bienio reformista   13
Bilbao   126, 127, 131
Bilbao, Crescenciano   208
Bilbao, Tomás   144
Blanco González, Segundo   123, 150–1
Blanco Valdés, Joaquín   24
BOC (*Bloc Obrer i Camperol*)   10, 33, 33n, 34, 34n2, 108
Bolshevik Triennium   8

Bombings of Catalonia 147–8, 164, 167
Bonet, Pere 119
  letter from prison 207–10
Bosch i Gimpera, Pere 73, 123
Bricall, Josep Maria 75–6, 83, 158
bullangues 6n5

Caballero, Largo 42, 97, 114, 118, 122, 122n13, 126n1, 127, 149, 220
  Unity Government 93–5
Calvet i Mora, Josep 41, 94, 104, 110, 110n22, 114, 123
Calvo Sotelo, José 16, 22
Cambó, Francesc 18, 57–8
Cánovas del Castillo, Antonio 7
Cantauri, Enric 47
Capdevila i Puig, Andreu 110
Carbó, Eusebi C. 76
Carlism (Carlist wars) 6, 6n2–3, 15n21, 23n1, 30, 56, 58, 70
Carlos Isidro 6n2
Carrillo, Santiago 150
Casado, Segismundo 168
Casanovas, Joan 3, 40–1, 85
Casares Quiroga, Santiago 20, 42
Catalan Communist Party 14, 33, 34, 108
Catalan Economic Advisory Council 76–8, 191
Catalan Federation (PSOE) 33, 34, 34n3, 40
Catalan League
  See *Lliga Catalana*
Catalan Left Republicans
  See *Esquerra*
Catalan Office of Internal Security
  See Committee for Catalan Internal Security
Catalan Proletarian Party 14, 33, 34
Catalan Republican Government
  See *Generalitat*
Catalan Socialist Union Party
  See USC
Catalan State Party
  See *Estat Català*
Catalonia, Battle of 161–5
Catalonia, under Franco 170–4
CEDA 9, 12, 13, 14n19–20, 15, 16, 18n25, 22
  Catalan CEDA 58
Central Committee of Anti Fascist Militias of Catalonia viii, ix, 35–40, 45, 50n8, 52, 57, 62, 84, 85, 95, 98, 183–5
  dual power 37–43
  regional committees 37, 39, 185

CENU 81, 82
Chamberlain, Neville 155
Chekas 124, 158, 210
Church 60–1
Civil Guard 45, 47, 50, 55, 56, 114, 133
  in military rebellion 22, 24, 27–30, 179–81
Closas, Rafael 94
CNT 8, 9, 17n22, 19, 70, 126n, 131, 149–51
  Fatarella incidents 200–3
  May Events 106–10, 112–6, 118, 119, 122, 123, 204–5
  military uprising and 23–5, 28, 30
  Militia Committees and 32–6, 38–43, 183
  militias and Aragon Front and 45, 46, 48, 50, 186–7
  public order and 57, 58, 62
  social and economic revolution and 70, 75, 76, 78, 80, 81, 83, 85, 191–2, 199
  Unity Government and 94–7, 99, 103, 104
Code of Military Justice 65, 68, 98–9
  under Franco 231–2
Codovila, Vittorio 123
collectivisation 75–81
Collectivisation and Workers' Control Decree 78
columna de muerte
  see Death column
Comitè Central de Milícies Antifeixistes de Catalunya
  See Central Committee of Anti-fascist Militias of Catalonia
Commission of Regional Militias (*Comissió de Milícies Comarcals*) 39
Committee for Catalan Internal Security 95, 97, 108n14, 188–9, 202
Committee of Public Health (*Comité de Salud Pública*) (Lleida) 67
Communist International 13, 34, 40
  See also PCE, PSUC
Communist Left
  see *Izquierda Comunista*
Comorera i Soler, Joan 34n3, 40, 68, 94, 123, 144
  and the May events 103–7, 110, 110n22
Companys, Lluís 18, 22, 33, 39, 40, 45, 47, 61, 61n15, 75n3, 87, 87n11, 92, 103, 106, 113, 114, 123, 134, 163, 164, 167, 199, 222, 225
  Generalitat's loss of autonomy 138, 139, 141, 142

Index • 241

July 1936 military insurrection and   25, 27–8, 34–6, 179
October 1934 insurrection and   9, 11, 17
Condor Legion   144, 145, 131
Confederación Española de Derechas Autónomas
See CEDA
Confederación Nacional del Trabajo
See CNT
Consejo Nacional de Defensa   168
Consell d'Economia de Catalunya
See Catalan Economic Advisory Council
Consell de l'Escola Nova Unificada
See CENU
Conservative Party   7
Cortada, Roldán   111
Costa i Déu, Joan   10
Council of the New Unified School
See CENU
Cultivation Contracts Law   10, 10n11, 12, 15, 17, 18, 59, 120, 143, 217
Cunill, José Maria   23

Dávila, Fidel   131, 145, 146, 161, 166
   occupation of Catalonia   226–8
Death column (*Columna de muerte*)   56
Decret de Col·lectivitzacions i Control Obrer
See Collectivisation and Workers' Control Decree
Defeatism   158
Deulofeu i Arquer, Joan   87
Díaz Sandino, Felipe   27, 41, 94, 98, 179
Díaz, José   109n20
Dimitrov, Georgi   13
Dollfuss, Engelbert   12
Dufoo, Julio   24
Duran, Expedit   38
Durán Rossell, Francesc   37
Durruti, Buenaventura   25
   Aragon offensive   45–8, 60, 80, 99, 101, 114, 186–7
   formation of Central Committee of Anti-fascist Militias   35–7

Ebro, Battle of the   153–7, 161, 162, 213–5
Eroles, Dionís   97, 201
Escofet, Frederic   11, 22, 23, 24, 25, 179
Escuder, José
   letter from prison   207–10
Espanya i Sirat, Josep Maria   22, 25n6, 41
Espinosa, Francisco   56

Esquerra   10, 14, 16, 32, 33, 34n3, 36, 38, 40, 41, 42, 46, 47, 49, 50, 57, 58, 76, 78, 82, 85, 94, 96, 103, 104, 104n26, 107, 108, 108n15–16, 109, 110, 114, 123, 142, 143, 151, 187, 204, 217
Esquerra Republicana de Catalunya
See *Esquerra*
Estat Català   25, 25n6, 46, 101, 101n13, 187
Esteve i Guau, Martí   41
Estivill, Ángel   10, 47

Fábregas, Joan P.   76, 77, 94, 103
Fabregat, Manuel   122
Fábregues, Tomás   36, 37
FAI   8, 33, 35, 36, 38, 39, 40, 41, 42, 43, 46, 57, 74, 75, 75n3, 76, 78, 97, 99, 101, 122, 126n, 131, 131n12, 150, 183, 187
   Fatarella incident   200, 201
   May Events   106, 108, 112, 113, 116, 204, 205
Falange Española Tradicionalista y de las Juntas de Ofensiva Nacional Sindicalista
See *FET y de las JONS*
Farré, Juan
   letter from prison   207–10
Fatarella   108, 200–3
Federació Estudiantil de Consciències Lliures
See Student Federation for Freedom of Conscience
Federación Anarquista Ibérica
See FAI
Federación Obrera de Unidad Sindical
See FOUS
Federalism   6
Fernández Burriel, Álvaro   21
   arrest and trial   56–7
Fernández, Aurelio   57, 97, 110, 122, 201
   Central Committee of Anti-Fascist Militias and   35–7
Fernando VII   6n2
FET y de las JONS   11, 22, 165–6, 172, 173, 227, 229n3, 231
   See also Phalangists
Figueres   24
Foment del Treball Nacional   22–3
Fontana Tarats, Josep Maria   23
FOUS   102, 102n17
Franco, Francisco   vii, xi, 2, 9, 11, 15n, 16, 20, 23n1, 52n12, 54, 55, 56n5, 58, 62, 63, 73, 74, 79, 92, 93, 95, 100, 108, 109, 117, 120, 121, 126n, 127, 136, 137, 140, 142
   Battle of the Ebro   149–59, 213

final months of the war 160–8, 224
imposes victory 169–74, 211–2, 212n, 226–32
September 1937 to August 1938 military campaigns 144–8
Summer 1937 military campaigns 131–5
French border 160–1, 166, 167
refugees from Catalonia 170–1
Fronjosà, Joan 76
Front d'Esquerres 14, 15, 16, 23, 34, 183
See also Popular Front

Galarza, Angel 42, 94
Gallego Salvador, Silverio 49
García Birlán, Antoni 76, 94
García Oliver, Juan (Joan) 25, 25n5–6, 26, 26n8, 35, 35n, 36–7, 47, 49, 51, 51n, 69, 85, 85n2–3, 95, 98–9, 114
García Ruiz, Luis 52
García Vivancos, Miguel 133
Garrido, Pere 45
Garsaball, Sebastià 38
Gassol i Rovira, Ventura 41, 94, 101
Gavilán Almuzara, Marcelino 56
General Front Inspection 48
General Health Council (*Consell General de la Sanitat*) 82
Generalitat ix, x, xi, xii, 3, 9, 11, 11n15, 15, 17, 18, 22, 24, 25n6, 26, 28, 43, 45, 46, 48–50, 52, 53, 53n15, 59, 60, 60n12, 62, 126, 149, 158, 165n14, 167, 170, 176, 178, 179, 181, 183, 184, 188, 202, 207
in crisis 32–43
economic transformations 76, 76n.5, 77–81
education reform 82, 159
formation of the Unity Government 95–104
justice system 65–9, 71, 72–3
loses power to Spanish Central government 137–44, 159, 216–9
May Events 106–11, 115, 121–5, 204–6
municipalisation of housing 190–9
war economy and industries 84–92
General Workers' Union
See UGT
Genovés, Dolors 120n7
Gerö, Ernö 124
Gil Robles, José María 12, 14n19–20, 15, 16, 18, 18n24
Giménez Arenas, Francisco 56
Giner de los Ríos, Bernardo 14, 42, 94, 118, 151

Giner de los Ríos, Fernando 8
Giral Pereira, José 42, 93, 94, 118, 151
Girona 24
Goded, Manuel 21, 27–8, 56–7, 176, 179, 181
Gómez, Julián
See Gorkín, Julián
Gómez Sáiz, Paulino 151
González Albadalejo, Salvador 36, 37
González Peña, Ramón 151
Gorkín, Julián 118, 118n4, 119
letter from prison 207–10
de Gracia, Anastasio 42, 94
Grijalbo i Serres, Joan 76
Grossi, Manuel 47
guardia civil
See Civil Guard
Guarner, Vicenç 22, 29, 49, 99, 129,

Hernández, Jesús 42, 94, 118, 120n7
Hernández, Miguel 156, 156, 157n10
Hernández Sarabia, Juan 164–5
Herrera, Pedro 104
Herrera, Pere 114
Hervás, Joan 121, 208
Hidalgo de Cisneros, Ignacio 119
Historical Memory Law 1
Hitler 9, 12, 33n1, 155, 160
Homage to Catalonia viii
Huesca 47–8, 127–9

Ibárruri, Dolores 149
Iberian Anarchist Federation
See FAI
incontrolados 55, 57, 63, 109n20, 188, 200
Insa Arenal, Amadeo 48
International Brigades Volunteers (International Brigades) 2, 123–4, 127, 129, 131, 134, 154, 155–7, 221–3
Irujo, Manuel 118, 122, 142–4, 151, 217, 220
Irurita, Manuel 60
Isabel II 6n2, 6n5
Isgleas Piernau, Francesc 104, 109, 110
Izquierda Comunista 33, 34

Jamància 6n5
Jané Jané, Benjamin 72
Jiménez de la Beraza, Ricardo 53, 87, 85
Jiménez Fernández, Manuel 12
Jiménez Pajarero, Luis 47
Jover, Gregorio 25, 47
Juan i Doménech, Josep 94, 104, 110
Juncadella, Emilio 23
Junta de Seguridad Interior de Cataluña

See Committee for Catalan Internal Security

Kléber, Emilio   129, 131, 131n12

Lacasa, Francisco   27, 56
Land and Freedom (film)   1
Landau, Kurt   121, 208
Lara del Rosal, Domingo   49
Law of Political Responsibilities   168, 171
League of Nations   155–6
Ledesma Ramos, Ramiro   11
Lerroux, Alejandro   13, 13n19, 14n19
Liberal Party (*Liberales*)   6
Líster, Enrique   130, 134, 146, 153
Llano de la Encomienda, Francisco   21, 27
Llei de Contractes de Conreu
   See Cultivation Contracts Law
Lliga Catalana   10, 15, 16, 18, 18n26, 23, 57, 58,
Llopis, Antonio   22
Loach, Ken   1
Local Trade Union Alliance (*Unión Local de Sindicatos*)   24
López, Juan   95
López Raimundo, Antonio   36
López Valera, Luis   21
Lukács, Pavol
   See Zalka

Macià, Francesc   40, 101n13, 172
Madrid   9, 19, 20, 24, 30
   arrest of POUM leaders and assassination of Nin   118–21, 208–10
   Caballero government   42–3, 50, 63, 64, 91, 95, 100, 101, 103, 127, 134
   government's move to Barcelona   138–9, 141, 145, 146, 168
Mallorca offensive   50–3
Manresa   24
Mantecón, José Ignacio   131
Manzana, José   45
Maragall, Joan   60
March, Juan   52, 52n12
María Cristina (de Borbón)   6n5
Marianet
   See Vázquez, Mariano R.
Martí Feced, Carles   114
Martí Pallarés, Manuel   87
Martín, Antonio   111
Martín Izquierdo, Marià   87
Martínez Barrios, Diego   20, 42

Martínez Peñalver, Ángel   24, 47
Marty, André   123
Mas, Valeri   114, 199
Maurín, Joaquín   13, 33, 34n2, 41, 208
May Events   70, 91, 91n21, 92, 104, 105–16, 126, 127, 138, 159, 204–6
   consequences   117–25
Meca, José   121
Medrano, Eduardo   47
Mena Burgos, Máximo   48
Mena, Marciano   208
Méndez Aspez, Francisco   151
Méndez, Rafael   142
Menéndez López, Emilio   116
Mera, Cipriano   168
Mestres i Albet, Pere   41
Miaja, José   161, 168
Military Investigation Service
   see S.I.M.
militias
   training of   49
   militarisation of   97–100
   anti-fascist committee and   186–7
   See also Central Committee of Anti-fascist Militias of Catalonia
Militias Committee
   See Central Committee of Anti Fascist Militias of Catalonia
Millán Astray, José   63
Ministry of Internal Security   205
Miravitlles, Jaume   36, 37
Miret i Musté, Josep   36, 110
Modelo prison   21, 66–7, 68, 72, 171, 209
Moderates (*Moderados*)   7n7
Modesto, Juan   153
Moix, Josep   144
Mola, Emilio   20, 55, 55n2
Monarchists   22
Montseny, Federica   35, 61, 95, 114, 115, 120, 122
de la Mora Maura, Constancia   119
Moragues, Manuel   183–5
Moroccan Corps   154
Morocco   8
Morrow, Felix   126n1
Mossos d'Esquadra   11, 21, 60, 179
Múgica, Mateo   137
Munich conference   155
municipalisation   190–9
Mussolini, Benito   11, 16, 155, 160

National Archive of Catalonia   3
National Defence Council   168

National Plan for Socialist
  Transformation   77–8, 80, 81
National Workers' Federation
  See CNT
Navarre   24
Negrín, Juan   42, 70, 71n21, 91, 92, 94, 118,
  120, 120n9, 123, 124, 125, 127, 130, 136–44,
  150–3, 158, 160, 163, 164, 167, 168, 225
  sending home international brigades
    155–7
  September 1938 speech before
    parliament   216–20
  'thirteen points' for victor   151–2
Negrín government   71, 136–44
Nel·lo, Oriol   39
Nin, Andreu   33, 34n2, 41, 65, 68, 76, 77,
  94, 97, 102n7, 109n17
  arrest and assassination   119–21
  in letter by POUM leaders   207–9

Obregón Blanco, Enrique   29
October 1934, general strike   22, 25
  See also Asturias
Olivar Daidí, Jordi   73
Oltra Picó, Josep   47
Operation Nikolai   119–20, 120n7
Orlov, Alexander   119–20
Ortiz, Antonio   46, 187
Orwell, George   viii, viii n1–2, 49, 126n1
Ovssenko, Vladimir Antonov   102–3

Pané, Josep   127
Partido Comunista Español
  See PCE
Partido Obrero de Unificación Marxista
  See POUM
Partido Republicano Radical   12
Partido Socialista Obrero Español
  See PSOE
Partit Català Proletari
  See Catalan Proletarian Party
Partit Comunista de Catalunya
  See Catalan Communist Party
Partit Socialista Unificat de Catalunya
  See PSUC
Pastor Velasco, Angel   91
patrullas de control
  See Security Patrols
PCE   7, 14, 74, 102, 109, 112, 129, 151
  Battle of the Ebro   149
  Central Committee   109n20
  conflict with Indalecio Prieto   149–50,
    153
  May Events   117, 119, 120n7, 123, 124

Peirats, José   83, 83n25, 104, 104n26
Peiró, Joan   63, 63n22, 79, 95, 118, 118n3,
  118
People's War School   49
Pérez Baró, Albert   78
Pérez Farràs, Enric   11, 45, 46, 48, 179, 181,
  186, 187
Pérez Salas, Jesús   47
Perramon, Llorenç   37
Peypoch, Ramon   76, 77
Phalange
  see FET y de las JONS
Phalangists (*Falangistas*)   17, 23, 56, 58,
  70, 133, 172, 173
Pi i Sunyer, Carles   96–7, 123
Pich i Pon, Joan   12
Pina Orce, Francisco   208
Pío Moa, Luis   11
Piqué, Jordi   65n6, 67
Pistolerismo   8
Pla de transformació socialista del país
  see National Plan for Socialist
    Transformation
Pla, Soler   60
Poblador, Josep María   23
Poch, Amparo   83
Pons, Juan   36
Popular Army   viii, 98, 99, 124, 127
Popular Front   14, 14n20, 15, 16, 34, 38,
  38n9, 43, 59, 64, 75, 117
  see also *Front d'Esquerres*
Popular-frontism (strategy)   13, 13n17,
  102, 112
Popular Olympics   46, 50
Portela Valladares, Manuel   12
Pou i Mas, Joaquim   76, 77, 114
POUM   7, 14, 16, 24, 25, 29, 57, 60, 62,
  65, 70, 71, 94, 96, 97, 99, 101, 101n15, 102,
  102n17, 102n18, 103, 103n22, 159, 187
  Anti-fascist Militia Committee and
    33–4, 36, 38–50
  May Events and   108–9, 112–29, 204
  repression against   207–10
  social and economic transformation
    and   74–6, 78, 81, 83
Pozas, Sebastián   115, 128, 129, 132, 134
Pretel, Felipe   150
Prieto, Indalecio   42, 63, 91, 94, 118, 122,
  130, 134, 140, 141n14, 149–50
  protests against   218
Prieto, Manuel   45
Primo de Rivera, José Antonio   11
Primo de Rivera, Miguel   8, 16, 58, 169
Progressive Biennium   6n5

Progressives (*Progresivos*) 7n7
pronunciamiento 7, 16, 23–24n2
Prunés i Sató, Lluís 41, 48, 85
PSOE 8, 11, 9, 13, 14, 16, 17n22, 18n25, 25n6, 33, 34, 34n3, 36, 40, 46, 74, 122, 122n13, 130, 149, 151, 187
PSUC ix, 34, 34n.4, 40–2, 47, 49, 50, 57, 68, 74, 75n1, 76, 78, 83, 94, 96, 99, 101–4, 129, 144, 149, 150, 224
   Fatarella 202,
   May Events 106–19, 122–4, 204
Puig i Ferreter, Joan 41
Puig i Pidemunt, Joaquim 76

Queipo de Llano, Gonzalo 20, 55
Quer, Juan
   letter from prison 207–10
Quero Morales, Josep 41, 87

Rabassaires (Rabassaires Union Party) 14, 16, 32, 36, 40, 41, 76, 80, 94, 96, 104, 110, 114, 123
Ramírez de Cartagena, Miquel 87
Rearguard Vigilance Militias 97
Redondo, Onésimo 11
Reformist Biennium
   see *Bienio reformista*
Refugees 100
   and food shortage 136–8, 141, 157–8
   in Catalonia 164, 166–7
Reig Tapia, Alberto 56
Renovación Española 22
Republican Catalan Action Party
   See ACR
Republican Government ix–xii, 11n16, 12, 13, 15n, 19, 20, 30, 30n, 44, 50, 52–3, 61, 68, 69, 71, 72, 79, 80, 89, 91, 91n23, 92, 95, 97, 99, 100, 115, 117, 119, 123, 126, 127, 131, 147, 149, 155, 165, 165n14, 167, 206, 207, 211, 216, 218–9
   in Barcelona 137–41, 143–4, 159
   See also Popular Front, *Generalitat*
Republican Military Union 22
Republican Radical Party 12
Requetés 23, 23n1
Revertés, Andreu 101
Revisionists 2
Revolutionary Sexenium (*Sexenio revolucionario*) 6, 7
Rey, David 119
   letter from prison 207–10
Rey d'Harcourt, Domingo 145
Rieger, Max 121
Roca, Francesc 81, 83

Rodríguez Dranguet, Alfonso 71, 71n20
Rodríguez Salas, Eusebi 107–8, 113, 116
Rodríguez Vázquez, Mariano
   See Vázquez, Mariano R.
Rofes, Cosme 76
Rojo, Vicente 132, 132n13, 134, 145, 153, 154, 154n7, 160, 160n1, 161, 161n3, 162, 162n6, 164, 164n10, 167
Romeu i Freixa, Darius, the Baron of Viver 23
Rosa, Carmel 25
Rosemberg, Marcel 124
Rouret i Callol, Martí 41
Rovira, Josep 36, 47, 119, 129
Ruiz, Antonio 48
Ruiz Funes, Mariano 42, 94
Ruiz i Ponsetí, Estanislau 40, 76, 77

Sabaté, Modest 10
Salanova, Manuel 46, 187
Sales Amenós, Ramón 58
Salses i Serra, Francesc 87
Sanjuán i Colomer, Alfred 87
Sanjurjo, José 8
Sanz, Gonzalo 25
Saravia, Hernández 145
Sbert i Massanet, Antoni Maria 104, 110, 114, 123, 136
Security Patrols 57, 97, 108, 109, 125, 185, 200, 201
Semana Trágica *see* Tragic Week
Semblancat, Angel 97
Serra i Pàmies, Miquel 123, 144, 150
Serrano Suñer, Ramón 211–2
Servicio de Investigación Militar
   see S.I.M.
Sesé, Antoni 114, 206
Seu d'Urgell 24
S.I.M. 71, 72, 73, 141, 141n14, 158–9
Solano, Wilebaldo
   letter from prison 207–10
Soler, Joan B. 76
Soria, Georges 121
Soviet Union 12, 13, 34, 40, 77, 101–3, 120, 120n7
   aid to Spanish communists 123–4
   conflict POUM vs. PSUC and 112, 160,
   role in repression of POUM 117–20
Spanish Federation of the Autonomous Right
   See CEDA
Spanish Military Union
   See *Unión Militar Española*

Spanish Republican Government
　See Republican Government
Spanish Socialist Workers' Party
　See PSOE
Spies in Spain 121
Stalin, Joseph 12, 101, 119, 123, 131n12
Stern, Manfred
　see Emilio Kléber
Student Federation for Freedom of Conscience 82

Tagueña, Manuel 153
Tarradellas i Joan, Josep 37, 43, 65, 78, 84–5, 87, 89, 94, 95–96n5, 104, 110, 114, 123, 142
Tarragona 24
Telefónica 29, 91n21, 113, 178, 181, 204–5
Teruel, Battle of 145–6
Togliatti, Palmiro 123
Tomàs i Piera, Josep 42, 94
Torralba, Pedro 127
Torrent, José María 137
Torrents, Josep 36, 37
Traditionalists (*tradicionalistas*) 14, 15n16, 22, 166
Tragic Week 8, 10n13, 58, 59, 60
Trepat, Jaume 121, 208
tribunals
　popular tribunals 64–77, 97–8, 143, 194, 208
　　Barcelona and 66–7
　　Girona and 67
　　Lleida and 65, 67–8
　　Tarragona and 67
　Catalan Espionage Tribunal 71
　Court of Espionage and High Treason 12, 71–3, 142
　emergency juries (*jurados de urgencia*) 68–9, 70, 71n21
　guard juries (*jurados de guardia*) 68–9, 71n21
　militarisation of 216–8
　'special courts' ('*justicia especial*') 70–3
　Special Guard Tribunals 71–3
Trienio Bolchevique 8
Trilles, Desiderio 62
Trueba, Manuel 47

UGT 8, 14, 17n22, 24, 36, 38, 40, 46, 57, 62, 76, 81, 96, 102–4, 144, 150, 151, 187, 191–2, 199
　Fatarella incidents 200–3
　May Events and 108, 108n15, 110, 114, 115, 122, 206
　popular militias and 48–9
UHP 106, 106n7
Unified Socialist Party of Catalonia
　See PSUC
Unió de Rabassaires
　See *Rabassaires*
Unió Socialista de Catalunya
　See USC
Unión de Hermanos Proletarios (Proletarian Brothers' Union)
　See UHP
Unión General de Trabajadores
　See UGT
Unión Militar Española 21
Unión Militar Republicana Antifascista 22
Unity Government, formation 93–5
Uribarri, Manuel 50–1
Uribe, Vicente 42, 94, 117, 118, 143n20, 151
Uruguay 56, 65
USC 14, 16, 33, 34, 34n3, 36, 40, 75n1
Utopian Socialism 6

Valdés, Miquel 94, 103, 104, 144
Valencia 6, 30, 48, 50, 51, 91, 100, 109n20, 116, 117, 119
　government's move from 137–139, 153, 154, 168
Vallejo, Eugenio 85, 87
Valls i Taberner, Ferran 57, 174, 174n4
Vázquez, Mariano R. 35, 114, 149
Vega, Etelvino 153
Velao Oñate, Antonio 151
Vidal i Barraquer, Cardinal 60, 137
Vidal, Germinal 29
Vidiella i Franch, Rafael 37, 40, 103, 104, 110, 114, 115, 123, 124, 124n18, 144, 199
Vilà, Joaquim 38
Vilar, Pierre 63
Villalba, José 47, 48

War Industry Commission 53, 85–92
war industries ix, 53, 84–92, 113, 125, 140, 142, 144, 147, 159, 205, 216–8
women
　alliberadors de prostitució 82, 82n23
　changes in role 46, 83, 170, 187
　Institute for Women's Professional Adaptation (*Institut d'Adaptació Professional de la Dona*) 82

Workers and Peasants' Bloc
  See BOC
Workers' Alliance (*Alianza Obrera*)   33, 33n1
Workers' Federation of Trade Union Unity
  See FOUS

Zalka, Matei   127
Zaragoza   45–8, 131–5
Zugazagoitia, Julián   63, 118, 122, 140, 142, 208